THE INTERNATIONALIZATION OF LAW AND LEGAL EDUCATION

IUS GENTIUM

Comparative Perspectives on Law and Justice

VOLUME 2

THE INTERNATIONALIZATION OF LAW AND LEGAL EDUCATION

Edited by

JAN KLABBERS

and

MORTIMER SELLERS

Springer

Editors
Prof. Jan Klabbers
University of Helsinki
Department of Public Law
Yliopistonkatu 3
FI-00014 Helsinki
Finland
jan.klabbers@helsinki.fi

Mortimer Sellers
University of Baltimore
School of Law
Center for International & Comparative Law
1420 N. Charles St.
Baltimore MD 21201-5779
USA
msellers@ubalt.edu

ISBN: 978-1-4020-9493-4 e-ISBN: 978-1-4020-9494-1

DOI 10.1007/978-1-4020-9494-1

Library of Congress Control Number: 2008939497

Printed on acid-free paper

9 8 7 6 5 4 3 2 1

springer.com

This book is dedicated to Johan Lauri Tuomola and
Cora Mary Stead Sellers.
multinational, multicultural, multitalented

Preface

The essays in this collection are based on papers originally presented at the sixth meeting of the European-American Consortium for Legal Education, held at the University of Helsinki, Finland in May, 2007.

EACLE is a transatlantic consortium of law faculties dedicated to cooperation and to the exchange of ideas between different legal systems and cultures. Each year the EACLE colloquium considers a specific legal question from a variety of national perspectives. The 2007 initiative on "The Internationalization of Law and Legal Education" was coordinated by the staff of the University of Helsinki Faculty of Law and the Academy of Finland Centre of Excellence in Global Governance Research. We would like to thank those who attended the 2007 meeting for their insightful remarks, and for their inspiration, suggestions, and encouragement in making this volume and the EACLE consortium so effective in fostering greater transatlantic cooperation on law and legal education.

Thanks are also due to the faculty, staff and students of the Center for International and Comparative Law who prepared this volume for publication, and particularly to Morad Eghbal, James Maxeiner, Kathryn Spanogle, Jordan Kobb, Astarte Daley, Suzanne Conklin, P. Hong Le, Pratima Lele, Nicholas McKinney, Shandon Phan, T.J. Sachse, Katherine Simpson, Toscha Stoner-Silbaugh, Björn Thorstensen, Ryan Webster, and Cheri Wendt-Taczak.

Helsinki, Finland — Jan Klabbers
Baltimore, MD, USA — Mortimer Sellers

Contents

Contributors

Larry Catá Backer Penn State Dickinson School of Law, Pennsylvania State University, Pennsylvania, USA

Claudio Grossman Dean, American University Washington College of Law, Washington, DC, USA

Jan Klabbers International Organizations Law, University of Helsinki; Academy of Finland Centre of Excellence in Global Governance Research, Helsinki, Finland

Candace Saari Kovacic-Fleischer American University, Washington College of Law, Washington, DC, USA

James R. Maxeiner Center for International and Comparative Law, University of Baltimore School of Law, Baltimore, MD, USA

Tyler T. Ochoa High Technology Law Institute, Santa Clara University School of Law, Santa Clara, CA, USA

Paul Przemysław Polański Department of European Law, Warsaw University Faculty of Law, Warsaw, Poland

Mortimer Sellers Regents Professor of the University System of Maryland; University of Baltimore Center for International and Comparative Law, Baltimore, MD, USA

Ida Staffans Institute for International Economic Law, University of Helsinki; Academy of Finland Centre of Excellence in the Foundations of European Law and Polity, Helsinki, Finland

Wibo M. van Rossum Department of Socio-legal Studies, Utrecht University School of Law, Utrecht, The Netherlands

Chapter 1
The Internationalization of Law and Legal Education

Mortimer Sellers

This volume is the product of international cooperation through the European-American Consortium for Legal Education (EACLE) and as such both a response to the internationalization of law and legal education and an example of the changed circumstances that it describes. The European-American Consortium for Legal Education came into existence in the millennial year, 2000, in response to a fourfold demand: students in American law schools and European law faculties were eager to spend some part of their formal legal education studying outside the legal systems in which they expected to be licensed; European and American law teachers wanted to broaden and improve their national laws and legal institutions through comparison and harmonisation with practices overseas; local governments wanted to support bilateral relations with other regional and local administrators; and the governing institutions of the United States and the European Union wanted to promote closer links (and increased harmony) between their legal institutions. Students, faculty, local jurisdictions and federal administrators were all eager to support broader transatlantic cooperation.

The EACLE came into being when it did because the pressures encouraging the internationalization of law and legal education reached a high point at the end of the 1990s. This was particularly true in Europe and the United States, but was part of a world-wide phenomenon. Not only lawyers, students, and law professors, but also judges, police officers, and politicians began to visit and exchange ideas across national and regional boundaries.[1] This florescence of legal globalization had three primary origins: *first*, in the

M. Sellers (✉)
Regents Professor of the University System of Maryland; University of Baltimore Center for International and Comparative Law, University of Baltimore, Baltimore, MD, USA
e-mail: msellers@ubalt.edu

[1] On this phenomenon, *see* Anne-Marie Slaughter, *A New World Order* (Princeton, 2004).

J. Klabbers, M. Sellers (eds.), *The Internationalization of Law and Legal Education*, Ius Gentium: Comparative Perspectives on Law and Justice 2,
DOI 10.1007/978-1-4020-9494-1_1,

astonishing success and prosperity of the European Union; *second*, in the ideological death and subsequent political dissolution of the Soviet Union; and *third*, in the obvious benefits of market or quasi-market institutions in all corners of the globe, but particularly in China and other formerly Communist and Socialist economies. At the end of the Cold War, as after the First and the Second World Wars, there was a worldwide turn to law, to trade, and to institution-building, in the hope of greater mutual understanding and lasting peace.

The European Union offered (and still offers) the most successful available model of widespread peace and prosperity through cross-border trade, based on legal and economic integration and harmonisation.[2] After the collapse of the Soviet Union, the Organization for Security and Cooperation in Europe seemed to present a similar promise to a broader array of peoples.[3] Above all, the World Trade Organization strengthened a structure through which many nations of the world sacrificed their economic independence in order to achieve what they hoped would be greater prosperity through freer trade.[4] Economic integration brought national laws and legal systems into closer contact with one another, but so did the greater migration, democratisation, and renewed commitment to universal human rights characteristic of the European Union and the new post-Soviet era.

This brief excursus into the ultimate and largely unexamined underlying causes of legal globalization at the beginning of the third millennium should not obscure the more immediate impetus towards academic integration, which arises from the personal enthusiasm of students and their teachers. At the same time that the United States government and the institutions of the European Union sought to promote harmony for political reasons,[5] and the European nations and American states sought closer links for economic reasons,[6] students and teachers sought to study and cooperate overseas for the sake of their own broader knowledge and the desire for cross-cultural understanding. If the internationalization of law is taking place primarily in response to economic self-interest (as with the W.T.O.) and moral pressure (as with universal human rights), the internationalization of legal education is taking place in large part because it is finally possible to fulfill the strong

---

[2] The Treaty on European Union speaks of "ending the division of the European Continent", establishing the principles of "liberty, democracy, and respect for human rights and fundamental freedoms and the rule of law", and "the convergence of their economies" to achieve "economic integration". (Preamble).

[3] *See* e.g. the *Budapest Document, 1994: Towards a Genuine Partnership in a New Era*.

[4] *See* the *Agreement Establishing the World Trade Organization* (1994) which sought "to develop an integrated, more viable and durable multilateral trading system".

[5] As with the European Union-United States Atlantis student exchange program.

[6] *See*, for example, the Baltimore-Rotterdam Sister City website at www.baltimorerotterdam.org

desire of young people and scholars to meet their counterparts from other parts of the world.

The European-American Consortium for Legal Education created an intercontinental network of law schools, and the EACLE has provided a model and example for similar networks between other continents and faculties of law. Five European Universities in Ghent, Helsinki, Parma, Rotterdam (Erasmus), and Warsaw and five United States Universities in Baltimore, California (Santa Clara), Georgia, New York (Hofstra) and Washington, D.C. (American University), created a consortium for the exchange of students and faculty, and for the pursuit of common research projects to improve the quality of law and legal education in Europe and the United States of America.

To some extent the EACLE partnership takes its inspiration from the European ERASMUS and TEMPUS programs, through which European law faculties have been exchanging teachers and students for many years. The European EACLE partners are participants in an existing ERASMUS network, and American partners benefit from the Europeans' greater experience. There is no reason in principle why the same model could not be extended to South America, Africa and to Asia, and indeed several of the participating universities already have very strong links with law faculties outside the current scope of the consortium, with whom they exchange teachers and students according to the same template used in the EACLE program.

The primary activities of the EACLE consortium have been: (1) the exchange of faculty every fall for week- or semester-long visits; (2) the exchange of students for semester-long visits; (3) an annual conference in May; and (4) the publication of the conference proceedings the following fall. Each academic year's exchanges focus on a particular research topic. Topics discussed have included Federalism (2001–2002), Security (2002–2003), Legal Personality (2003–2004), Agreements (2004–2005), Autonomy (2005–2006), and Internationalization (2006–2007). The professors exchanged in the fall discuss and lecture on the chosen topic, and the spring conference and resulting publication present the results. This structure is not so rigid, however, that other exchanges and visits cannot take place where appropriate.

Each year different European and American schools are paired, following a five-year scheduled rotation, to make the primary exchanges of one faculty member and at least two students. Other exchanges have also taken place each year by agreement between the schools involved. The emphasis has been on flexibility, to accommodate the needs and interests of students and professors. In the ninth year of the program, most members of the EACLE consortium now have annual bilateral exchanges with each of the other partners, in addition to the rotating exchanges established by the EACLE framework.

One key to the success of the EACLE exchanges have been their very limited expense. Students exchanged through the program pay only those costs and tuition that are normally required by their home institution. Faculty members pay only for the costs of their travel. Other expenses are borne by the host institution. Typically European students study in the United States during their final year of legal education. American students visit Europe during the third year of the J.D. program or during the second semester of their second year of their legal studies.

The partners in the EACLE consortium are convinced that the future of legal education will require greater integration between law faculties across borders, and more frequent exchanges of faculty and students. This will work best through closer partnerships in multinational webs of cooperation, which will give students the greatest possible flexibility, and more strongly encourage their transnational experience. Too often highly cohesive national or (in the United States) state or local bars develop eccentric and unjust legal structures through the gradual accretion of self-interest or the accumulation of ill-considered custom and precedents. Federal institutions and transborder cooperation within Europe and between the United States since the Second World War have moderated the close-mindedness of national or state laws and legal education within both continents. Now the time has come to achieve similar cooperation across the oceans. Asia, Africa and South America made striking advances in their legal institutions at the end of the twentieth century by making themselves more open to the reception of foreign ideas. Europe and North America have much to gain by becoming similarly open-minded.

The European-American Consortium for Legal Education has been a vehicle through which American and European law scholars and students have escaped the confines of their own local discourse to improve understanding both of their own national institutions and of those of their foreign partners. This has led both to local reforms and to better international cooperation. More important, however, has been the lasting change in worldview that students and faculty have enjoyed as a result of their participation.

The internationalization of law and of legal education are the inevitable result of changes in technology and communication that make global contacts and cooperation more possible, and therefore more likely to occur. Like most cultural changes, these developments may have negative as well as positive implications. The internationalization of law follows inevitably in the wake of globalization, for good or ill. But the internationalization of legal education proceeds at the more deliberate pace of the scholarly enterprise. The difference is that while legal cosmopolitanism may be difficult and threatening to some lawyers, educational cosmopolitanism is eagerly sought and happily received by most students and teachers. Law can be narrow and parochial, while universities from their inception have been attractive to foreigners and oriented towards the wider world.

The internationalization of legal education is the happiest and most amiable face of the internationalization of law, but it has a very serious aspect. As the aims of law should be justice and the common good, so the aims of the university should be truth and freedom of thought. These shared values animate the academic enterprise and should guide the study of law, as much as any other object of inquiry. The greatest eras of university education have been the periods of greatest mobility and international exchange, as in the years of the *ius commune* in Europe, or in the United States after the Second World War. These have also been the periods of the greatest advances in government and law.

Let us hope that the rising era of greater global integration will also become an era of greater global justice. Law and lawyers will need the full engagement of the universities to bring this better world to life.

Chapter 2
Reflections on Globalization and University Life

Jan Klabbers

Many years ago, the British comedic team Monty Python staged a football match between a team of Greek philosophers and a team of German philosophers. After a lot of inconsequential dallying about (clearly, the philosophers had little understanding of the game), the match was won by the Greeks. Archimedes saw the light, shouted "eureka", and dribbled the ball into the net – without meeting much resistance.

The sketch is a painful reminder that it may be difficult to discern, in philosophy or scholarship, whose technique is best. While it might be a nice parlor game to try to decide, with the assistance of well-chosen alcoholic beverages, whether the Greek philosophers would have beaten the German philosophers, or to discuss the relative merits of French post-structuralism and the English analytical school, clearly, as Monty Python reminds us, such comparisons should not be taken too seriously.

Yet, in today's academic world, they are taken seriously – very seriously. Every year some organization or other presents a new ranking of how universities fare against each other or, more entertaining still, how various specialized schools fare in comparison to each other. The law school rankings in US News and World Report are a modern classic – and, for its publisher, no doubt, a huge commercial success.[1] Alternative rankings, such as those compiled by Brian Leiter,[2] may be more specific (by ranking separately in each area of specialization, or separating faculty quality from student quality), but they still engage in the same unpersuasive comparisons and are seemingly based on the same premise: that somehow it may be worthwhile to compile such rankings.

J. Klabbers (✉)
International Organizations Law, University of Helsinki; Academy of Finland Centre of Excellence in Global Governance Research, Helsinki, Finland
e-mail: jan.klabbers@helsinki.fi

[1] Available at http://www.usnews.com (visited 5 September 2007).
[2] Available at http://leiterlawschool.typepad.com (visited 5 September 2007).

J. Klabbers, M. Sellers (eds.), *The Internationalization of Law and Legal Education,* Ius Gentium: Comparative Perspectives on Law and Justice 2,
DOI 10.1007/978-1-4020-9494-1_2,

The interest in rankings and comparisons owes much to globalization. Globalization, whatever else it may be, usually includes a tendency towards greater competition across boundaries. Where once the University of Helsinki would strive to be the best institution of higher learning in Finland, and later took pride in picturing itself as one of the best in the Nordic world, these geographical limitations have lost much of their plausibility. Intuitively, it makes little sense to strive to be the best in Finland if the general level of education in Finland is below par. To be Finland's finest means something, however, if Finland itself is also seen as having a high level of education. Thus, globalization stimulates a natural coalition between education policy makers and the universities. Ministry of Education bureaucrats wish to boost Finland's relative position among all the world's educators. (And have met with considerable success: Finland typically does very well in the elementary school investigations known as PISA).[3] Officials seek to advance the nation's relative position, partly for reasons of status, but also because a high level of education usually supports a high level of development. Finnish universities have similar ambitions, again partly for status' sake, but also because a high ranking may help to generate income in the form of consultancy assignments or public funding. The OECD, home of the PISA rankings, puts it unapologetically: "The prosperity of countries now derives to a large extent from their human capital, and to succeed in a rapidly changing world, individuals need to advance their knowledge and skills throughout their lives."[4]

Still, those rankings give rise to some surprising results. Thus, Dutch students might be dismayed to find that their perennial favorite (according to regular rankings carried out by the weekly magazine Elsevier),[5] Tilburg University, does not make it to the top 200 of some of the competing rankings – and is one of only two Dutch universities ranked outside the top 200. Indeed, in the Shanghai rankings of 2007,[6] it is the only Dutch university not listed among the top 500. Likewise, universities doing well in one ranking may fare poorly in another. It all depends on how things are measured and compared, and on what exactly is being measured and compared.

Still, the relative quality of rankings aside (which ranking ranks best?), there is a deeper issue at stake, relating to the very phenomenon of ranking

---

[3] This stands for Programme for International Student Assessment, and is an initiative of the OECD. Typically, Finland ranks among the top five (this covers the OECD member states plus a number of affiliated states) in the three areas which are measured: reading, science and mathematics, with a subscription on top spot in reading. For more details, *see* http://www.pisa.oecd.org (last visited 22 August 2007).

[4] The words are taken from the foreword to OECD, *Learning for Tomorrow's World: First Results from PISA 2003*, at 3, available at http://www.pisa.oecd.org (last visited 22 August 2007).

[5] Available at http://www.elsevier.nl (visited 5 September 2007).

[6] Available at http://ed.jstu.edu.cn (visited 22 August 2007).

in academia. It is not just a matter of academic output being difficult to measure and compare within disciplines: many might that feel Karl Marx contributed more to economic theory than, say, Joseph Stiglitz, but the latter has won a Nobel prize while the former, had he lived now, would most likely have been purposefully overlooked, and never had a university appointment to begin with. Nor is it just a matter of comparing across disciplines: is Stiglitz better than Francis Crick – or better than political theorist Bernard Crick, for that matter?

This way of putting the issue already suggests one of the deeper problems with ranking universities or even, more modestly, ranking individual departments or schools (as in the law school rankings): we don't ask whether Columbia University's Economics Department is better than the Politics Department at Edinburgh University or the Chemistry Department at the University of Groningen, and indeed, the question would make little sense. Part of the problem is that the status of a school or department is always dependent, to some extent at least, on chance, mainly related to the accidental presence of gifted individuals: Leiden has a famous law school because, once upon a time, Grotius happened to teach there; Uppsala's fame owes much to the coincidence of having had Linnaeus on the faculty – as indeed Uppsala's advertisements never tire of reminding us.

This sort of thing gets lost in the rankings, of course, which do not look at individuals but rather at institutions. But had Grotius been working in Antwerp, just across today's border with Belgium, or Münster, located just inside Germany, the University of Leiden would still be viewed as middling parochial institution; not unlike Orléans where Grotius did his doctoral work.[7]

The deeper problem is not just that rankings tend to overlook the role of individuals; but that they foster the competitive desire to do better, to improve. This holds true no matter what the ranking is about. A revealing little item in *Helsingin Sanomat*, Finland's leading newspaper, published sometime in the summer of 2007, listed the most expensive cities in the world, and did so in a tone which suggested that the author of the item was disappointed with Helsinki's performance: it should do better, i.e., become more expensive – however ridiculous this may sound.[8] This seems to be the sentiment that rankings inspire: a continuous drive to improve, to do better, to climb, no matter what the rankings and regardless of whether improvement (as with living in an expensive city) would actually be desirable.

---

[7] A wonderful account of the influence of Leiden's law school on the birth of New York (and the US at large) is Russell Shorto, *The Island at the Centre of the World* (2004) (arguing that the civic spirit prevailing in 17th century New York owed much to the presence and influence of Adriaen van der Donck, who had read law at Leiden and enthusiastically disseminated Grotian ideas).

[8] Under apologies to Blue Book aficionados, I must concede that I have been unable to retrieve the article in question.

There are two obvious methods of improving academic rankings. One is, simply, to purchase recognized talents. This is what some of the wealthier private universities in the US do – they simply lure talents from elsewhere with promises of large salaries, generous research budgets, great teaching facilities, first-rate students to work with, and the absence of administrative burdens. This might help explain how the United States came to be represented by 18 universities among the top 25 in the 2007 Shanghai rankings.[9]

The cash-strapped public institutions in Europe cannot, however, employ this strategy. They must rely on a second way of trying to improve their rankings: by conscious policy. University managers in Europe do their best to improve the relative position of their institutions, in much the same way that business managers continuously strive to make their organizations grow and prosper in a competitive setting.[10] But where in business life, growth and competitiveness appear in the profits, and can be measured through sales figures and the like, no such instruments are available to universities, at least not in any meaningful way. For one thing, universities in Europe often have a regional function: the University of Lapland attracts students from the north of Finland who are keen to stay relatively close to home; likewise, the University of Amsterdam attracts students from the Amsterdam region for convenience, rather than because of the quality of its teaching or research. Moreover, there are always linguistic concerns: Oslo University might be the best worldwide in neurobiology,[11] but that is of little competitive use for those of us who do not speak Norwegian. Linguistic studies, local history, and the study of law, tend to be accessible only for those with specific language skills – and this influences the competitive landscape.

European universities typically strive to "improve" themselves through internationalization strategies, growth strategies, and all sorts of other strategies, much like their counterparts in the business world. The basic assumption underlying this strategizing is the misguided idea that academic work (teaching and research) can be managed, and directed, in a meaningful way. Administrators imagine that increased output can be stimulated if only we have a proper strategy; students can be attracted if only we have a proper strategy; and while private funding remains largely a pious hope, at least the university can do well in competitions for public research

---

[9] *Supra* note 6.

[10] Incidentally, university managers are also increasingly receiving salaries commensurable with the business world: the best-paid university managers in the Netherlands, so the daily *De Volkskrant* reports, earn some 250.000–300.000 euros per year; quite a bit more, it may well be presumed, than the best-paid professors. *See* "Meer topverdieners in het hoger onderwijs", available at http://www.volkrant.nl (visited 5 September 2007). Likewise, the salary scaling at the University of Helsinki has a certain ceiling for brilliant professors, and a significantly higher ceiling for university managers.

[11] Hypothetically, of course; I have no idea whether this is the case, and cannot provide a source.

funding – provided we have the proper strategy in place. Indeed, more and more research is funded in this way: by means of competitive tenders.

2.1

The results of this struggle for status through rankings have been quite obviously disastrous. Academic work responds no better to management than does painting, music, or literature. Indeed, as every half-decent academic knows, most academic achievement depends on processes that are more easily compared with artistic processes than with industrial processes. What distinguishes the very good from the good scholar, and the good scholar from the mediocre scholar, has a lot to do with such factors as inspiration and talent, especially in the humanities and social sciences. At best, administrators could create the right conditions for academics to do their jobs by providing peace and quiet, limiting administrative tasks, and encouraging the sort of teaching that advances research work. This is what university management should be seeking to achieve (after hiring the right people.) In fact, the opposite has occurred. Instead of doing research in peace and quiet, academics are involved in all sorts of time-consuming paperwork and lengthy meetings involving a variety of committees, subcommittees and working groups, and useless administrative burdens (useless since they are supposed to aid the administration, rather than have the administration function in the service of academic work, and useless in that they are often self-referential discussions of the outcomes of last month's meetings). Academics often find that they can only pursue their research work in the evenings or during the weekend – if then.[12]

Much research funding is based on similar strategic notions: funding agencies seek to stimulate certain branches of scholarship (not uncommonly those with industrial or commercial applications) or, more generally, to stimulate research at the expense of teaching, in the expectation that a strong research reputation will result in a stronger competitive position for the local economy. As a result, funding is redirected from university departments to funding agencies (Academies of Science, typically), and much funding is based on individual or collective applications to these funding agencies. The results, however, are not always felicitous, and are often, counterproductive.[13]

---

[12] How's this for an anecdotal irony: the competitive drive entails that prominent guest lecturers are invited to speak: their glory rubs off, if only a little bit, on the institution inviting them. Yet, I am usually unable to attend those lectures, as I am either sitting in a meeting, preparing for one, or (rarely) so happy not to have a meeting that I think I should use my time doing some reading or writing.

[13] Not to mention other considerations: typically, if funding comes in the form of scholarships (as is often the case), the researcher concerned will not build up any pension rights, will not have health insurance, and will have no safety net to cover possible

Here it is perhaps useful to introduce what I would call the Case of the Wittgensteinian Application. Ludwig Wittgenstein had an enormous influence on twentieth-century philosophy – but he spent much of his lengthy academic career writing two difficult books: the early *Tractatus Philosophicus*, and the later *Philosophical Investigations*. It would have been difficult enough for him, had he lived and worked now, to acquire funding for the first: an attempt to present a comprehensive philosophy, especially one giving a prominent place to logic, would probably have been deemed "unrealistic" and "over-ambitious" by his peers, or perhaps even as utter gibberish, by university administrators less gifted than Wittgenstein himself.

But imagine the chances of attracting funding for the *Philosophical Investigations*: "Dear Sirs, I hereby apply for a grant so as to refute my own work published some time ago. I feel I was wrong then, and need considerable funding to investigate my own mistakes." No responsible funding decision-maker would be willing to sponsor such a work, especially not when taking into account Wittgenstein's rather erratic working methods (he was known to wander off from time to time, for instance, which would create problems of its own in respect of reporting to the funding agency).[14]

Now, Wittgenstein might be an extreme case, but other path-breaking work would also have a hard time attracting outside funding. Martin Heidegger, that other twentieth century giant, would have encountered problems of a radically different nature after 1945. Thomas Kuhn's work on the structure of scientific revolutions would have probably been judged far too radical by funding agencies, and it seems fair to suppose that someone like Michel Foucault would also have met with serious obstacles had he tried to find outside funding for projects on governmentality and the like. In short, much of the work we now take for granted and consider as paradigmatic (the very word itself only came in vogue with Kuhn) could, in all likelihood, only have been produced inside a protected university structure, free from all sorts of concerns about marketability, or utility, and that sort of thing.

This competition for funding creates a number of minor and major irritants. For one thing, highly qualified professors spend a lot of their time writing applications for funding, rather than doing actual research. Instead, much of their research is outsourced to doctoral students. This may not be a bad thing in educational terms: one of the better ways of learning is by working with, or under supervision of, a more established and experienced colleague. As Michael Oakeshott put it with his customary lucidity and flair:

---

unemployment once the project is finished. The universities, therewith, have been among the first places to contribute to the breakdown of the welfare state, and stimulate a huge degree of inequality: the position of an unproductive (note the word) professor with tenure is many times better than that of the young but productive researcher who has to make a living on scholarships.

[14] On Wittgenstein, *see* the magnificent biography by Ray Monk, *Ludwig Wittgenstein: The Duty of Genius* (London 1990).

> To work alongside a practiced scientist or craftsman is an opportunity not only to learn the rules, but to acquire also a direct knowledge of how he sets about his business (and, among other things, a knowledge of how and when to apply the rules); and until this is acquired nothing of great value has been learned.[15]

But useful as it may be for young scholars to follow the work of more experienced colleagues close-up, it is quite a different thing if those more experienced scholars end up spending all their time writing funding applications and filing administrative paperwork. Often, funding requests must be accompanied by bureaucratic statements that there will indeed be an office available for candidates X, Y and Z in the unlikely event that funding will be forthcoming, and somehow the funding agencies will also need to be convinced of the appropriateness of candidates X, Y and Z as funding recipients, which in turn entails that supervisors write endless streams of character references and recommendations.[16]

It also entails that many of the applications will be written with a view not so much to what would make academic sense, as to what would lead to the application being successful; and indeed, one almost has a moral obligation to do so, for an unsuccessful application means that people (good, talented, hard-working people) may have to be let go, or give up on promising academic careers before their promise has come to full fruition. Thus, when applying for funding, one has to take the funder's views into consideration, with the result that scholarship and research no longer begin with trying to figure out how the world works and how best to understand it, but rather with an attempt to understand the motives and emotions of funding agencies.

The importance of grant applications has the secondary effect of burdening prominent academics with a huge amount of peer review. Funding agencies need academic evaluators from within the disciplines they are funding. This leads to corruption, because academics must cultivate friendships and develop alliances with any colleague who might conceivably be in a position to evaluate their grant application. Review articles and book reviews become over-generous, because academics fear to arouse the animosity of their colleagues.[17]

---

[15] *See* Michael Oakeshott, "Rational Conduct", reproduced in his *Rationalism in Politics and Other Essays* (London 1962), 80–110, at 92.

[16] And sometimes to no avail, even formally. By way of illustration: for one of the researchers working under my supervision, we recently applied for funding under an EU-sponsored scheme. We had not, in all haste, noted the need for a declaration of institutional support and, when asked to provide one later, we did so forthwith. Imagine our surprise when nonetheless we received a formal answer that the added statement could not be included as part of the application, which, no doubt, will render the application unsuccessful. The big question is this: if later additions are not allowed, then why were we asked to send one?

[17] Dutch historian and essayist Bastiaan Bommeljé observes much the same among Dutch historians, speaking of "protectionism" in peer review. More generally, he suggests

The reviewers, themselves also soon realize that there is no point in being honest. A solid, decent proposal launched by a solid, decent colleague will have to be rated as "excellent" in order to stand any chance of survival; after all, having been reviewed, it will have to compete with other proposals from other fields and disciplines, and if someone else has decided that a poor proposal is "excellent", then one cannot avoid doing the same thing. The marks "good" or even "very good", however well-deserved, will kill off the application immediately, because of descriptive inflation. The surprising result is that many, many proposals come out of the review process labeled "excellent", with the obvious result that the funding agency still has little or no academic basis for its ultimate decisions. Decisions must then be made using non-academic criteria: if researcher X was funded last year, perhaps he or she will be passed over this time around; or attempts will be made to spread funding equitably among universities, or among disciplines; or somehow project Y fits in more nicely with the policy demands of the state supporting the funding agency than project F; or somehow project Z might be considered better-equipped to attract co-funding. But if this is the case, why not use these non-academic criteria to begin with? Why go through all the hoops of a lengthy and time-consuming peer review process if, in the end, decisions do not depend upon them?[18]

2.2

The same result-orientation is also present when it comes to matters of teaching and the curriculum. Typically, university funding is made dependent, at least in part, on output, measured by the numbers of lawyers, doctors, or engineers produced.[19] This too, however understandable perhaps

---

that the professionalization (he uses a Dutch word that roughly translates as "scientification") of the discipline has lead to a great increase in detailed, technically sound but bland and uninspiring studies, lacking the spark with which earlier generations could write. *See* his essay "Geschiedschrijving in Nederland", reproduced in Bastiaan Bommeljé, *De sfinx op de rots: over geschiedenis en het menselijk tekort* (Amsterdam 1987) 143–171. esp. at 166–169.

[18] And yet, it is also clear that this sort of decision probably has to be taken by some committee of peers; the alternatives might be decidedly worse. The classic rendition of the argument that such things cannot be left to courts is Lon L. Fuller, "The Forms and Limits of Adjudication", 92 *Harvard Law Review* (1978) 353–409.

[19] This sort of "commensuration" (reducing everything into quantitative terms) is a more general phenomenon, which also such plagues such issues as policy-making at the UN. *See*, e.g., Jan Klabbers, "Redemption Song? Human Rights versus Community-building in East Timor", 16 *Leiden Journal of International Law* (2003) 367–376 (arguing that community-building became reconceived in measurable (quasi-)human rights terms precisely because this facilitates measurement); the term "commensuration" is gratefully borrowed from Eva Illouz, *Cold Intimacies: The Making of Emotional Capitalism* (Cambridge 2007), esp. at 33.

from a historical perspective, has a few unpleasant and, so to speak, counterproductive side-effects.

One of them is that we start treating our students as children, and are therewith bucking the trend according to which children are increasingly treated as adults.[20] Our university students, typically, are in their late teens or early to mid-twenties. They are allowed to buy alcohol in most countries (and guns in those where gun possession is legal); they can get married; drive cars; fight wars on our behalf; buy pornographic materials; if they were to commit a crime, we would try them as adults; and if convicted, we would mete out adult punishment. We even let them vote in elections and therewith trust their public judgment enough to let them, through their elected representatives, run our countries, and thus also our lives. In short, people of the university-going age are treated, in all walks of life, as fully grown up adults – except at their universities. The latest invention in the place I work in is to make each student, together with a responsible professor, draw up an individual study plan, outlining in some detail when he will take which courses, and how much time he intends to spend writing his thesis. We no longer trust them to make their own study plans and plan their own lives; it has to be done under supervision. By the same token, the number of exam opportunities is steadily increasing, and the importance of exams is blown all out of proportion. Exams, ideally, should be a method for the teacher to measure the student's progress, and to gain an understanding of what the student's weaker and stronger points are. Instead, exams have degenerated into the ultimate measure of performance, the result being that much of the teaching is geared towards helping students to pass exams rather than helping them to become good lawyers, doctors, or engineers. Duncan Kennedy, writing a quarter of a century ago, emphasized much the same point: if law schools were to re-channel some time and money "into systematic skills training and committed themselves to giving constant detailed feedback on student progress in learning those skills, they could graduate the vast majority of all the law students in the country at the level of technical proficiency now achieved by a small minority in each institution."[21] Instead, as Kennedy argued, through examinations and class rankings (as well as other modalities), law schools tend to reproduce the existing hierarchy.[22]

Another example of this paternalistic line of thinking, according to which students are to be treated as young children, can be discerned in the call made in the summer of 2007 by the president of the Dutch universities league, suggesting that many of the Dutch university programs adhered to

---

[20] For a useful discussion, *see* Benjamin Barber, *Consumed* (New York 2007).

[21] *See* Duncan Kennedy, "Legal Education and the Reproduction of Hierarchy", 32 *Journal of Legal Education* (1982) 591–615, at 600.

[22] Ibid.

meager intellectual standards (which may well be the case) and that the solution to this would be to intensify teaching,[23] by requiring more hours of teaching per week. The intention also seems in part to be to prevent students from drifting away, by imposing some structure on an academic career that might otherwise all too easily succumb to the temptations of college sociability and big city life. Again, though, the underlying assumption about students is that they are helpless, immature creatures, who need discipline and structure more than anything else; and that once discipline and structure are provided, output will rise. Often, there seems to be little attention paid to the kind of person delivered at the end of the line: what matters is the production of doctors, lawyers, and engineers *per se*, rather than the production of good, mature, independent, doctors, lawyers, and engineers.[24]

But there is a bigger problem that arises from the push for greater production, a problem which is often completely overlooked. This arises because education should, ideally, serve two functions: it should prepare the student for professional life, but also for public life – for life as a citizen. Yet, public life has been completely forgotten: to the extent that we educate our lawyers, doctors, or engineers, we educate them to be technically competent. We have forgotten, that we ought also to be teaching them to acquire the basic values of citizenship: the ability to listen and to discuss the public good in a more or less rational and polite manner, to respect other people's opinions, and to accept the value of human plurality. Ethics courses for lawyers or doctors do not serve this purpose. These focus on the codified ethics of the profession, but stop short of addressing the responsibilities of public life. Low voter turn-out, simpleminded partisanship, irresponsible political leadership and public apathy, are all to some extent the result of inadequate citizenship education. We no longer teach our students to care for our common world – we only teach them to care for themselves.[25] An increased focus on the output of higher education will only stimulate further apathy about all things public. Perhaps it is time to revert to the idea of education as *Bildung*, which should provide people not only with technical professional competence but also with a sense of what it means to live together in a common world.

When education is a public affair, paid for out of public funds and paying attention to public virtues, public education is particularly important – and particularly likely to be successful. The growing privatization of education

---

[23] *See* note 8 above.

[24] *Et plus ca change*...: almost four decades ago the young Duncan Kennedy, a law student at Yale at the time, wrote a passionate piece urging law schools to pay more attention to the sort of persons they produced. *See* Duncan Kennedy, "How the Law School Fails: A Polemic", 1 *Yale Law Review of Law and Social Action* (1970) 1.

[25] For some stimulating perspectives, *see* Mordechai Gordon (ed.), *Hannah Arendt and Education: Renewing our Common World* (Boulder CO, 2001).

through the influence of the WTO or other market forces will undermine the commitment to citizenship, by separating universities from the public good. But then again, where public universities behave as if they are operating in private markets, fueled by an imaginary competition; perhaps the differences between public and private should not be exaggerated: neither does much, at present, to take care of our common world.

2.3

In a globalizing world, lawyers will need to be educated in such a way as to make it easy to move across jurisdictions, across specializations, and to move across employment opportunities.[26] Few lawyers will have one and the same employer throughout an entire legal career. Instead, lawyers typically spend some time in general practice; they may work for a multinational company for a while, and also do a stint with an intergovernmental organization. Those different positions bring with them different sets of professional demands and different attitudes. As a result, legal education should, ideally, be fairly general in nature: the lawyer who knows her Finnish criminal code by heart but not much else will have a hard time surviving professionally, and might be better off having an understanding of the principles underlying the criminal code rather than the details of that code itself. This might make it easier for her to move abroad, or do a stint with the International Criminal Court. Legal education, in other words, should focus on general principles and a broad understanding rather than, as is so often the case, on detailed rules and memorization. For this reason, topics such as public international law (so broad that it is forced to focus on general principles) and legal theory will be extremely useful, in addition to general skills such as knowing how to work with deadlines, to write without typos, to structure an argument, and to do legal research in an actual library (as opposed to relying on computer search engines).[27]

This emphasis on general principles will benefit the future lawyer and, therewith, his or her employer: it is also vital for the self-preservation of the discipline. If the traditional curriculum, in Duncan Kennedy's happy phrase, was built around the "ground-rules of late nineteenth-century laissez-faire capitalism"[28] (he singled out contracts, torts, property, criminal law, and civil procedure), today's curriculum should come to terms

---

[26] *See* generally also Adelle Blackett, "Globalization and its Ambiguities: Implications for Law School Curricular Reform", 37 *Columbia Journal of Transnational Law* (1998–99) 57–80 (advocating a combination of attention for the global with the local).

[27] I have discussed this in greater detail in Jan Klabbers, "Legal Education in the Balance: Accommodating Flexibility", 56 *Journal of Legal Education* (2006) 196–200.

[28] *See* Kennedy, "The Reproduction of Hierarchy", note 21 above, at 597.

with the ground-rules of global capitalism, including such things as the law of world trade, and perhaps foreign investment law and conflicts of law.

It is very important in a globalizing world, that students should also be educated as global citizens.[29] Some attention should be paid to the institutions of global governance (such as the UN and the WTO). Some attention should be paid to universal human rights. Thinking about such issues might help instill a sense of global citizenship and induce future lawyers to feel some responsibility for our common global world, but only (ironically, perhaps) by insisting on this political function of human rights, rather than a focus on the technicalities or on "rightsism". By the same token, and in much the same way as in domestic settings, respect for different opinions and an acceptance of human plurality are great goods. Most of all, students should be re-educated in the art of questioning received wisdom, and questioning authority. For if there is one thing that university-level education should try to instill in its students, it is the faculty of thinking: independently and preferably without blind spots – "thinking without banisters", as Hannah Arendt so felicitously put it.[30] Or as Richard Rorty once observed: while education generally may consist of socialization, at universities and colleges the happy few must be given the opportunity to question things and (should a utilitarian justification be required) therewith provide societies with a fresh impetus.[31]

The big irony, of course, is that it is precisely this fresh impetus which may help societies to achieve economic progress and welfare. Today's managerial, technical approach, with its focus on output and neglect of critical faculties, is bound to backfire. Although it is intended to stimulate economic progress, over-administration actually undermines the driving force of economic progress. And as far as university life is concerned, the very drive to manage research processes, with its emphasis on meetings and strategies, implies that actually, very little research is being done. While many things may get published (and it seems that the number of things published is growing all the time), much of the writing tends to be repetitive, and either a bit sloppy, a bit superficial, or simply poor. The managing of science, then, shoots itself in the foot – or feet perhaps: every minute spent in a meeting, devising a strategy, or writing an application, is a minute

[29] For a discussion among political scientists along similar lines, *see* Benjamin Barber et al., "Internationalizing the Undergraduate Curriculum", *PS: Political Science and Politics* (January 2007) 105–120.

[30] The correspondence between her students Elizabeth Young-Bruehl and Jerome Kohn, under the title "What and How we Learned from Hannah Arendt: An Exchange of Letters" and recorded in Gordon, note 25 above, 225–256, suggests that she too brought this into the classroom and instilled a lifelong habit in them.

[31] *See* Richard Rorty, "Education as Socialization and as Individualization", reproduced in Richard Rorty, *Philosophy and Social Hope* (1999) 114–126.

not spent on research, on reflection, or on teaching; every minute spent on academic management is a minute effectively wasted.

Last but far from least, the focus on output in teaching creates entire generations of students who do well at tests and exams – that is, after all, what we prepare them for. But the public world, the world of politics and citizenship, gets lost in the process. Perhaps it is time that we seriously reconsider what on earth we are doing to ourselves and to our children, mindful of Arendt's wise words:

> Education is the point at which we decide whether we love the world enough to assume responsibility for it and by the same token save it from that ruin which, except for renewal, except for the coming of the new and young, would be inevitable. And education, too, is where we decide whether we love our children enough not to expel them from our world and leave them to their own devices, nor to strike from their hands their chance of undertaking something new, something unforeseen by us, but to prepare them in advance for the task of renewing a common world.[32]

[32] These are the closing words of Hannah Arendt, "The Crisis in Education", reproduced in Hannah Arendt, *Between Past and Future: Eight Exercises in Political Thought* (1961), 173–196, at 196.

Chapter 3
Building the World Community Through Legal Education

Claudio Grossman

Today we are witnessing dramatic global transformations that call into question both the content and the methodology of legal education. These changing processes have been well documented and extensively discussed elsewhere.[1] They include global trade, foreign investment, the breakdown of authoritarian political structures, the emergence of new nations, and the presence of new international actors such as individuals, multinational corporations, and non-governmental organizations (NGOs).[2] Crucial problems that challenge humankind cannot be solved solely by individual states. Instead, this growing trend demonstrates the need for greater international cooperation.[3] This need is particularly pressing in the case

C. Grossman (✉)
Dean, American University Washington College of Law, Washington, DC, USA
e-mail: grossman@wcl.american.edu

[1] This chapter reiterates views expressed in the author's earlier publications in 18 *Dickinson Journal of International* Law 441 (2000) and 17 *American University International Law Review* 815 (2002). See Alberto Bernable-Reifkohl, *Tomorrow's Law Schools: Globalization and Legal Education*, 32 San Diego L. Rev. 137 (1995) (arguing that changing economic and political world order, including major shifts in trade patterns, internationalization of financial markets, and post Cold War political structure, call for adjustment of legal education). *See also* W. Michael Reisman, *Designing Law Curricula for a Transnational Industrial and Science-Based Civilization*, 46 J. Legal Educ. 322 (1996) (arguing that legal education must accommodate globalization by implementing the notion of a comprehensive transnational legal system rather than autonomous national systems).

[2] *See* Claudio Grossman and Daniel D. Bradlow, *Are We Being Propelled Towards a People-Centered Transnational Legal Order?*, 9 Am. U. J. Int'l. L. & Pol'y 1 (1993) (arguing that new actors include individual voices who implement change through non-governmental organizations and have played a monumental role in developing transnational alliances towards securing human rights, consumer protection, social justice and sustainable environment, thus garnering transnational affiliations and making their voices heard).

[3] *See* Reisman, *supra*, note 1, at 323–24 (contending that increasing acts of political violence, transnationalization of crime, and economic monopolization render the individual

J. Klabbers, M. Sellers (eds.), *The Internationalization of Law and Legal Education*, Ius Gentium: Comparative Perspectives on Law and Justice 2,
DOI 10.1007/978-1-4020-9494-1_3,

of transboundary problems such as the proliferation of nuclear weapons, widespread poverty, environmental degradation, international terrorism, and war crimes. The growing importance of such issues confirms that a new world reality is emerging and is here to stay. Society must now ask how these phenomena will affect legal education.

For rhetorical purposes, we can identify two main schools of thought that consider the implications of these global changes and their effects on legal education. The first school contends that the transformations taking place are of minimal concern because lawyers deal primarily with domestic issues. This theory seeks to preserve the status quo in legal education, believing that the practice of law deals primarily with domestic interests and issues that are exclusively within one nation's borders. Proponents of this viewpoint further allege that the modification of legal education is unnecessary because the global questions are "merely a matter of translation." For example, a real estate lawyer in the U.S. Midwest who engages in the development of agricultural land will need a language translator if a foreign party is involved in a transaction, but need not employ different legal concepts. Accordingly, because the basic concepts underlying the transaction remain the same, the traditional concept of legal education should remain intact.

The second school of thought goes beyond translation, arguing that more is required to prepare lawyers for the seismic changes currently taking place beyond mere language interpretations and translation. Proponents of this school of thought regard translation alone as an ineffective means of establishing a continuous relationship with a client. They believe that knowledge of the client's cultural values is also of great importance when developing a professional relationship. This group believes that legal education needs to be modified by increasing global exposure, achieved by adding courses, hiring more international faculty, sponsoring more international academic programs, opening research centers with global connections, and augmenting the number of formal international linkages. Unfortunately, this group only makes quantitative changes to legal education. The actual law school experience would still not undergo any basic transformation.[4]

Standing alone, neither of these two approaches produces the paradigm shift required to educate lawyers in the new world reality. Both schools of thought appear to underestimate the breadth of the changes currently taking place, as one simply maintains the status quo and the other advocates making only surface changes to legal education. What is needed, instead, is a profoundly different approach, one that advocates a *qualitative* rather

---

state unable to protect public order and, therefore, increase the need for intergovernmental cooperation).

[4] This approach further neglects the fact that crucial international legal dilemmas in recent times have concerned "non-Anglo-Saxon" nations (e.g., international tragedies such as war crimes in the former Yugoslavia and Rwanda, human rights violations in the form of disappearances and state-sponsored terrorism in Latin and South America, female genital mutilation in Africa, and the Bhopal environmental disaster in India).

than a *quantitative* change in legal education. The aim of this paper is to push the debate in that direction and to explore ways to reconceptualize legal education in accordance with current global transformations.

3.1 The Case Method, Sovereignty, and International Law

The belief that Christopher Columbus Langdell's[5] case method should be the only way to teach law in the United States continues to be questioned.[6] Theoretically, opponents view the case method as a way to instill a false ideology, and others criticize only limited aspects of its implementation.[7] Additionally, those that advocate the movement towards clinical education and experiential learning allege that the case method teaches neither the values nor the skills that are necessary for the practice of law. They further assert that this method limits students because they are only engaging with one type of material. This longstanding criticism has led to the general acceptance of clinics, although most schools still do not offer all their students a clinical experience.[8]

---

[5] Christopher Columbus Langdell became the Dean of Harvard Law School in 1870. Langdell was largely responsible for creating the case method, and establishing it and the Socratic method as the primary methods for the study of law. *See generally* Robert Stevens, Law School: Legal Education in America from the 1850s to the 1980s (1983).

[6] *See* Reisman, *supra* note 1, at 323–24. *See also* Anita Bernstein, *A Feminist Revisit to the First-Year Curriculum*, 46 J. Legal Educ. 217 (1996) (discussing a seminar at Chicago-Kent College of Law that offers an alternative method of legal education; six first year courses are taught from a feminist perspective such as sexual fraud as a tort, prenuptial agreements as contractual issues, intramarital crime, and exclusion of jurors on the basis of sex). *See also* Ann Shalleck, *Feminist Theory & Feminist Method: Transforming the Experience of the Classroom*, 7 Am. U. J. of Gender & Law 229 (1999) (describing how feminist theory can be brought into classes through role playing exercises).

[7] *See* Walter Otto Weyrauch, *Fact Consciousness*, 46 J. Legal Educ. 263 (1996) (criticizing the case method as an ineffective means of teaching students and emphasizing the misplaced importance law schools place on doctrinal logic derived from the case study method of teaching law since cases are often heavily edited in the interest of stressing particular doctrinal issues rather than actual facts or observations of events).

[8] The American Bar Association does not require law schools to provide experiential learning opportunities to all of their students. *See* ABA Standards for Approval of Law Schools §3.02(d) ("A law school shall offer live-client or other real-life practice experiences. This might be accomplished through clinics or externships. A law school need not offer this experience to all students."). Of the 160 law schools that are members of the Association of American Law Schools (AALS), 144 of those schools currently have at least one clinical program. This fact does not guarantee, however, that *all* students will have the opportunity to take advantage of these programs. This statistic was obtained through an informal survey conducted by the American University Washington College of Law's Office of the Dean (hereinafter "WCL Informal Course Survey"). The Office reviewed the course offerings, as posted on school official websites and through phone interviews with law school administrators.

The case method is also criticized as being incapable of developing a theoretical understanding of the law, and the historic processes that shape it.[9] These criticisms, however, have not come from "a world point of view." Indeed, these criticisms have failed to examine the extent to which the case method is linked to a focus on domestic law and consequently to outmoded concepts of national sovereignty. There has been limited, if any, criticism directed at the case method's relevance to the study and practice of international law.[10] Minimal attention has been given to the relative unimportance of the case method in teaching interpersonal and negotiation skills that transcend cross-cultural differences, including the importance of linguistic diversity. Nor does the case method illuminate the ways that a historical and theoretical understanding of the world should inform the value choices confronting lawyers.

The outmoded value of the case method in legal education is most clearly seen when evaluating the development of international law since the days of Langdell. The case method was born in an era dominated by the principle of national sovereignty. In fact, the Permanent Court of International Justice (PCIJ) reflected the principles of this era in the 1927 *S.S. Lotus* decision.[11] The majority opinion in *S.S. Lotus* held that individual states could extend the application of their laws to persons and acts committed on the high seas because such undertakings were not prohibited by international law.[12]

---

[9] *See* Stevens, *supra* note 5, at 156–57 (discussing the 1930s realist movement that criticized Langdellian notion that law consists of a series of objective principles, and questioned the case method's ability to teach law within a political, historical, and cultural context).

[10] *See* Alfred Zantzinger Reed, Training for the Public Profession of the Law, 1 (1921) (criticizing the case method for its limited relevance and effectiveness as a teaching methodology and its failure to equip law students with experiential training necessary to practice law within a domestic order).

[11] *See* S.S. Lotus (Fr. V. Turk.), 1927 P.C.I.J. (ser. A) No. 9 (Sept. 7). In *S.S. Lotus*, the PCIJ confronted the issue of whether international law allowed Turkey to implement Turkish law in criminal proceedings against a French lieutenant, after a French steamboat, the *S.S. Lotus*, collided with a Turkish steamboat, the *Boz-Kourt*. *See* (*id.*) at 13.

[12] *See* id. at 22–31. "International law governs relations between independent States. The rules of law binding upon States therefore emanate from their own free will . . . [r]estrictions upon the independence of States cannot therefore be presumed. [A State] may not exercise its power in any form in the territory of another State . . . every State remains free to adopt the principles which it regards as best and most suitable." *See* id. In accordance with this belief, states retained absolute freedom of action in the absence of specific obligations. *See* Detlev Vagts & Harold G. Maier, *State Immunity: An Analytical and Prognostic View*, 80 Am. J. Int'l L. 758–5 (1986) (reviewing Gamal Moursi Badr, *State Immunity: An Analytical and Prognostic View* (1984)) ("The principle of absolute sovereign equality is fundamental to international legal theory, in which community consent is the only limit on the absolute sovereign rights, a proposition clearly stated in the *Lotus* case."). *See also* Alan Neale, *Jurisdictional Conflicts Arising from Antitrust Enforcement*, 43 Antitrust L.J. 761,766 (1985); Nicholas R. Koberstein,

S.S. Lotus appeared to espouse the state-centered view that "if it is not forbidden, you can do it."

S.S. Lotus embodied the prominent theoretical framework of its era during which national sovereignty was viewed as the fundamental principle from which all international rules were derived.[13] Limited constraints, if any, were agreed upon by the states.[14] Attuned to these isolationist global conditions and largely dissociated from the context of a "distant" world,[15] American legal scholars of this era shaped the study of law in accordance with domestic concerns. These early legal educators found it unnecessary to look to the outside world to teach U.S. law students.

When Christopher Columbus Langdell became the Dean of Harvard Law School in 1870, he equated the study of law with the study of science. Langdell believed that the law is derived from a logical set of objective principles that, in turn, were arrived at through appellate decisions.[16] This scientific approach to the study of law was better suited to a domestic reality that was searching for order, consistency, and certainty.[17] The era in which Langdell lived however, was far from consistent in its legal interpretations, partially due to the isolationist tendencies of nations in the nineteenth and early twentieth centuries.

Langdell redirected the study of law to accommodate a political culture which confined the practice of law to national borders.[18] The acceptance of this approach amounted to the acceptance of the then-present notion of absolute sovereignty. International law was seen as a set of ethical aspirations

---

Without Justification: Reliance on the Presumption against Extraterritoriality in Sale v. Haitian Centers Council, Inc., 7 Geo. Immigr. L. J. 569, 580 (1993).

[13] *See* Mark W. Janis et al., International Law, Cases and Commentary 1, 87 (1997).

[14] These restraints could limit a state's freedom to act, resort to war, and assert colonial rule. However, the restraints could also limit a state's refusal to grant minimum standards of treatment for all individuals. *See* Burns H. Weston et al., International Law and World Order 1, 47 (1980); Ian Browlie, Principles of Public International Law 291 (1990). Notwithstanding the presence of such restraints, few were ever applied.

[15] *See* Stevens, *supra* note 5, at 52.

[16] *See* id. ("Law as a science is a body of fundamental principles and of deductions drawn therefrom in reference to the right ordering of social conduct...[t]he intellect in deriving legitimate deductions from the principles follows the legitimate process of logic, over which the will has no control, and which are always and everywhere the same, whatever may be the subject of the investigation."). Langdell once wrote that law, considered as a science, consists of certain principles or doctrines and "to have such a mastery of theses as to be able to apply them with a constant facility and certainty to the ever-tangled skein of human affairs, is what constitutes a true lawyer." *See* Lawrence M. Friedman, A History of American Law 613 (1985).

[17] *See* Lawrence M. Friedman, A History of American Law 613 (1985).

[18] *See* Stevens, *supra* note 5, at 52. Langdell argued that the study of law must be limited to principles discovered in U.S. appellate court opinions in order to remedy judicial deviations and create a system of law that was self-contained, unitary, and, thus, capable of erecting principles that could then be applied to each new case.

that would bend to domestic notions of self-preservation and self-aid. The wanton destruction caused by two world wars and the subsequent development of even more lethal means of mass destruction demonstrated the limits of the principle that absolute sovereignty would guarantee the well-being and survival of humankind. The absence of restrictions on individual nations, and the use and threat of force on international relations,[19] could no longer be accepted after the development of weapons of mass destruction. Equally, war crimes and genocide made it clear that international norms and procedures would be necessary in order to protect individuals from governmental actions. After World War II, numerous states convened in an effort to regulate the use of force; to develop an international bill of rights; and to create and strengthen international organizations that would foster cooperation, peacefully resolve conflicts, and provide states with a universal body of civil administration.[20]

This process has continued since World War II. Nearly all areas of human activity—trade, investment, crime, and the environment—have expanded beyond purely domestic jurisdiction, such that no state can independently solve the complex issues of contemporary society. The walls and curtains built during the Cold War certainly limited the unfolding of this process. However, even the Cold War could not destroy the need for cooperation, even if this cooperation was used mostly to avoid the proliferation and use of atomic weapons. The end of the Cold War and the fall of the Soviet Union helped to further the widespread recognition that human rights and governmental structures can no longer be seen as purely domestic matters. The change from the bipolar world power structure of the Cold War to the present reality in which multiple nations wield influence has necessitated the cooperation of states in order to accomplish global changes.

---

[19] The use of force by a state is, in itself, a traditionally acceptable use of a sovereign state's power. "It always lies within the power of a State to endeavor to obtain redress for wrongs, or to gain political or other advantages over another, not merely by the employment of force, but also by direct recourse to war." 2 Charles Cheney Hyde, International Law Chiefly as Interpreted and Applied by the United States §597 (1922). After the devastation of World War I, however, states agreed that war in an advanced technological age was too costly, both in terms of dollars and lives. In the Kellogg-Briand Pact, the United States and fourteen other countries agreed to avoid war as a solution to international conflict or "as an instrument of national policy." The Kellogg-Briand Pact, Aug. 27, 1928, 46 Stat. 2343. Again, states pooled their interest in avoiding war in the Covenant of the League of Nations, June 28, 1919, 225 Consol. T.S. 188. Of course, these agreements did not prevent the start of World War II and the Holocaust.

[20] The devastation of World War II led to the creation of the United Nations. In the United Nations Charter, the member states agreed that "[a]ll Members shall refrain in their international relations from the threat or use of force against the territorial integrity or political independence of any state, or in any other manner inconsistent with the Purposes of the United Nations." U.N. Charter art. 2, para 4.

If *S.S. Lotus* represented the era of absolute sovereignty, the *North Sea Continental Shelf*[21] cases presented a new paradigm.[22] Through the *North Sea* cases, the International Court of Justice (ICJ) rejected the principle that "if it is not forbidden, you can do it" and introduced the possibility of "obligation without acceptance" upon states. In doing so, the ICJ challenged the notion of absolute national sovereignty.[23] Indeed, the ICJ conceptualized new legal approaches more suited for an increasingly independent world order.[24] Specifically, the court held:

> [The Geneva Convention] has constituted the foundation of, or has generated a rule which, while only conventional or contractual in its origin, has since passed into the general *corpus* of international law, and is now accepted as such by the *opinio juris*, so as to have become binding even for countries which have never, and do not become parties to the Convention. . . .[I]n the case of general or customary law rules and obligations which, by their very nature, must have equal force for all members of the international community, and cannot therefore be the subject of any right of unilateral exclusion exercisable at will by any one of [the States] in its own favor. . . .[P]arties are under an *obligation* to act in such a way that, . . .*equitable* principles are applied.[25]

By recognizing a general norm of customary international law over the treaty regime, the ICJ generated rules of obligation that became binding even for countries that were not parties to the Convention.[26] Through the *North Sea* cases, the ICJ abandoned early international law, which dealt mainly with bilateral relations between sovereign states, and encouraged the governing regimes to embrace a new coherent system of world order that focused on interdependence and accountability. This new system espoused the belief that global governance, economic development, and human existence must be approached from an international perspective.[27]

---

[21] North Sea Continental Shelf (F.R.G. v. Den.; F.R.G. v. Neth.), 1969 I.C.J. 3 (Feb. 20).

[22] *See* id. Although the specific factual background of these cases is beyond the scope of this article, it is important to delineate the norms and ideological principles that emerged from the *North Sea Continental Shelf* cases. The ICJ was asked to address the principles and rules of international law that were applicable to the removal of limitations between the Parties regarding the continental shelf areas that belonged to each of them, located beyond the partial boundary determined by the Continental Shelf Convention. In pursuit of the decision requested by the ICJ, the governments of the Kingdom of Denmark, the Federal Republic of Germany, and the Netherlands delimited the continental shelf in the North Sea by agreement.

[23] *See* Jonathan I. Charney, *Universal International Law*, 7 Am. J. Int'l L. 529–30 (1993).

[24] *See* id.

[25] *North Sea Continental Shelf*, 1969 I.C.J. at 138–39, 140.

[26] *See* id. at 140, 143. The ICJ asserted that it "is unacceptable in this instance [that] a State should enjoy continental shelf rights considerably different from those of its neighbors merely because in one case the coastline is roughly convex in form and in the other it is markedly concave, although those coastlines are comparable in length." Id.

[27] Grossman and Bradlow, *supra* note 2, at 4.

3.2 Legal Education in an Interconnected World

Despite the past century's numerous philosophical changes in international law, the curricula of law schools continue to focus on a domestic agenda. A study conducted by the American Society of International Law (ASIL) found that during the Langdellian era (1870–1895) there were only twenty-three educational institutions that offered international law in the United States.[28] Surprisingly, the contemporary law student is only slightly more likely to have taken a course in international law than her counterpart in 1912.[29] Moreover, although international law is offered more widely in today's law schools,[30] the full incorporation of the subject into legal training remains marginal. For example, there are still no questions on any bar exam concerning international law, no mandatory international law courses, and generally no first-year exposure to the study of international law.[31] This disregard of international law has been particularly disheartening with regard to the teaching of international human rights law. In 1979, only fifteen law schools offered a course or seminar on the subject, and only twenty schools offered such a course in 1990.[32] Despite strides being made to disseminate information and prosecute the perpetrators of human rights violations—events such as state-sponsored terrorism, ethnic genocide, and war crimes such as rape, torture, and the conscription of child soldiers—the subject has yet to become an accepted element in the traditional law school curriculum.[33]

The first-year curriculum in most law schools consists of standard "core courses," including torts, contracts, property, civil procedure, criminal law, and constitutional law. Furthermore, many professors continue to rely on the traditional case method for instruction. A brief look at Langdell's curriculum at Harvard indicates that changes to the first-year legal training have been moderate at best. At the end of the nineteenth century, the primary first-year course of study consisted of:

---

[28] *See* Reed, *supra* note 10, at 301.

[29] *See* Richard B. Bilder and Valerie Epps, *John King Gamble's Teaching International Law in the 1990s*, 87 Am. J. Int'l L. 686, 688 (1993) (book review).

[30] *See* WCL Informal Course Survey, *supra* note 8. One hundred fifty-two (152) of the 160 AALS schools offer a general international law course. *See* id.

[31] *See* id.

[32] *See* Richard B. Lillich, *The Teaching of International Human Rights Law in U.S. Law Schools*, 77 Am. J. Int'l L. 855, 856 (1993).

[33] *See* id. Despite the increase in institutions offering a course or seminar on international human rights law in the 1980s, only 11.9 percent of the 168 schools then listed by AALS offered courses in human rights law. As of March 2000, over half of American law schools offer a course that studies human rights law, but fewer than twenty percent of schools offer more than one course on the topic. *See* WCL Informal Course Survey, *supra* note 8.

1. The Law of Merchants, Contracts
2. Equity
3. Pleading, Practice, and Evidence
4. Criminal Law
5. Real Property[34]

The continued focus on standard courses that remain inextricably attached to domestic concerns is inadequate to prepare lawyers for a new world reality.

Lawyers practicing within this new reality will be challenged by rapidly developing international economic and political links. Rising global technologies, such as satellite communications, establish greater transparency between global actors. The internet and high-tech computer networks now connect the world with the click of a button. Authoritarian political systems are being dismantled and societies are becoming more open.

These changes in the world have impacted what is needed from law schools, calling for a fundamental reconceptualization of legal training. Exclusive reliance on the Langdellian ideology, which treats law as a science in which legal principles are derived by studying selected cases, will not adequately prepare law students for the contemporary world.[35] New forms of communication such as e-mail, the internet, and teleconferencing have exploded onto the scene, enlarging the scope of dialogue and questioning the integrity of legal training. The classical ingredients of legal training—consisting of faculty, students, appellate decisions, and research centers—underestimate the scope of legal training that is demanded by the new world paradigm. The world is now immersed in multiple networks with ever-growing interconnectedness, redefining the needs of legal education.[36]

Inasmuch as individual states can no longer isolate themselves from the international community, legal training can no longer be enveloped within the four walls of a law school. Instead, law schools must connect themselves with the outside world and reconstruct their academic agendas to work with actors in the international community, such as NGOs, multinational

---

[34] Reed, *supra* note 10, at 454.

[35] *See* Weyrauch, *supra* note 7, at 263–63 (emphasizing that although the Langdellian teaching method is still largely adhered to, it nonetheless precludes students from observing facts and understanding social norms).

[36] *See* Grossman and Bradlow, *supra* note 2, at 10.

It is becoming less tenable to classify issues as "international" and therefore as inside the boundaries of international law or as "domestic" and therefore within the jurisdiction of each sovereign state. All issues now have both international and domestic features, in the sense that they influence or are influenced by developments in both the domestic and international arenas. This collapsing distinction between domestic and international calls for a reconceptualization of international law so that these issues can be addressed in their totality and free of the constraints that are created by the artificial distinction between domestic and international issues. Id.

corporations, governments and the legal systems of other countries. In addition, while the study of case law continues to provide an indispensable vehicle for legal training, we now know the importance of expanding legal training beyond this unidimensional approach.

Today, new skills are required in legal education as exemplified by the development of practical and experiential training methodologies. Clinical programs, moot court competitions, study-abroad courses, debate clubs, and an increased reliance on non-legal disciplines such as economics, psychology, political science, anthropology, and sociology have made the study of law based exclusively on readings cases obsolete. Today's law school graduates must have the skills to play the role of facilitators and problem solvers in international transactions. They must also be able to act as liaisons between and among formally organized legal systems with differing national histories, customs, and experiences. Put simply, the philosophical foundation of Langdell's case theory is insufficient to prepare law students for the world they will encounter.

3.3 An Innovative Model of Legal Education

What can be done with regard to the disconnection between domestic-oriented legal training and the global-oriented world system? One approach may be simply to make quantitative changes by sponsoring more research programs, stressing the importance of linguistic diversity, and augmenting the number of international students, faculty, and courses. However, this additive approach does not necessarily provide the typical law student with the diverse interaction that is needed to operate in the new world. In addition, law schools should adopt a qualitative, process-oriented approach that sets into motion the dynamics necessary to transform the traditional, domestically-oriented legal training into training that is interconnected with the world. The building blocks of this approach consist of the following: (A) establishing links between the study of domestic and international law; (B) focusing on different legal systems; (C) including cultural issues in the academic agenda; (D) incorporating the perspectives of other academic disciplines into the study of law; and (E) promoting social change and international awareness through purpose-oriented programs outside of the curriculum.

3.3.1 Establishing Links Between the Study of Domestic and International Law

Virtually every lawyer practicing in the twenty-first century, regardless of his or her practice area, will encounter issues of international law. This reality requires a curriculum that incorporates international law concepts from the very beginning of the law school experience. International law concepts should be woven into courses that have traditionally been thought of as "domestic."[37] For example, international legal research is a necessary element in any introductory course teaching the fundamentals of legal research and writing to first-year students. In the same way, the large first-year introductory doctrinal courses can be made to incorporate elements of the international legal system. Students should be exposed simultaneously to issues that have traditionally been classified as either "domestic" or "international." For example, the first-year torts class at American University's Washington College of Law addresses the "international" components of tort law, such as liability for international crimes. The interplay between "international" and "domestic" spheres is presented to the class in a historical perspective with the aim of showing that their interconnection permeates the law. Students in this first-year class are introduced to the *Paquete Habana* case, a U.S. Supreme Court case decided on the basis of customary international law.[38] The students also study cases brought by foreign nationals in U.S. courts under the Alien Tort Claims Act. These cases help students understand the outer limits of the application of U.S. laws abroad as well as the application of treaty law and customary law within the United States.

Washington College of Law has also adapted traditional law school teaching methodologies to incorporate this global perspective, for example, in the annual Inter-American Human Rights Moot Court Competition.[39] The Competition, based on the jurisprudence of the Inter-American System for the Promotion and Protection of Human Rights, includes foreign students from Spanish and Portuguese speaking law schools.[40] This competition provides the opportunity for students to develop oral argumentation skills and an understanding of human rights issues. The competition is also an innovative way for all students to gain first-hand exposure to international

---

[37] This process also purports to avoid possible conflict between the "domestic" and "international" law school faculty by asserting that this academic division is increasingly untenable.

[38] The Paquete Habana, 175 U.S. 667 (1900). The Paquete Habana was a boat owned by a Cuban fisherman who was a subject of the Spanish crown. During the Spanish-American War, the ship was stopped by an American blockade, condemned as a war prize, and eventually sold at auction despite the protests of the owner that customary international law forbade nations from capturing fishing vessels as prizes of war. The U.S. Supreme Court recognized the binding nature of customary international law, even though the U.S. Constitution fails to mention what authority international law should have in the United States.

[39] The Inter-American Moot Court Competition began in 1996. Since then, more than 500 students and faculty have participated in these annual competitions. The next competition will be held May 17–22, 2009.

[40] According to the competition's rules, only one team can represent each law school. Teams consist of two law students who can be accompanied by a professor or other person who has assisted in the development of the team.

jurisprudence.[41] The Human Rights Moot Court enhances the students' research skills by allowing them to learn to work with a cross-cultural legal team and enabling them to develop friendships with law students from other parts of the hemisphere and the world. Students involved in the competition are also afforded the opportunity to meet current leaders in the field of human rights who serve as judges for the competition.[42] In addition to those students participating in the competition, approximately sixty students are involved in planning the conference each year, including drafting the problem and organizing seminars for participants.

United States law students can also participate in international competitions, such as the annual René Cassin Human Rights Moot Court Competition in Strasbourg, France.[43] The René Cassin competition is based on the European Convention for the Protection of Human Rights and Fundamental Freedoms. The oral phase of the competition takes place in the official Council of Europe courtrooms before judges from the European Court of Human Rights.[44] Competitions such as these teach students to work with legal concepts and procedures outside of the traditional U.S. system.

The convergence of domestic and international law becomes apparent when law schools offer LL.M. programs for foreign lawyers or international law LL.M programs for U.S. law graduates. By uniting American and foreign lawyers such programs demonstrate to both the unity of the national and international systems of law.

3.3.2 Focusing on the Different Types of Legal Systems that Exist Around the World

In addition to understanding the international laws and norms that regulate the conduct of nation states, lawyers practicing in the global environment

---

[41] Each year, competing teams grapple with a hypothetical problem that explores human rights issues, such as women's rights, freedom of expression, states of emergency, amnesty laws, due process guarantees, torture, exhaustion of domestic remedies, and the legality of detention.

[42] The final round of the competition has been judged by such distinguished jurists as Carlos Reina, President of Honduras; Stephen G. Breyer, Associate Justice of the U.S. Supreme Court; ambassadors from the Organization of American States; and members of the Inter-American Commission on Human Rights.

[43] The René Cassin Moot Court Competition is one of the most prestigious competitions in Europe. Each year, over sixty teams from all over the world compete, debating human rights law issues. Teams must submit written legal memoranda before beginning the oral argument phase of the competition. The competition is named after René Cassin, the 1968 Nobel Peace Prize Award winner who helped found UNESCO and was the president of the U.N. Commission on the Rights of Man.

[44] Prior to 1999, judges from the European Commission heard the final oral arguments for the René Cassin competition.

must understand the legal traditions that influence other countries. This requires more than an understanding of the substance of the law, but also an understanding of the legal culture, whether it is common law, civil law, religious law, or customary law. Special courses examining these various traditions, either singly or in comparison, and study abroad opportunities in countries with different legal traditions, give students the opportunity to put the peculiarities of their own legal system into perspective. Such courses provide a knowledge base on various international legal traditions; however, an additional set of courses should be developed to examine the ways in which legal issues can be resolved between parties from countries with different legal systems. Such courses might include: International Conflict of Laws; Judicial Assistance in Transnational Litigation; State Responsibility for the Protection of Foreign Investment; and International Litigation and Arbitration.

Study abroad programs provide further opportunities for students to study and work in countries with different legal traditions. Students can study subjects such as international trade, international human rights, international environmental law, and comparative law in a setting that reinforces their importance. Overseas externship experiences in a host country law firm or an NGO give students perspectives that would not be available at home.[45]

3.3.3 Including Cultural Issues in the Academic Agenda

Lawyers practicing in today's interconnected world must have an understanding of how culture affects the action of individuals and their relationship with a legal system. Study-abroad programs are one of the means of exposing students to these cultural issues by affording them the experience of living, working, and studying in a different culture, but similar opportunities should also be made available through the regular curriculum. For example, the Washington College of Law has an International Human Rights Law Clinic (IHRLC), which focuses on issues of international law and offers an unprecedented opportunity for students to represent individuals, families, or organizations alleging violations of recognized or developing human rights norms. Casework involves international human rights claims before international and domestic tribunals, including those of the Organization of American States (OAS), the United Nations, and the United States.[46] Clinic

---

[45] International externships are supervised through the International Externship Program, *supra* page 24.

[46] In 1998, IHRLC student attorneys assisted both the Spanish court and the British Crown prosecutors in preparing the case against former Chilean dictator General Augusto Pinochet. WCL clinic students drafted legal memoranda on the interaction of international human rights law and domestic legal issues in national courts. During the

students also represent clients in domestic asylum cases before the U.S. Immigration and Naturalization Service, the Executive Office for Immigration Review, the Board of Immigration Appeals, and U.S. federal courts. IHRLC student attorneys are challenged by language and cultural barriers involved in representing clients from foreign countries. Thus, IHRLC students learn the skills that are necessary for the practice of law, but they also learn to apply these skills in an international setting.

Students also benefit from opportunities to work with clients in a multicultural setting through supervised externship programs. Participation in such programs with faculty supervision, allows students to connect their classwork to real-world situations,[47] develop a critical understanding of today's multicultural legal world and gain insights into how the law works in practice.

New technology now makes it possible for students to participate in externships abroad. While overseas, students can stay in touch with their law school teachers through internet communication.

Finally, students can be exposed to cultural issues through their interactions with faculty and students in a diverse law school community. LL.M. students bring diverse experiences to the classroom. While the J.D. student population in U.S. law schools comes primarily from the United States, J.D. students can integrate with LL.M. students in upper-lever classes, ensuring that the multicultural aspect of the school is present in both the J.D. and the LL.M. programs.

3.4 Conclusion

It is vital that we adapt legal pedagogy that reflects the global nature of today's legal reality by rejecting the traditional focus on an autonomous domestic system. In this approach to legal education, new skills will be

---

initial hearing on whether Pinochet should be entitled to immunity as a former head of state, two WCL students traveled to London to assist barristers in the Crown Prosecutor's Office with their legal arguments.

[47] WCL offers subject-specific externship seminars, specializing in areas such as administrative law, public interest law, international human rights, and public international law. If a student does not wish to concentrate her externship in one of these fields, WCL also holds general externship seminars, addressing issues such as the role of lawyers in society or the relationship of feminism to legal practice. In addition to performing their fieldwork assignments and attending seminar classes, externship students are required to keep a daily journal of their work activities and write a paper relating to their externship area. Students are also required to meet frequently in small groups or individually with the faculty member to discuss the progress of their externships. *See* Susan Carle, Peter Jaszi, Marlena Valdez & Ann Shalleck, *Experience As Text: The History of Externship Pedagogy at the Washington College of Law, American University*, 5 Clinical L. Rev. 403 (1999).

identified, social change and awareness will be emphasized, and a cross-cultural perspective will be sought. By experimenting with new and innovative forms of education, the curriculum must break down barriers between LL.M. and J.D. students; between faculty and students; between domestic and international law; between men and women; and among racial and ethnic groups. The consistent encouragement of hands-on interaction with faculty, and interaction with students from all over the world, will sensitize students to different cultural realities, and increase their understanding of the problems confronting the world. This approach seeks to shape an environment that is not restricted to only one view of the world. The law school curriculum should embrace the emerging transnational legal order to create a more open and forward-looking legal education that truly participates in the wider world with which law graduates will have to engage, to pursue successful legal careers.

Chapter 4
Integrating Practical Training and Professional Legal Education

James R. Maxeiner

Reform of legal education is a hot topic. Talk today focuses on practical training. While similar issues are present in every legal system, this discussion will concentrate principally on the three systems of legal education that I know best: the legal systems of the United States, Germany and Japan. All three systems face the problem of how to integrate theory and practice in professional education.

Recently, in the *United States*, the Carnegie Foundation for the Advancement of Teaching released a study, *Educating Lawyers: Preparation for the Profession of Law*. The Foundation castigates American legal education for paying "relatively little attention to direct training in professional practice"[1] and contrasts this with American medical education where there is "growing recognition that medical science is best taught in the context of medical practice. . . ."[2]

At more or less the same time, in *Germany*, the German Lawyers' Association proposed a new legal education law that would completely overhaul

J.R. Maxeiner (✉)
Center for International and Comparative Law, University of Baltimore School of Law, Baltimore, MD, USA
e-mail: jmaxeiner@ubalt.edu

[1] William M. Sullivan, Anne Colby, Judith Welch Wegner, Lloyd Bono and Lee S. Shulman, Educating Lawyers: Preparation for the Profession of Law (The Carnegie Foundation for the Advancement of Teaching Preparation for the Profession Program, 2007) [hereinafter Sullivan]. *See generally* James R. Maxeiner, *Educating Lawyers Now and Then: Two Carnegie Critiques of the Common Law and the Case Method*, 35 Int'l J. Legal Info. (2007); Josef Redlich, The Common Law and the Case Method in American University Law Schools: A Report to the Carnegie Foundation for the Advancement of Teaching, Bulletin No. 8 (1914). Both are reprinted in James R. Maxeiner, Educating Lawyers Now and Then: An Essay Comparing the 2007 and 1914 Carnegie Foundation Reports On Legal Education (Lake Mary Fl: Vandeplas Publishing, 2007).
[2] Sullivan, supra note 1, at 192.

J. Klabbers, M. Sellers (eds.), *The Internationalization of Law and Legal Education*, Ius Gentium: Comparative Perspectives on Law and Justice 2,
DOI 10.1007/978-1-4020-9494-1_4,

post-university legal education there[3] in order to bring about "practical lawyer-training" (*praktische Anwaltsausbildung*).[4]

In 2004, *Japan* actually did completely overhaul its system of legal education. But it *reduced* the practical internship to one year from two years and introduced two-to-three years of law school education between historic undergraduate legal education and practical training.[5]

In all three of these countries legal education, and in particular the practical component of legal education, had been stable for a long time: for a half century in Japan, nearly a century in the United States, and more than a century-and-a-half in Germany. But stability is about the only trait that the three systems shared. In particular, the practice component varied.

Practical training is an issue in legal education because legal education does more than convey legal knowledge: it prepares students for professional practice. Knowledge of law is essential to becoming a jurist. Yet knowledge of law alone is not enough; becoming a lawyer, judge or other legal professional also requires professional skills. Learning substantive knowledge of the law is usually denominated "education," while acquiring practical skills is ordinarily called "training." Legal educators ponder the proper proportions and proper places for legal education and for practical training in the preparation of legal professionals.

In the United States, by the twentieth century, a system of purely professional law school studies replaced a system of purely practice apprenticeship that had prevailed in the first part of the nineteenth century. In twentieth century Germany, even the Nazi dictatorship did not displace the nineteenth-century Prussian system of university study followed by practical court-supervised training in the courts, other government offices and law firms. In Japan, until 2004, the system followed a modified German model.[6] Then Japan moved in the direction of the contemporary

---

[3] *Entwurf eines Gesetzes zur Einführung einer Spartenausbildung in der juristenausbildung: Gesetzentwurf des Deutschen Anwaltvereins* (DAV), 2007 Anwaltsblatt 45.

[4] Hartmut Kilger, *Wie der angehende Anwalt ausgebildte sein muss*, 2007 Anwaltsblatt 1, 3.

[5] *See* James R. Maxeiner and Keiichi Yamanaka, *The New Japanese Law Schools: Putting the Professional Into Legal Education*, 13 Pac. Rim L. & Policy J. 303 (2004).

[6] The old Japanese system had its origin in adaptation of the corresponding German system of the late nineteenth century. Jiro Matsuda, *The Japanese Legal Training and Research Institute*, 7 Am. J. Comp. L. 366, 368 n. 7 (1958). Similarities to the German system remain substantial. *Cf.* Luke Nottage, *Reform, Conservatism and Failures of Imagination in Japanese Legal Education*, Zeitschrift für Japanisches Recht, No. 9, 23, 27 n. 11 (2000). In both systems, aspiring lawyers typically study law at a university for four years after completing secondary (high) school. They then take an examination and, if successful, are admitted to a practical training program to become qualified as judges. Practical training begins with classroom-type instruction in the skills of a judge and continues with several-month apprenticeships at the courts and other legal institutions. Following completion of this practical training period, students take a second bar examination. Those who pass with few exceptions become judges, prosecutors or private

American model, reduced practical training from two years to one, and introduced professional law school study between university study and practical training.

Today's models of legal education in Germany and the United States may now change just as the historic model in Japan recently has. In the United States the Carnegie Foundation, which has proposed changes, has an impressive history of catalyzing change in medical education.[7] In Germany legal education is changing in any case to accommodate the harmonizing Bologna model of the European Union.[8]

4.1 Reasons for Comparative Study of Legal Education

Each of these recent innovations in the United States, Germany and Japan seeks to address the same problem of combining legal knowledge with practical training. Comparing these efforts can help us better to understand the problem at hand, and further improvements that we might make to our own systems of law and legal education.

Still, we should be the first to recognize that legal education is as culturally-determined as any field of professional study. If we didn't know that already, the experiences of the World War II generation of refugee professionals made it clear. I am old enough to have known refugees from the professions of law, medicine and engineering. It is no coincidence that refugee physicians and engineers had more portable careers than did their legal counterparts. The former needed only minor retooling; the latter began the study of their discipline completely anew.

Notwithstanding the national focus of legal education, an understanding of its varied offerings throughout the world today helps us contemplate the options available to each system. Differences in legal and educational systems are so profound that anything resembling a transplant is unlikely. But ideas travel more easily than institutions. Hence it is worthwhile to look at professional legal education comparatively.

This comparison considers three questions central to the integration of legal practice and legal education:

---

attorneys. John Owen Haley, The Spirit of Japanese Law 50 (1998). There is, however, one crucial difference between the systems of lawyer training in Japan and Germany: in Japan the number of candidates admitted to practical training is severely limited.

[7] *See* Molly Cooke, David M. Irby, William Sullivan & Kenneth M. Ludmerer, *American Medical Education 100 Years after the Flexner Report*, 2006 N. Engl. J. Med. 355: 1339.

[8] For the Bologna program and German legal education generally, see Der Bologna-Prozess an den Juristischen Fakultäten (G. Fischer & T. Wünsch, eds., 2006). For another view of current developments in the same three systems, see Martin Kellner, *Legal Education in Japan, Germany, and the United States: Recent Developments and Future Perspectives*, 12 Zeitschrift für Japanisches Recht 195 (2007).

1. Which type of legal professional is being trained?
2. Which skills should practical training teach?
3. Does practical training require apprentice practice?

It must eschew consideration of other questions, as well as detailed consideration of these three.[9]

4.2 Three Questions About Practical Training

4.2.1 Which Kind of Legal Professional is Being Trained?

Fundamental to integrating theory and practice in legal education is deciding which kind of legal professional is to be trained. The answer to this question influences or even determines what constitutes practical training and who should control it.

It is not a question that we think about often in the United States, where we train all students to be lawyers and by tradition our students are not judges until they have been lawyers for years. In Germany one thinks about it more, since in Germany all students are trained to qualify as judges, even if most become lawyers. The situation in Japan has been similar to that in Germany, but in Japan there is great demand for *more* lawyers.

All three systems of legal education share the attribute that their end product is a single type of jurist, potentially suitable for all applications, although trained principally for one. The German language even has a term for it: *Einheitsjurist* or "unitary jurist."[10] None of these systems produces different classes of legal professionals, say judges, lawyers, prosecutors and so on. Nor do they produce lawyers specialized in particular areas such as in criminal law, civil law, or intellectual property law, although the German system does offer some possibilities for specialization in studies.

The choice of which type of jurist should be the focus of legal education has importance beyond the pedagogic. It permeates legal life. In the United States, where all persons who wish to become legal professionals, whether as lawyers or as judges or otherwise, are trained as lawyers, the image of the lawyer-advocate is the ideal-type of legal professional. In Germany, where all persons who wish to become legal professionals, whether as lawyers or

---

[9] Of particular interest are the political and social questions that accompany decisions about practical training, e.g., regarding access to the bar and funding. In Germany, trainees are paid for the period of practical training. In Japan, under the old system that was the case, but now, they must pay for law school. In common law countries, trainees pay for practical courses that precede apprenticeship "articling" where they are paid. Similarly of great interest is how practical training requirements can be used to restrict access to the bar.

[10] *See* Annette Keilmann, *The Einheitsjurist: A German Phenomenon*, 7 German L.J. 293 (2006).

as judges or otherwise, are trained as judges; the image of the judge is the ideal-type of legal professional.[11]

A unitary approach is not, however, essential to legal education. While the German system has long educated all jurists to be judges, the old communist East German system provided not only separate practical training, but also separate university training for lawyers, judges, prosecutors and government lawyers.[12] Until 1947 the Japanese system trained lawyers separately from prosecutors and judges.[13]

Medical education in the United States, which the Carnegie Foundation Report holds up as *the* model for integrating theory and practice, provides highly specialized training. While all American physicians have four years of medical school education in common, they have separate periods of "residency," i.e., practical training, of three or more years, in more than thirty different career paths, where they train to become surgeons, oncologists, gynecologists, and so forth.

4.2.2 The Dilemma of Practical Training: On Which Skills Should It Focus?

Emphasis on practical training gives rise to a dilemma: the more practical training becomes, the less general application it has. While every legal position requires practical skills, those skills are not always the same. Practical training that is useful for one trainee may be useless for another, who pursues a different career path.

American medical education deals with this dilemma by providing more than thirty different courses of practical training. Since these paths are very long—three to seven years—and follow four years of medical school, integral to their success are the perception of participants and the reality that jobs at the end are practically guaranteed.

Unless legal education is able to provide similar guarantees, it should be short in duration and general in scope. Training of short duration minimizes the opportunity costs of the trainees; training that is general in scope

---

[11] *See* Thomas Raiser, *Reform der Juristenausbildung—Förderung von Beratungs- und Gestaltungsaufgaben als Ziel der Juristenausbildung*, 2001 Zeitschrift für Rechtspolitik 418, 422 (observing that German judges are seen to stand above the parties, to be neutral, to not work for money, but selflessly for truth and justice, while attorneys have a more complicated role that requires that they both work in their clients' interests and yet also for justice).

[12] Daniel J. Meador, Impressions of Law in East Germany: Legal Education and Legal Systems in the German Democratic Republic (1987).

[13] Maxeiner, *The New Japanese Law Schools, supra* note 5, at 315 n. 48.

maximizes the chances that what they learn in training will be useful in professional practice.

An oft-cited American report on legal education, the "MacCrate Report," lists ten "Fundamental Lawyering Skills" for future American lawyers. In short form these are:

1) Problem solving
2) Legal analysis
3) Legal research
4) Factual investigation
5) Communication
6) Counseling
7) Negotiation
8) Litigation and Alternative Dispute Resolution
9) Administrative skills necessary to organize and manage legal work
10) Recognizing and resolving ethical dilemmas.

The MacCrate Report describes these as skills for lawyers and not as skills for other legal professionals, such as judges, but for this discussion, we can use them as a stand-in for the practical skills necessary in all areas of the legal profession.

While the MacCrate Report states these skills in general terms, not all of them are equally *transferable*. Some of them, such as communication, counseling and negotiation, and even factual investigation, are highly dependent upon the people for whom they are exercised. Does the lawyer speak the clients' language (literally or figuratively)? Does the lawyer understand their business relationships? Does the lawyer understand the science or craft that underlies their business? Other skills, such as problem solving, legal research and litigation, become ever easier the more a trainee or later professional is familiar with the fields of activity concerned. How well can the lawyer handle transactions of particular importance to these persons? Study of the hiring of experienced lawyers (*i.e.*, lateral hiring) demonstrates the diversity of skills sought in the practice of law. Often, lawyer recruiters look less for the best performers among all candidates, than for very good lawyers with unusual skill sets that fit specific employers well. These skill sets usually include experience with the industry or with specific technical tasks. They often have nothing to do with law.

Of the ten skills just mentioned, the one that is most transferable, the one that is most useful to all jurists, is what Americans term "legal analysis" or "thinking like a lawyer," what Japanese call the "legal mind"[14] and what Germans refer to as "legal thinking." Legal analysis combines theory and practice. It is the teaching and learning of legal methods. "Legal methods" in this context include devices used to relate abstract legal rules to factual

---

[14] Haley, *supra* note 6 at 91.

situations in order to decide concrete cases.[15] This extends to the creation as well as to the implemention of legal rules.[16] Legal methods include: law-making, law-finding, and law-applying.[17]

Legal methods are different in different legal systems. Within these different systems they are taught in different ways and in different places. Whether legal methods pertain to the theory or to the practice of law is subject to contrary conclusions.

In the United States legal methods are taught principally in the first year of professional law school. In Germany legal methods achieve their greatest importance in the first year of training at the courts. In Japan, under the old system, legal methods were taught at the Legal Research and Training Institute in Tokyo; it remains to be seen where they will be taught in the new system.

When and where should learning to think like a lawyer be taught? In 1914, an Austrian law professor, Josef Redlich surveyed American legal education on behalf of the Carnegie Foundation. He concluded that American university law schools had succeeded in incorporating into their curricula one of the most important of practical skills. Redlich asserted that teaching the case method itself constitutes "methodical preparation for the practical calling of law."[18] As proof of the success of the case method, he observed that the best law offices preferred to hire case method trained applicants over all others.[19]

Ironically, so successful were the law schools in bringing legal methods into law school instruction, that 93 years later, the current Carnegie Foundation Report, with no reference to Redlich's report, sees the case method as part of the theory rather than as part of the practice of law.[20]

In Germany it is frequently urged that since 80% of law graduates become lawyers, it is foolish that they all train to be judges.[21] Yet it is in the trainee stage in Germany that legal methods are inculcated into students. During the internship period, they learn the *Relationstechnik* of relating facts to law and of crafting judgments. Judges as classroom teachers didactically teach classes that lay out the fundamentals of this technique, while individual judges, at least in theory, tutor the aspiring legal professionals, the

---

[15] 1 Wolfgang Fikentscher, Methoden des Rechts in Vergleichender Darstellung 13–15 (1975).

[16] *Cf.* Jan Schapp, Hauptprobleme der juristischen Methodenlehre (1983) (relating statute, case, and judicial decision).

[17] *Cf.* Hart, Concept of Law 61 (2nd ed. 1994). Richard B. Cappalli, *The Disappearance of Legal Method*, 70 Temp. L. Rev. 393, 398 (1997).

[18] Redlich, *supra* note 1, at 35.

[19] Id.

[20] Sullivan, *supra* note 1.

[21] German law requires that to become lawyers, candidates must establish their suitability to be judges (*Befähigung zum Richteramt*).

trainees, as apprentice judges. The interns learn how to make use of the substance of the law they learned at the university, how to conduct legal proceedings to determine facts, and how to justify in legal judgments their correct determinations of how law applies to particular cases.[22] In short, they learn to do what a judge has to do in applying the law. And it is the mastery of the techniques of applying law to facts (*Relationstechnik*) that defines the judge.[23]

The German bar is now urging separate tracks for practical training. It sees the training for the profession of judge as something apart from training for the profession of lawyer. Not everyone agrees. The *Relationstechnik*, the most important feature of practical German legal education, is a skill of utmost importance in the daily life of every type of legal professional. It is the mastery of this technique that primarily accounts for the high regard in which German jurists are held the world over. This technique has been a central element in the development of German legal science. The drafters of German laws are all masters of the *Relationstechnik*.

4.2.3 Does Practical Training Require Apprentice Practice?

The most practical of practical training is to learn as a trainee under supervision what one does later as a professional. The Carnegie Foundation Report points to medical education as proving that practice "*comes alive* most effectively" when students personally experience the responsibilities of the profession.[24] In Germany the system of practical training anticipates that trainees, as much as possible, act in their own responsibility."[25]

Pure learning by doing—even after education in theory—however, creates problems of *pedagogy* and of *feasibility*.

The *pedagogic problem* is that professional education should be comprehensive. It should enable trainees to deal with the complete range of problems, at least within a specific field, even if they will never see some of these are problems in practice. Professional practice, on the other hand, mirrors the vagaries of life. It is not comprehensive, but spotty. Not all problems arise. If practical training were to rely exclusively on practice experience, it would miss some problems.

---

[22] *See* Wolfgang Fikentscher, *The Evolutionary and Cultural Origins of Heuristics That Influence Lawmaking, in* Heuristics and the Law 207, 216–19 (G. Gigerenzer and C. Engel, eds., 2006).

[23] *Accord*, Alfred Rinken, Einführung in das juristische Studium 135 (1977).

[24] Sullivan, *supra* note 1 at 197.

[25] Ausbildungs- und Prüfungsordnung für Juristen (JAPO) § 44(2), 2003 Bayerisches Gesetz- und Verordnungsblatt 758, 770, *available at* http://www4.justiz.bayern.de/ljpa/japo/JAPO_2003_Bayern.pdf. [hereinafter JAPO].

One way that practical training programs deal with this pedagogic problem is to include a classroom component. In Bavaria, where there is mandatory practical training, and probably elsewhere in Germany, each step in that practical training includes an introductory classroom component.[26] In Japan, one function of the new professional law schools is to provide this classroom component that previously the Institute conducted. In England, where admission to legal practice requires a two-year practical training period of "articling," the Law Society requires between university education and articling a one year "Legal Practice Course."[27] In the United States, where there is no mandatory practical training for admission to practice, there is mandatory continuing legal education or "CLE". It takes place almost exclusively in classroom settings.

The *feasibility problem* is that there must be productive work for trainees to do; it must be work that they are capable of doing, and it should be work that they later will do as professionals. To solve this problem American medical education brings trainees inside the hospital, where it provides plenty of menial work for even the least-experienced among them, and then gradually, through the system of residency, provides them with ever more challenging work under ever less supervision, which is work that they later will do as professionals.

Do the systems of legal education that we are discussing share the effectiveness of American medical education? The American system does not. The situation is less clear in the German and Japanese systems.

In the United States formal law office training disappeared when law offices, thanks to nineteenth century innovations in office technology such as the typewriter, no longer had copying work for clerks to do.[28] While informal training, *i.e.*, non-mandatory training provided by law firms to their own associates, continues, it is under ever-greater cost pressures to dispense with training. Only the strongest law firms have high value work, such as "due diligence" and "discovery," that can be done by bright, but inexperienced trainees. While this work is useful, it is not all directly relevant to the work lawyers will do as they enter positions of greater responsibility.[29]

---

[26] JAPO § 50(1).

[27] Legal Practice Course Written Standards, *available at* http://www.lawsociety.org.uk/documents/downloads/becominglpcstandards.pdf.

[28] *See, e.g., Untitled Note*, 43 Albany L.J. 490 (1891) ("The law clerk gets but little law in this busy age, especially since the introduction of those labor-saving devices, the stenographer, typewriter and phonograph."); William V. Rowe, *Legal Clinics and Better Trained lawyers—A Necessity*, 11 Ill. R. Rev. 591, 600 (1917) ("The general introduction, since 1880, of telephones, stenographers, typewriters, dictating and copying devices, and improvements in printing...has made students not only unnecessary but also undesirable in most of the active law offices.")

[29] A similar trend is noted in training of medical residents: as medical treatment has become more specialized and hospital stays shorter, residents have less opportunity to

Since the disappearance of formal law office training, American law schools have tried to fill the gap. They use legal clinics to give trainees work in a practice setting. While they have not moved the law school into the courthouse, they have brought clients into the law school.[30] Law school clinics provide legal services to people who would not otherwise receive legal services, by employing law students to do legal work under the supervision of lawyers. While this is not dissimilar to medical education, there are two major differences.

One difference is that public money pays for the medical, but not for legal treatment, of the subjects of service. In academic health centers clinical medical education funds itself; it does not take resources from the classroom. In law schools, on the other hand, not only does clinical legal education not fund itself, it disproportionately takes resources from the classroom, for it is much more labor intensive and expensive than traditional instruction.

Another difference is relevancy. When medical trainees treat those who would otherwise not receive services, they are doing as trainees the tasks that they later will do as professionals. Only the particular patients, but not the tasks, will change. When legal trainees, on the other hand, provide legal services to those who otherwise cannot afford them, they are not providing the same services that most trainees later will provide as professionals. Their clients as professionals will not just be a different type of person; they often will not be natural people at all, but rather legal persons. Legal persons have different legal problems and require different legal services than do natural persons. Already in 1917 one skeptic of legal clinics claimed: "The instruction cannot . . . be skilled instruction. It prepares a student only for a petty practice, and lays no foundations other than technical ones. It is very wasteful of the student's time."[31] One need not accept the characterization of clinical work as "petty" to recognize that its relevance for work in other practice areas is less than in the case of its medical counterpart. No wonder that few law schools have ever made clinical legal work mandatory, while medical schools all require clinical experience.

In Germany and in Japan practical legal training more closely approaches the model of American medical education. Much as American academic health centers provide practical medical training, German and Japanese "law centers," *i.e.*, the courts, provide practical legal training. In Japan, where numbers of trainees are low, finding work for trainees does not seem to have been a problem. In Germany, until recently, there have been

---

learn. *See* Institute of Medicine, Academic Health Centers: Leading Change in the twenty first Century (2003) at 82, available at www.iom.edu.

[30] *See, e.g.*, E.M. Morgan, *The Legal Clinic*, 4 Am. L. School Rev. 255 (1917); Rowe, *supra* note 28. *Compare Law Apprenticeships*, 5 Alb. L. J. 97 (1872).

[31] O.L. McCaskill, *Methods of Teaching Practice*, 2 Cornell L.Q., 299, 312 (1917). *See* Maxeiner, *Educating Lawyers, supra* note 1, text at notes 130–132.

opportunities enough to keep trainees busy. As office technology improves and the number of trainees increases it may become more difficult to find meaningful tasks for them to do. German judges now often use dictaphones or enter their own data directly into personal computers. All the while, the number of trainees has increased substantially.

Another advantage that German and Japanese practical legal training share with American medical training is institutional. Ministries of justice and academic health centers, i.e., hospitals, are relatively large bureaucratic entities. That situation makes it easier for them to set and enforce standards of trainee instruction. They can dedicate personnel to trainee instruction. When practical training is the province of the bar, the maintenance of standards is inherently more difficult. Practical training is likely to be more uneven in quality. Indeed, uneven quality is already a problem in Germany with respect to the law office side of existing practical training.

Even if the German system can continue to find enough useful work for trainees to do to justify the public funding of their modest stipends, can the system provide work that is relevant to their later activity as professionals? A focus of present day criticisms of German practical education is that it is not sufficiently directed to the requirements of legal practice. That argument, of course, assumes that judicial training is not relevant to practice as a lawyer. The correctness of that assumption depends upon which skills are taught to trainees.

4.3 Conclusion

We are all prisoners of our experiences. American lawyers, who have not received formal practical training, may be skeptical about its usefulness.

Even so, it is not difficult to see the value of the first year of German practical training. Although some in Germany consider the *Relationstechnik* to be merely a workmanlike skill, its rigor is what makes German legal science possible. Moreover, the German state ministries of justice seem to do a good job of conveying this valuable skill to all German jurists. Similarly, the first year of American law school teaching, while somewhat detached from reality, has many benefits, among which is providing a good crash-course introduction to American legal methods. Whether these skills are denominated as theory or practice, they are essential to the legal enterprise and to every professional jurist of whatever type.

Beyond this, however, there are obvious limits to the benefits of formal practical training for future lawyers. The greatest value of medical practical training is that trainees do actually learn by doing. But that system more-or-less presupposes that the trainees who learn by doing end up as professionals doing the same things. It expects a degree of specialization that is yet to be found in most legal practice.

Lawyers can and do definitely learn by doing. Anyone who has ever practiced law can testify to this reality. I myself practiced law as a government prosecutor, a litigation law firm associate, and an in-house counsel. There were many practical skills that I needed in practice that I did not learn in law school. Many of these skills I learned before I went to law school; many I learned after law school while in practice. I spent more than 14 of those years working for just four legal persons. Had I known in law school the form that my career would take, I could have made study plans accordingly. But I knew then neither that I would be working for these four persons nor what I would be doing for them. Had I prepared myself more for them, that preparation would have been largely wasted had I worked for almost any other employer. Upon reflection, I am hard-pressed to identify practice skills that I could reasonably have learned in a practical training setting that I did not learn in the six hours of practice courses that I had.

This personal experience illustrates the nature of the problem. The difficulty lies not so much in the integration of theory and practice as in integrating practical training and practice. The aspiring professional is going to learn by doing in any case. The principal issue is whether that learning by doing takes place in a formal or in an informal setting. The aspiring professional will be disappointed and bored if practical training can not be directly related to what he or she later does in practice.

Chapter 5
Internationalizing the American Law School Curriculum (in Light of the Carnegie Foundation's Report)

Larry Catá Backer

5.1 Introduction[1]

Over a century ago, influential members of the public began to worry about the social order. In the face of large numbers of immigrants with no cultural connection to English social and political values,[2] and significant class distinctions arising as a consequence of the great revolution in American

L.C. Backer (✉)
Penn State Dickinson School of Law, Pennsylvania State University, Pennsylvania, USA
e-mail: lbacker@tulane.edu

[1] A note on footnoting for this essay, placed, ironically enough, in a footnote: I have deliberately attempted to avoid over-footnoting or footnoting exhaustively. For many, pedantic footnoting may serve as a sort of proxy for assurance that the author has read all the appropriate sources and has been appropriately schooled in the proper boundaries of the debate in which she is participating. While there is a certain logic to these assumptions in specific contexts—the Ph.D. dissertation, and perhaps even the pre-tenure "masterpiece"—my object here is to duplicate neither experience. *See* Arthur D. Austin, *Footnote Skullduggery and Other Bad Habits*, 44 U. Miami L. Rev. 1009 (1990). I am also mindful of Alan Watson's astute observation of the danger of losing the power of insight in bloated articles. *See* Alan Watson, The Shame of American Legal Education (Lake May, FL: Vandeplas Publishing, 2005).

[2] *See*, e.g., Morton Borden, Jews, Turks, and Infidels (Chapel Hill, NC: University of North Carolina Press, 1984); Ellen Condliffe Langemann, The Politics of Power: The Carnegie Corporation, Philanthropy and Public Policy (Chicago, IL: University of Chicago Press, 1992). The author profited greatly from the insights offered to him by his many colleagues at the Tulane Law School who were part of the *Educating Lawyers* reading group. He also profited from discussions with colleagues at Penn State and other law schools, especially Professors Tiyanjana Maluwa (former legal advisor to the Office of the United Nations High Commissioner for Human Rights and the first legal counsel to the Organization of African Unity), William Butler (formerly chair in comparative law at the University of London and founder and director of the Vinogradoff Institute in Moscow), S. Beth Farmer (former director of Penn State's overseas program for students in London), and Melissa Tatum (Tulsa Native American and international programs). I am grateful to my former student, Gregory Alvarez (Penn State '06) for insightful perspectives from that other critical group of stakeholders in the law school enterprise. My research assistant

J. Klabbers, M. Sellers (eds.), *The Internationalization of Law and Legal Education,* Ius Gentium: Comparative Perspectives on Law and Justice 2,
DOI 10.1007/978-1-4020-9494-1_5,

business and industry,[3] all sorts of groups arose to help "fix" the problems that might have been viewed as threatening the Republic.[4] This was the age of the Progressive Party and a new sort of Enlightenment progressivism in the United States committed to the idea that social problems could be fixed and made better, and that the application of "scientific" or "rational" principles could overcome any difficulties.[5]

Among the more pressing issues of the early twentieth century was the training of lawyers. The late nineteenth century saw a revolution in the legitimacy of methods for the training of lawyers. Abandoning the traditional system of training in customary (common) law systems, the new scientific age successfully gave rise to a new science of law and legal training based in the University and not (as before) in the offices of practicing lawyers.[6] By the early twenty-first century, the law school stood triumphant atop a system of certification for entry into legal practice in the United States. But that triumph has not gone without a certain amount of criticism. On the one hand, some critics have suggested that the present system may not be up to reflecting the change, actual or hoped for, within American society.[7] Others have suggested the need for a more rigorous academic training.[8] Still others have suggested the need to reform the legal profession itself rather than its system of legal education.[9]

Yet other influential groups, almost from the inception of the turn to academic legal education, have suggested a certain danger in the increasingly

---

Augusto Molina Roman (Penn State '09) did excellent work above and beyond the call of duty. Of course, the views expressed here are strictly those of the author.

[3] *See*, e.g., Mink, Gwendolyn, Old Labor and New Immigrants in American Political Development Union, Party, and State, 1875–1920 (Ithaca, NY: Cornell University Press, 1986).

[4] *See* Haas, Garland A. The Politics of Disintegration: Political Party Decay in the United States, 1840–1900 (Jefferson, N.C.: McFarland & Co., 1994); Paul Kleppner, The Third Electoral System, 1853–1892: Parties, Voters, and Political Cultures (Chapel Hill, NC: University of North Carolina Press, 1979).

[5] *See*, e.g., Harold Howland, Theodore Roosevelt and His Times: A Chronicle of the Progressive Movement (New Haven, CT: Yale University Press, 1921).

[6] *See*, e.g., William P. Lapiana, Logic and Experience: The Origin of Modern American Legal Education (New York, NY: Oxford University Press, 1994).

[7] *See*, e.g., Noel Lynn, Inside Law School: Two Dialogues about Legal Education (Calgary, Alberta, Canada: University of Calgary Press, 1999).

[8] *See* Alan Watson, The Shame of American Legal Education (Lake May, FL: Vandeplas Publishing, 2005) (Most law professors are plumbers, but they wish to be regarded as philosophers, hence, they are poor plumbers).

[9] *See* Deborah Rhode, In the Interests of Justice: Reforming the Legal Profession (New York, NY: Oxford University Press, 2000) ("This mismatch between what law schools supply and what law practice requires argues for a different approach. The diversity in America's legal needs demands corresponding diversity in its legal education. Accreditation frameworks should recognize in form what is true in fact. Legal practice is becoming increasingly specialized. It makes little sense to require the same training for the Wall Street securities specialist and the small town matrimonial lawyer." Id. at 190).

academic character of legal training. Among the most persistent and influential of this group has been the Carnegie Foundation.[10] Over the course of the last century, it has fought a losing battle to alter the course of American legal education. It has sought to recognize the class divisions in American legal practice by a corresponding diversity in the forms of legal education offered.[11] Additional studies of legal education, important in their time, were produced in the 1970s and 1990s.[12]

The Carnegie Foundation has now published the results of its latest study of legal education in the United States. That study "involved a comprehensive look at teaching and learning in American and Canadian law schools today. Intensive field work was conducted at a cross-section of 16 law schools during the 1999–2000 academic year."[13] Published in book form as *Educating Lawyers: Preparation for the Profession of Law*,[14] the study is bound to have serious impact, though whether that impact will be successful or permanent remains to be seen. *Educating Lawyers* is supposed to provide "an opportunity to rethink 'thinking like a lawyer'—the paramount educational construct currently employed, which affords students powerful intellectual tools while also shaping education and professional practice in subsequent years in significant, yet often unrecognized, ways."[15] The principal thesis is that academic law is losing touch with both its roots in the practice of law and its mission to educate lawyers for practice. However, through practical application of the techniques offered, grounded in a change in the fundamental conception of the nature of the legal education enterprise, legal

---

[10] The Carnegie Foundation for the Advancement of Teaching was founded in 1905 and chartered in 1906 by an act of Congress. The Carnegie Foundation for the Advancement of Teaching is an independent policy and research center with a primary mission "to do and perform all things necessary to encourage, uphold, and dignify the profession of the teacher and the cause of higher education." Carnegie Foundation for the Advancement of Teaching, The Carnegie Foundation, available at http://www.carnegiefoundation.org/ (last accessed Feb. 1, 2008).

[11] *See* Alfred Z. Reed, Training for the Public Profession of Law (New York, NY: Carnegie Foundation, 1921) (also noting the race, religious and ethnic divisions cemented or privileged by that division).

[12] *See* Herbert Packer and Thomas Ehrlich, New Directions in Legal Education (1972); and Ernest Boyer, Scholarship Reconsidered (1990). For a history of the Carnegie Foundation's efforts, *see* Ellen Condliffe Langemann, Private Power for the Public Good; A History of the Carnegie Foundation for the Advancement of Teaching (New York: College Examination Board, 1999).

[13] Carnegie Foundation for the Advancement of Teaching, Program Areas, Legal Education Study, available at http://www.carnegiefoundation.org/programs/index.asp?key=1819 (last accessed Jan. 28, 2008).

[14] William M. Sullivan, Anne Colby, Judith Welch Wegner, Lloyd Bond, Lee S., Shulman, Educating Lawyers: Preparation for the Profession (San Francisco, CA: Jossey-Bass, 2007) [hereafter *Educating Lawyers*].

[15] Carnegie Foundation for the Advancement of Teaching, Program Areas, Legal Education Study, available at http://www.carnegiefoundation.org/programs/index.asp?key=1819 (last accessed Jan. 28, 2008).

education can be appropriately redirected. What is new is the suggestion that the ends of legal education ought not to be confined to the teaching of legal doctrine and analysis, but should also include an equal dose of "the several facets of practice included under the rubric of lawyering"[16] and a broad "emphasis on inculcation of the identity, values, and dispositions consonant with the fundamental purpose of the legal profession,"[17] a purpose left substantially undefined.

Ironically enough, at about the same time over a century ago, many groups and institutions engaged in the education of lawyers were beginning to face the realities of the importance of transborder activities, especially of activities arising from the creation of national markets and practices within the United States. Some reacted by digging more deeply into their traditional state-oriented curricula and methods of training. Others, including what emerged as key groups of academic legal educators, embraced the challenge of this new reality. By the last third of the twentieth century, most law schools, more or less enthusiastically, had embraced a "national law practice" model as the foundation of their teaching and research missions.[18] Though the foundations of that model have been challenged as perpetuating the power of wealthy elites and contributing to the subordination of ethnic, religious and racial groups,[19] and though some sectors of legal education have sought to avoid its pull,[20] there are few who deny

[16] *Educating Lawyers, supra* note 14, at 194.

[17] Id.

[18] For a general history of legal education in the United States, *see*, e.g., Robert Stevens, Law School: Legal Education in America from the 1850s to the 1980s (Chapel Hill, NC: University of North Carolina Press, 1983). The national model is reinforced by the American Bar Association through its role in the accreditation process. For materials on this process, *see* the materials at American Bar Association, Section on Legal Education and Admission to the Bar, available at http://www.abanet.org/legaled/ (last accessed Feb. 14, 2007). It is also cultivated through the production of sets of acceptable cultural norms for the providers of legal education articulated through the organs of the collective representative organizations of American legal education, such as, the Association of American Law Schools. *See* Association of American Law Schools, What is the AALS?, Purpose and Description, available at http://www.aals.org/about.php (accessed on or before Mar. 30, 2008) ("The AALS is a non-profit association of 168 law schools. The purpose of the association is 'the improvement of the legal profession through legal education.' It serves as the learned society for law teachers and is legal education's principal representative to the federal government and to other national higher education organizations and learned societies." Id.).

[19] *See*, e.g., Jerold S. Auerbach, Unequal Justice: Lawyers and Social Change in Modern America (New York, NY: Oxford University Press, 1977) (suggesting that the elite nature of the profession and its emphasis on serving its business interests served to exclude participation by minorities).

[20] And, indeed, there are law schools within the United States that remain substantially unchanged—focusing deliberately on a curriculum limited by the territorial boundaries of the state in which they are established, or on educating traditionally underserved communities. In a bar admission context grounded on licensing by states, this approach

the power of the "national model" as the dominant ideology of law school education.[21]

Today, law schools that embraced the national law model face a challenge similar to that confronted a century ago.[22] Instead of confronting the challenge of a "national" practice, legal education now confronts the realities of multi-jurisdictional practice, sometimes described as the internationalization of law and legal practice, with little more than a heavily traditional set of approaches to teaching and scholarship.[23] Legal practice, traditionally grounded in the laws of states from which American lawyers are licensed, and substantially overlain with national rule systems affecting virtually every aspect of legal relations in the United States, now increasingly includes activities dependent on the application of rule or norm systems beyond that of the state or nation. Everything from large-scale global business activity to the movement of goods, people and services on even the most modest scale involves the influence of issues that require familiarity with norms and legal systems other than the one from which a lawyer derives her license to practice law. Greater possibilities for the free movement of lawyers, as well as the provision of legal services, across borders are becoming a larger reality in the market for legal services. Indeed, some within the legal academy have begun to recognize the necessity that legal education confront the realities of the international and transnational multi-jurisdictional market in which law graduates will practice their profession.[24]

Most law schools are not completely unprepared to respond to these challenges. Many have some faculty, and some programs, focusing on one

---

offers some schools a limited advantage in attracting students who are sure about where and what they wish to practice. California and Georgia, are examples.

[21] Even its critics suggest that any necessary deviation from the dominant normative model is "costly." Many arguments, then, are based on the idea that specific benefits from deviation are greater than its detriments. *See*, e.g., Marina Lao, *Discrediting Accreditation?: Antitrust and Legal Education*, 79 Wash. U. L. Q. 1035, 1075 (2001). Others have suggested less drastic deviations from the "one size fits all model." For a discussion, *see* Daniel J. Morrissey, *Saving Legal Education*, 56 J. Legal Educ. 254, 277–280 (2006) (technology based changes and education through law school consortia drawing on collective strengths).

[22] *See* Harold Hongju Koh, *Luncheon Address* (May 17, 2006), in American Law Institute Remarks and Addresses 83rd Annual Meeting, Washington, D.C., pp. 65–89.

[23] Academics have noted the coming of this reality for a number of years. *See*, e.g., Louis F. Del Duca, Vanessa P. Sciarra, *Developing Cross-Border Practice Rules: Challenges and Opportunities for Legal Education*, 21 Fordham Intl. L. J. 1109 (1998); Roger J. Goebel, *Professional Qualification and Educational Requirements for Law Practice in a Foreign Country: Bridging the Cultural Gap*, 63 Tul. L. Rev. 443, 447 (1989).

[24] *See*, e.g., Laurel S. Terry, *GATS' Applicability to Transnational Lawyering and its Potential Impact on U.S. State Regulation of Lawyers*, 34 Vand. J. Transnatl. L. 989, 995 (2001). Some have suggested a value "in itself" of such an education. *See* Jan Klabbers, *Legal Education in the Balance: Accommodating Flexibility*, 56 J. Leg. Educ. 196 (2006).

or another component of multi-jurisdictional practice beyond national borders. The great organs of the production of legal education culture also have begun to emphasize the importance of this maturing, but still largely nascent reorientation of legal practice.[25] How law schools confront the challenge posed by the realities of human activity, and by legal systems that no longer respect the niceties of the political borders of nation-states, will determine the shape of legal education for the future. Law schools that fail to conform their educational mission to the realities of law and the practices of the great global legal actors—merchants, immigrant communities, nongovernmental organizations, economic entities, banks and other users of legal services—will find themselves playing a limited role in the future of the development of law and the production of law and lawyers for the global marketplace. Certainly the bar has begun to recognize this reality, even well outside the centers of traditional internationalist practice.[26]

In a number of forward looking law schools, or law schools looking to leverage niche competence into reputation gains within the legal academy, faculty have begun to examine this problem with a view to developing a comprehensive analysis of matters related to the multi-jurisdictional "component" of their law schools.[27] In some cases, that analysis is tied to the development of relationships with other related faculties of the universities in which the law school is resident. For example, some universities have established schools of international affairs, international relations or foreign service, with curricular objectives that might run parallel to those being

---

[25] The current round of cultural production was kicked off in 2000 in the context of a Conference of International Legal Educators, hosted through the AALS, the contributions for which may be accessed at http://www.aals.org/2000international (last accessed Feb. 7, 2007). The AALS then noted that the Conference "represents its strong commitment to foster more cooperative efforts among law schools throughout the world. The time has long since past that anybody can be educated members of society and the legal profession without developing an understanding of other cultures and legal systems." Id. This was followed by a widely touted conference, hosted in Hawaii in 2004 by the AALS, entitled Educating Lawyers for Transnational Challenges, the proceedings of which are available at http://www.aals.org/international2004/ (last accessed Feb. 8, 2007). The conference was "designed not only to bring about a dialogue concerning the education of graduates for a transnational law practice, but also to consider formulating a possible curriculum outline for a law school that seeks to educate its graduates for such a practice." Id.

[26] *See*, e.g., Janet H. Moore, *Going Global: A Guide to Growing an International Practice*, 69 Tex. B.J. 998 (Nov. 2006). Texas, like other border states, has a long history of dealing with law that crosses national borders. *See*, e.g., Chris Wolfe, April A. Strahan, *An Overview of the History of Foreign Legal Consultants Between the United States and Mexico*, 47 S. Tex. L. Rev. 557 (2006).

[27] *See* discussion, e.g., Jeffery Atik and Anton Soubbot, International Legal Developments in Review: 2001; *Public International Law, International Legal Education*, 36 Intl. Law. 715, 717 (2002).

contemplated for the international and transnational focus of a law school. The creation of formal relationships with such existing institutions might provide an efficient means to incorporate a transnational element into legal education.[28] In other cases, it may be tied to a leveraging of established programs of graduate legal education for foreign lawyers.[29]

Basic to any such analysis is a consideration of core pedagogical issues, such as the courses offered and their content.[30] In addition, other important components would have to be identified and considered, including programs for foreign students, the addition of masters and SJD programs in international law and related disciplines for law students and others who qualify, other degree offerings, affiliations (both formal and informal, and both institutional and personal) with foreign institutions, and the institution of other programs abroad for law students, foreign or "domestic," including certificate programs and summer and semester programs abroad.[31] Even clinical programs can become international.[32]

Thus two great movements in legal education have been gaining momentum and legitimacy within the legal academy. On the one hand, there is the century-long dialogue about the nature of legal education and its connection to the bench and bar within the United States. On the other

---

[28] At Penn State, for example, the Penn State Board of Trustees at its January 19, 2007 meeting approved an affiliated School of International Affairs for implementation. *See* Pennsylvania State University, *Penn State Establishes New School of International Affairs Intimately Linked with Law School*, available at http://www.dsl.psu.edu/news/IntlAffairs.cfm (accessed on or before Mar. 30, 2008).

[29] *See*, e.g., Carole Silver, *Internationalizing U.S. Legal Education: A Report on the Education of Transnational Lawyers*, 14 Cardozo J. Intl. Comp. L. 143 (2006) ("Law schools experience financial and reputational gains from their graduate programs for foreign law graduates. These programs internationalize the student bodies of law schools, which schools use as evidence of their international and even global characters. While the international character of a law school may stem from its LL.M. program, the significance of the international label addresses a law school's ability to attract applicants for its J.D. program as well." Id. at 154).

[30] This can be a difficult issue, even in well-defined areas of law. *See*, e.g., Larry Catá Backer, *Human Rights and Legal Education in the Western Hemisphere: Legal Parochialism and Hollow Universalism*, 21 Penn St. Intl. L. Rev. 115 (2002). For a discussion of the development of special courses targeted specifically to teaching or introducing the transnational dimension in US legal education, *see*, e.g., discussion *infra* at notes 124–134.

[31] For certificate programs in legal education, *see*, Larry Catá Backer, *General Principles of Academic Specialization By Means of Certificate or Concentration Programs: Creating a Certificate Program in International, Comparative and Foreign Law at Penn State*, 20 Penn St. Intl. L. Rev. 67 (2001).

[32] *See* Karen Barton, Clark D. Cunningham, Gregory Todd Jones, Paul Maharg, *Valuing What Clients Think: Standardized Clients and the Assessment of Communicative Competence*, 13 Clinical L. Rev. 1 (2006); Dina Francesca Haynes, *Client Centered Human Rights Advocacy*, 13 Clinical L. Rev. 379 (2006); Richard J. Wilson, *Training for Justice: The Global Reach of Clinical Legal Education*, 22 Penn St. Intl. L. Rev. 421 (2004).

hand, there is the half-century-long search for the expansion of the core areas of law that ought to form part of the basic instruction in American law schools, and the practice of the bench and bar. But these two great movements have been developing in parallel streams. There has been little in the way of communication between these two tendencies. They do not take cognizance of each other. Yet they have great potential for fruitful co-operation. This paper will advocate greater communication between these two schools of thought.

The conversation grows naturally out of the Carnegie Report on *Educating Lawyers*. The Carnegie approach rests on certain basic assumptions about legal education. These assumptions both frame and may limit the suggestions for change. The nature of the limitations inherent in the foundational assumptions of the study provide important insights into the scope of the proposals set out in *Educating Lawyers*. The attitude changes proposed in its Introduction and Chapter One are elaborated as practice models in the remaining chapters of the work. Yet for all of its theoretical insights, the reality of the practical suggestions made in the Carnegie Report will have little effect on the drift of legal academic education. This is inevitable in the context of great changes in American law itself, as it departs ever further from its common law roots and embraces in theory and in fact a different framework for understanding law and the relationship between law and lawyers. There are significant lacunae in the Carnegie approach. The most prominent of these omissions appears as an assumption of the purely domestic nature of the law in which American law students must be trained. The dangers of modifying an ancient approach for modern times are the likelihood that the foundational frameworks within which these constructions are offered have been altered. This is also true of the content of the law that American lawyers must practice. Just as the law among states within the union was at the frontier of American legal education in the early part of the twentieth century, so now are the laws among nation-states and the law of a variety of communities of states at the frontier of American legal education in the twenty-first century. The failure to consider the impact of these changes marks a significant weakness in *Educating Lawyers* that will limit its utility. Yet the insights of *Educating Lawyers* ought to be applicable in the expanding context of the law to be taught, a consideration taken up in Section 5.4 of this study.

Section 5.3 critically examines several strands of proposals for the incorporation of aspect of transnational legal education in the curricula of American law schools. The paper suggests an analytical framework for evaluating these interaction proposals and for evaluating the ways in which these methods seek to incorporate the international and transnational element in law school curricular, research and service activities. Specifically, Section 5.4 will offer a possible structure for the analysis of the value of integrating transnational elements within law school teaching, research and service. The proposals themselves can be divided into five categories—three are modifications or extensions of traditional approaches to curricular issues. The three traditional models—the integration, aggregation and segregation models—each seeks to modify existing resources and teaching/research models to incorporate a transnational element into the curriculum. Each model offers a number of benefits but also has some weaknesses. Two other approaches, an immersion model and a separation model, are best understood as departures from traditional curricular models in legal education. The immersion model applies the lessons of economic globalization to the business of legal education. Its success depends on the ability of a law school to forge effective networks with law schools in other states. The separation model is based on the idea that the transnational element in law is distinct enough to merit a substantial treatment in its own right. Grounded in the notion that international and transnational law is somehow different from traditional practice, the separation model would extract all international and transnational legal studies—teaching and research—from the undifferentiated law school curriculum and place it within associated or affiliated departments of international law or international affairs that are more than just a separate law department, providing the focus for a multi-disciplinary pedagogy built around the study of legal regimes that cross borders.

Section 5.4 considers these models of integration in light of the foundational model of apprenticeship proposed in *Educating Lawyers*, suggesting the great tensions between the approaches to integrating transnational law into American legal education and integrating practice elements from *Educating Lawyers*. It will also describe the possibilities of integrating the apprenticeship models of *Educating Lawyers* within frameworks for integrating transnational legal education into American law schools.

5.2 Educating Lawyers and a Reconstituted Framework for Preparation for the Profession of Law

Educating Lawyers is meant to respond to a crisis of professionalism.[33] "For professional education, the question is how to provide a powerful experience of what it means to take up a profession."[34] That question is the core problem taken up by the study. The providers of legal education have lost touch with the ethical objectives of the profession.[35] The Carnegie Reports make a number of core assumptions about the relationship between

---

[33] *Educating Lawyers, supra* note 14, at 29–33.

[34] Id. at 30.

[35] "Ethics in a professional curriculum ought to provide a context in which students and faculty alike can grasp and discuss, as well as practice, the core commitments that define the profession." Id. at 31.

academic legal education and its stakeholders. *Educating Lawyers* starts with a presumption that the principal stakeholder of legal education is the bar, and that the bar has assumed a critical role in the functioning of the American state.[36] It interrogates this function through what it describes as "an unusual angle of vision."[37]

Law schools and the legal profession, however, have never worked together as a harmonious whole. They have never fully shared the same set of norms, tasks, goals and incentives. Perhaps before the creation of law schools, lawyers and law instructors were fungible and interchangeable and shared a common culture, with similar objectives, frames of reference, professional incentives and the like. Law instructors may have served the interests of the bench and bar, as then constituted. Once law schools replaced apprenticeship as the primary form of legal education, the aims and interests of law instructors and other legal professionals began to diverge.[38] The authors of *Educating Lawyers* somewhat charitably describe this split as producing a "hybrid institution." This hybrid blends two distinct and not necessarily complementary communities—that of the ancient traditions of the common law bar, and that of the so-called modern research university.[39] But what should have been a happy union has gone bad—"as American law schools have developed, their academic genes have become dominant."[40] Thus, the overall goal of *Educating Lawyers* is to give greater influence to the practicing bar.[41] To achieve that purpose, *Educating Lawyers* proposes a unitary framework for education through which the doctrinal, practical and ethical elements of legal practice can be integrated[42] within the normative context of a university environment in the form of a set of three related apprenticeships of professional education.[43]

The question remains whether this sort of hybrid unity is possible within the context of an enterprise (university sourced professional education) that is neither fish nor fowl. Part of the problem, well identified by the authors, is described by them as a set of powerful "external factors."[44] But what the authors characterize as external factors are in reality a set of internal factors—internal, that is, to the values and practices of the academic community within which law schools operate. These include the

---

36 "Thus, the focus of this book is on the preparation of lawyers, more particularly on their preparation in law school—the crucial portal to the practice of law." Id. at 1.
37 Id. ("[f]ocusing on the daily practices of teaching and learning through which future legal professionals are formed." Id. at 2–3")
38 Id. at 4–7.
39 Id. at 4.
40 Id.
41 Id. at 12–15.
42 Id. at 194–197.
43 Id. at 27–29.
44 Id. at 33–34.

disciplinary mechanism of ranking by outsiders[45] and the costs of providing the sort of education that students are willing to pay for.[46] It is difficult, though, to understand why those factors are external to the university as such. Whatever their demerits, the standards used represent in large measure the decision taken both by industry leaders (the so-called top schools) and the consumers of those services (the bar and potential students). They serve as a significant disciplinary tool for the organization of academic communities and affect decisions with respect to the allocation of resources and the competition for faculty in ways that are internal to legal education as part of a university community.[47]

At least some of the factors identified by the Carnegie Report could be seen as "external." Teaching to the test (the bar examination) might be considered to be external to the law school[48]—but that analysis fails if we adhere to the initial assumption that law schools are hybrid institutions. The bar examination may be external to the law school as an academic institution, but it is hardly external to the law school in its role as part of the community of the bar. The bar examination, in that sense, is no more external to the law school than an examination in any course offered within the institutional framework of the university. Likewise, the hiring practices of the leading law firms are hardly external to the institution grounded in its principal relationship with the bar.[49] Decisions of the legal academy's principal stakeholder (as identified in *Educating Lawyers*) here serves an appropriate disciplinary role, but one internal to the institution itself. Hybridity, in this context, makes for complexity. But the extent of the external impediments may be far smaller, and contain more internal contradictions, than that in non-hybrid systems.

The greater problem is normative and might be insurmountable. The authors spend a bit of time identifying, and then ignoring, the crucial dilemma of legal education: the nature of law and the function of the legal profession within it. Since the mid nineteenth century there has been a contest in the United States for the "soul" of law.[50] The progressive nature of American culture began to see the customary law as increasingly obsolete, or at best an impediment to progress. Scientific principles that began to seem more important in all of the social sciences eventually found form in the

---

[45] Id. at 33.

[46] Id.

[47] "Within academic circles, legitimacy and respectability accrued to whatever could be assimilated to the model of formal, science like discourse." Id. at 6.

[48] Id. at 33.

[49] Id.

[50] *See* Larry Catá Backer, *Reifying Law: Understanding Law Beyond the State*, 26 Penn St. Intl. L. Rev. 511 (2008).

science of law.[51] That science, founded on a need to make sense and give order to law (in the sense understood in the great codification efforts in Europe, and especially Germany), produced a great movement toward positivism that has, to some extent, overcome the ancient foundations of the self-conception of the bench and bar, and the understanding of its mission within the American legal framework.[52] "Law entered the American [u]niversity at a time when attempts to blend academic and practitioner traditions of legal training resulted in what was, in some respects, less a reciprocal enrichment than a protracted hostile takeover."[53]

The problem is not merely methodological—as assumed by the proposals in *Educating Lawyers*—but part of a complex contest for the control of the production of knowledge, and especially for control of the understanding of law in the United States. The contest between the bar and the university represents, in symbolic form, a larger contest between the customary law origins and culture of the early American Republic, with the needs and aspirations of a positive law state into which the United States is evolving. This contest, now over a century old, has been decided for all practical purposes—and the traditional bench and bar, as guardians of the customary law, have lost.[54] In this respect, *Educating Lawyers* fails before it starts, at least with respect to the grand vision of restoring balance between the bar and the university communities represented in legal academic education. The bar is now necessarily a junior partner in the enterprise. So the critical mission now becomes much more modest: to preserve some sort of role for the bar within an academic enterprise that serves the interests of a positivist legal order in which lawyers have a more pervasive but much diminished role.

"In the world of legal theory, this new spirit was exemplified in the efforts of legal positivists, who viewed law as an instrument of rational policymaking—a set of rules and techniques rather than a craft of interpretation and adaptation embedded in the common law."[55] Nothing has changed. Although *Educating Lawyers* may lament this passage of power from the bar to the legislator and the academic, it does not propose

---

[51] The authors of *Educating Lawyers* put it less provocatively. *See Educating Lawyers, supra* note 14, at 5.

[52] *See* Id. ("All this spelled the eclipse of traditional forms of practitioner-directed apprenticeship by academic instruction given by scholar teachers." Id.).

[53] Id.

[54] Indeed, the authors of *Educating Lawyers* suggest this in their reminder of the century long struggle of the Carnegie Foundation against the tide of the reconstruction of legal education (Id. at 18–20) in the face of the imperatives of membership in university communities ("Thanks in part to the development of legal scholarship, the law schools of the leading universities no longer fear being dishonored as 'mere trade schools.' " Id. at 7), and in the contest for reshaping the meaning of law and the place of lawyers within American society.

[55] Id. at 5.

revolution. And so, the bulk of the study reduces itself to an intense review of micro concerns—methodology for the most part.[56] The focus is on urging the university to incorporate a broader methodology that nods in the direction of the bar, without seeking to undo the shift in power over law. The law school is now to focus not only on the development of conceptual knowledge, but also on skills and ethics.[57] The purpose is to socialize the law students to the realities of law today, but it is not to shift power back to the bar or to turn back the clock on the primacy of the common law. The academy has won in this sense, and the only object left is to ensure that they find of way of training lawyers to function within the new realities more effectively.[58] In a sense, the roles of the bar and the university reverse their relationship of a hundred years ago. "Law schools can help the profession become smarter and more reflective about strengthening its slipping legitimacy by finding new ways to advance its enduring commitments."[59] The forms of the old partnership are to be maintained—thus the emphasis on the apprenticeship models as metaphors for the methodological suggestions in *Educating Lawyers*,[60] but the focus is now on the construction of a lawyer better suited for the times.[61]

Yet methodology can be important, and sometimes even acquire a normative dimension.[62] *Educating Lawyers* first focuses on the Socratic method as the core of legal education's signature pedagogy and its utility to the goals of extending the law school teaching objectives to skills and ethics.[63] It then explores the teaching of legal skills,[64] and the place of law school as a site for professional formation.[65] It ends with a set of

---

[56] "The focus of such attention naturally falls on teaching practices that enable learners to take part in the basic features of the professional practice itself." Id. at 9.

[57] Id. at 12–14.

[58] Id. at 23–24. Thus perhaps the emphasis on signature pedagogies as a method of specialization. Id. at 23. These are understood in the manner of disciplinary techniques. *See*, Michel Foucault, Discipline and Punish: The Birth of the Prison (Alan Sheridan, trans., 1977, NY: Vintage Books, 1995) pp. 195–228.

[59] *Educating Lawyers, supra* note 14, at 128.

[60] Id. at 25–29.

[61] Id. at 31–32.

[62] *See* Larry Catá Backer, *Global Panopticism: Surveillance Lawmaking by Corporations, States, and Other Entities*, 13 Indiana J. Global Legal Studies – (forthcoming 2008).

[63] *Educating Lawyers, supra*, note 14, at 47–86 ("In this chapter we attempt to unlock the secret of the learning process in the case-dialogue method and place it within the overall process of preparing legal professionals." Id. at 47).

[64] Id. at 87–125 ("In this chapter we look at some current promising experiments in the preparation of students for legal practice. In doing so, we hope to call attention to the largely unrealized potential that these models offer for addressing many criticisms of today's law schools, those of the profession and the public." Id. at 88–89).

[65] Id. at 126–161 ("We show how virtually all forms of the teaching that takes place in law schools,. . .are pedagogies that can be used to shape professional identity." Id. at 128).

implementation recommendations.[66] Consequently, methodology may play a critically important role in the naturalization of new areas of legal study within the American academy. In this sense, *Educating Lawyers* provides a powerful framework for understanding a basis for the incorporation of new practice areas that will maximize their utility to the bench and bar, while both satisfying the institutional needs of the university and remaining connected to their own sources. It is with this in mind that will be reviewed the implementation proposals set forth in Chapters 1–4.3 of *Educating Lawyers*.

Methodology focuses on socialization. Law schools teach doctrine well, but could do a much better job of teaching individuals to "think like a lawyer."[67] This involves more than the transmission of doctrine. It involves the socialization of the individual into the mores and habits of a community, and in doing so more consciously takes up the role once reserved to the bar and bound up in its transmission of the "craft, judgment, and public responsibility"[68] of lawyers. That socialization focuses on the case dialogue method of instruction.

While the authors of *Educating Lawyers* place much positive value on the case dialogue method as the signature pedagogy of legal education, they suggest the possibility of broader application. While the case dialogue method, as classically developed, is a superb instrument of socialization within a core mission to inculcate doctrinal knowledge, it has not been effective in inculcating professional values.[69] Lawyers need training, not only as legal technicians, but also as moral agents.[70] This points to the need for education beyond doctrine.

Education beyond doctrine can serve as a valuable bridge between education and practice. The Carnegie Report confronts the realities of the class hierarchies that are inevitable within the normative structures of university culture. The authors refer to this as the "problematic legitimacy" of clinical legal education.[71] "The standard is so securely established that there are few leverage points from which to effect change to the model."[72] Certainly such change is impossible if it is inconsistent with the value structure of university organization. The authors, drawing on earlier reforming efforts,[73] propose to change the dynamic indirectly by changing the way in

---

[66] Id. at 162–184 ("In this chapter we look closely at assessment in legal education—how it is done, how it might be done." Id. at 164).
[67] Id. at 47.
[68] Id. at 4.
[69] Id. at 56–58. (This is value understood as both ethics and a direction toward the "right" result.)
[70] Id. at 84.
[71] Id. at 89.
[72] Id. at 90.
[73] Id. at 91–95.

which clinical education is valued, and then integrating this segment of legal education within the doctrinal mainstream.[74] The core of the argument is based on a privileging of teaching case theory,[75] that is "the lawyer's task of understanding the client's needs and constructing a strategy to address those needs."[76]

The last building block of an integrated approach to legal education focuses on issues of professional identity and purpose. Lawyers are demoralized and their reputation is diminishing. The authors ascribe this to a disconnection between legal practice and the morals and values on which the profession ought to be grounded.[77] But it is also possible that the demoralization arises as a consequence of the instability in the self-identification of a profession that no longer serves, as in Coke's day, as the guardian of the common law against both the state and the individual. Instead, as agents of a state which has increasingly absorbed lawmaking power, the lawyer finds herself between professions. In a sense, *Educating Lawyers* acknowledges both this transitional dilemma and the ultimate new source of equilibrium—grounded in the mission of the university law school to shape the lawyers it produces for their new role in society.[78] This requires a dialogue between the moral and the legal, for which the authors provide an example from contracts law.[79] Uniting cognitive, practical and ethical-social development requires a broad range of courses that take students from an initially passive role as the imbibers of doctrine to externship courses that permit them to try out what they have learned.[80]

Finally, *Educating Lawyers* tackles issues of measurement. There is a bit of irony here. For it is measurement, in part, that has brought the profession (and by that is meant the profession of legal education) into its current confusion. Numerous private attempts to rank law schools have had a significant effect on legal education. Hierarchy, subordination, and judgment are key features of academic culture. It is no wonder that they carry over to the pedagogy offered to train students. Without reform in the way in which law schools create their own hierarchies, there can be little real hope for change in the way law schools assess their own work products. Still, *Educating Lawyers* makes a case against the single end of semester

---

[74] Id. at 100–111.

[75] Id. at 124–125.

[76] Id. at 122.

[77] Id. at 126–131.

[78] Id. at 131–132.

[79] Id. at 142–144.

[80] Id. at 147. The relationship between these integrative approaches based on both the infusion of ordinary classes with social and ethical issues and the development of more ethically charged courses radiating from out of the traditional course in professional responsibility is explored. Id. at 151–158.

examinations[81] and the practice of grading on the curve.[82] Drawing from related professions, *Educating Lawyers* makes a case for change.[83] The Carnegie Foundation's study favors what its authors call institutional intentionality: "linking feedback to students with feedback from students about how well they are achieving the learning goals for the course."[84]

Putting this all together, the authors of *Educating Lawyers* warn against treating their suggestions as an additional component to be added to the curriculum of legal education. They warn against segregating the professional and ethical components in legal education.[85] Instead, an integration model is preferred; "we endorse a different strategy, which we call *integrative* rather than *additive*. . . .The core insight behind the integrative strategy is that effective educational efforts must be understood in holistic rather than atomistic terms."[86] For this purpose, "the common core of legal education needs to be expanded in qualitative terms to encompass substantial experience with practice, as well as opportunities to wrestle with the issues of professionalism."[87] In that context, educational climate matters. "The goal should be to create a campus culture that is a positive force."[88] It is clear that this can be done. But again there is cognitive dissonance. Law schools will have to pay attention to reforming the climate among faculty and between faculty and administration, if they mean to be successful in changing the educational climate generally. Faculties are likely to reproduce for their students the academic climate in which they operate. What seems like an innocuous and separable component, thus suggests complexities untouched by the authors of *Educating Lawyers*.

Yet, integration is costly. The authors of *Educating Lawyers* tacitly acknowledge the power of the university model in describing the skill sets necessary to implement the integrative model they propose.[89] A principal effect of the move to a university norm set has been to denigrate the practice experience of applicants for teaching positions. In many cases, too much experience is deemed to poison the candidate for an academic career. The idea, seems to be that people too long in practice have too deeply imbued the values and norms of the bar and will not be able to successfully

---

[81] Id. at 167.

[82] Id. at 168–170.

[83] Id. at 171–179.

[84] Id. at 180.

[85] Id. at 190–191. The case for clinical legal education is made. Id. at 120–122.

[86] Id. at 191 ("Legal scholarship has generated a succession of bold, even radical, new ways of understanding the law, but this kind of scholarly innovation has proved entirely compatible with a stable, even conservative orientation toward educational practice and is part and parcel of an orientation that privileges the cognitive apprenticeship in its present, stand alone configuration." Id. at 192).

[87] Id. at 195.

[88] Id. at 183.

[89] Id. at 202.

transition to the norm structure of the university, which requires a focus on doctrine and writing. Thus, "Faculty development programs that consciously aim to increase the mutual understanding of doctrinal and lawyering faculty of each other's work are likely to improve students' efforts to make integrated sense of their developing legal competence."[90] All must come to accept a common educational purpose and bend their efforts to that objective. Faculty with different strengths must "work in a complementary relationship."[91]

The study ends with a suggestion of steps law schools might take to go in the "right direction." The models proffered include that of New York University and CCNY, which in different ways seek "to bring the three aspects of legal apprenticeship into active relation."[92] One alternative seeks to leverage the de facto division of talent (doctrinal faculty who are not lawyers, and lawyers who are in charge of clinical courses) within the university to construct webs of courses that are linked in a way that privilege the three areas of legal training.[93] That approach works for large law schools with substantial resources and an institutional framework that permits an adequate administration of programs of this sort of complexity. Cost is certainly an obstacle.[94] Moreover, this sort of leverage is necessitated by the privileging of the normative structure of the university that tends to privilege "a distinguished well-published faculty that includes leaders of the field."[95] Another alternative involved a greater investment in integration within the curriculum. That approach required less attention to leveraging differences in talents and more on broadly changing the focus of the curriculum.[96] Yale is cited for its decision to reduce the number of doctrinal courses "and encouraging students to elect an introductory clinical course in their second semester."[97] This is said to point to an intermediate strategy, "a course of study that encourage students to shift their focus between doctrine and practical experience not once but several times, so as to gradually develop more competence in each area while, it is hoped, making more linkages between them."[98]

---

[90] Id. at 196.

[91] Id. at 197.

[92] Id.

[93] Id. The programs at N.Y.U. are described in some detail. Id. at 38–43.

[94] *See* Id. at 198.

[95] Id. at 38. Of course, the field no longer necessarily includes the bench and bar, but the community of academic scholars. *See*, e.g., Larry Catá Backer, *Defining, Measuring and Judging Scholarly Productivity: Working Toward a Rigorous and Flexible Approach*, 52 J. Legal Educ. 317 (2002).

[96] Id. at 197. The programs at CCNY are described in some detail. *See* Id. at 34–38.

[97] Id. at 197.

[98] Id. The programs at Southwestern Law School are also identified as falling in this category—these involve some curricular changes. Id. at 198.

Reduced to its essence, *Educating Lawyers*, as a theoretical exercise, seeks to find a space within university-centered and positivism-focused academic law for the new realities of law and the responsibilities of the profession. It embraces the critical ideas that law schools are important as a site for the rapid socialization of law students into the standards of legal thinking that they will carry into the profession.[99] For this purpose, law schools have relied on a single, if powerful, pedagogy: the case-dialogue method.[100] Though powerful, the case-dialogue method produces unintended consequences, principally making legal education remote from the context in which law will be practiced.[101] This remoteness is compounded by an undeveloped system for assessing student learning, one grounded in the traditions of the academy but not on the lived realities of the profession and its needs.[102] Lastly, legal education tends to be conservative and tradition-bound within the boundaries of its own institutional imperatives.[103] Incrementalism and conservatism tend to produce a preference for gestures toward change in place of actual change. Substantive changes follow formal changes, though the appearance of change may make greater or deeper change less likely.[104] It is the appearance of change without substantial change that the authors of *Educating Lawyers* seek to avoid.

More importantly, as methodology, *Educating Lawyers* seeks to privilege certain specific principles of legal education. Foremost among them is the integrative principle of education over an additive or compartmentalized approach to legal education. Also important is the tacit acceptance of significant class divisions within legal education—what may be appropriate for "top tier" schools may be beyond the abilities, or even the ambitions, of lower ranked schools. To each class of law school belongs a different level of acceptable approaches to integration. Adopting the language of *Educating Lawyers*, for every New York University, there is a CCNY, for every Yale Law School there is a Southwestern Law School. For those who still cling to the principle of equality among law schools—of horizontal rather than vertical professional organization, this might be disquieting, but only makes explicit what has been implicit for years. As a consequence, there is a bit of flexibility. Yet, this flexibility is grounded in academic reputation and resources. Lastly, *Educating Lawyers* acknowledges that law schools are incapable of great changes in short order—they can act only incrementally.[105] Changes

---

99 Id. at 185.
100 Id. at 186.
101 Id. at 187.
102 Id. at 188.
103 Id. at 189.
104 Id. at 190–191.
105 Id. at 189–191.

have to be adapted to that reality, but ought not to settle for incrementalism as a goal in itself. Partial changes must lead to a holistic objective.[106]

Still, *Educating Lawyers* seeks to modify the framework within which academics speak about education. It is meant to remind the academy that legal education is not a closed autonomous system running exclusively on the basis of its own imperatives to feed the desires of the professorate (and increasingly more importantly of the bloating superstructure of administrators that purport to serve them and the institutions for which they work).[107] *Educating Lawyers* is meant to remind legal academics and their keepers that they are not necessarily the only stakeholders in the provision of legal education, nor is the educational experience necessarily meant to focus on the educators. Because of the key role played by the bench and bar, *Educating Lawyers* seeks to integrate lawyers and educators, as well as doctrine, practice and professionalism—a noble gesture. Before it is possible to consider the impact of *Educating Lawyers* on the integration of transnational law in the American law school, it is necessary to understand the dynamics of that integration movement in its own right.

5.3 How Law Schools Go About Incorporating Global Law in American Legal Education

Just as the ideas articulated in *Educating Lawyers* have been developing for a century, so too those animating the movement to incorporate international and transnational multi-jurisdictional law within the law school curriculum have acquired their own dynamic. Reviewed on its own terms, it is clear that the patterns of development in the discourse of incorporating international and transnational law in law schools has significant parallels with the discourse of the integration of professionalism and ethics in university-centered legal education. This section first considers this incorporation movement on its own terms. In Section 5.3.1, the focus is on the contemporary framework within which law schools tend to assess the impact of international and transnational issues on law school stakeholders. Section 5.3.2 turns to the traditional framework structures for incorporating the international and transnational element into law school curricula, research and service. These include an integration, segregation and aggregation model of incorporation. Section 5.3.3 then considers emerging framework structures: an immersion model for incorporating the international and transnational element in law school curriculum, research and service.

---

[106] Id. at 191.

[107] *See* essays in Autopoietic Law: A New Approach to Law and Society (Gunther Teubner ed., 1988).

No consideration of the problem of integrating international and transnational practice issues into the operations of law schools can be adequately addressed without a reasonable framework for analysis. That analysis must focus on three things: (A) what are the realities of law-making and practice; (B) how do those realities relate to the mission of a particular law school; and (C) what are the resources and resource constraints of that institution. On the basis of that analysis, it becomes easier to approach the assessment of the objective: the manner, if any, in which a particular law school will choose to embrace (and support) international and transnational elements in its teaching, research and service. The structure of analysis ought to work from "big picture" issues to the minutiae of implementation. Unworkable dreams are distractions worth avoiding.

5.3.1 Assessing the Impact of International and Transnational Issues on Law School Stakeholders

The assessment of the impact of international and transnational issues on law school stakeholders is not made in a vacuum. It involves an assessment of the impact of a variety of factors. The stakeholders are not hard to identify: faculty, students, employers, administrators and institutional actors in the field of the production of legal culture (courts, government, norm makers). However, factors and assumptions underlying stakeholder choices are less apparent. These bear careful examination before choices are made.

The factors affecting assessment are far more difficult to apply. First, there is the issue of time. It is tempting to assume that the character, desires, and practices of stakeholders *today* ought to serve as the basis for assessment. One can then simply determine the form of that reality and conform one's analysis to that reality as thus conceived. Yet in a context in which such character, desire and practice is likely to change in the future, such assessment guarantees obsolescence even before implementation. Does one plan for the current context or a future context? If one plans for a future context, with what degree of certainty can one assess the characteristics of that future on which such assessments are to be made?

Second, there is an issue of identity. This is, of course, related to the issue of time. Today's student pool may not resemble tomorrow's pool. A realistic assessment of the character and general potential of students is necessary before any analysis. Many schools tend to avoid this issue—falling back on more or less empty rhetoric, or using the opportunity to reaffirm notoriously hortatory goals. A law school that deliberately (or which out of necessity) recruits a student body whose interests remain focused on state, local or even national practice, may tend to misallocate resources to international and transnational practice and research issues.

Or it may not. The desires, objectives and values of law school stakeholders may not be congruent. Indeed, they might cut in irremediably inconsistent directions. Consider the law school whose students are focused on state and local practice issues, and who serve an employer base that reflects those preferences. These students may be taught by a faculty whose predominant interests and strengths (including reputation with bench, bar and other academics) are national, rather than state and local. But this institution may operate in a broad academic context in which reputation among elite academic institutional players is increasingly dependent on allocation of resources and emphasis on international and transnational law and legal issues (international, comparative, foreign and transnational law). Such an institution's administrators, with the support of university administration, may be committed to a course of action the object of which is to secure a certain reputation among elite academic institutional players. Knowledge of stakeholder interests, in this context, provides little comfort. Information—knowledge—does not necessarily suggest choices.

In this context it is important to be realistic and honest. Unstated premises are dangerous things. Context is critical: both current and future context must be assessed realistically. For example, if very few of a law school's graduates will practice in the area of international human rights, talking about the pedagogical value of that aspect of international and transnational practice may be somewhat disingenuous, but less so if the faculty becomes committed to devoting resources to attract students (and employers and research focus) in that field. At this point in the development of a consensus of its general utility within American legal academic culture, it is also important to recognize that faculty preference and interest, as well as the "market" for students, drive the extent and manner in which international and transnational issues may be incorporated into a law school's mission. Once the importance of the professional interest of the faculty is understood, and its relationship to pedagogical need honestly stated, it is more likely that a law school can intelligently and openly discuss how to facilitate the work of all faculty.

In addition, there is the issue of substance (or taxonomy). The traditional division of fields touching on transborder issues—international law, comparative law and foreign law—now may no longer realistically define the field. An assessment bounded by current or past understanding of the definition of the "fields" contained within the objective (incorporating transborder legal issues within the curriculum) may substantially miss the mark. But this discussion, usually heated in many places, tends to reinforce the academic nature of the dispute, and works against the framework advocated in *Educating Lawyers*.

Moreover, change itself is costly. Inertia is not merely a matter of economics at least reduced to the monetary cost of change. It also affects social structures, power relationships and communal norms within a law school.[108] Old approaches are powerfully defended in part because of their legitimacy—their traditional value. But they are also defended because those members of institutions that had embraced them have derived a certain amount of power—financial, reputation, influential—within and outside the institution on the basis of that institutional structure, and the resultant allocation of things of value. Change threatens those relationships, and that power. People thus threatened will do what they must, using whatever language or devices available, to retain their position. Change this costly should not be lightly undertaken, nor should it necessarily be avoided. The proud saddle maker in 1930 could look with a certain amount of satisfaction at his ability to avoid losing status when she was able to successfully thwart plans to incorporate an automotive division within her saddle making firm, but she is the poorer for the experience, and her institution the more irrelevant for the choice. There is always a call for saddle makers, at least as long as people ride horses. A good saddle maker will always be in demand, but saddle making, like horse transport in general, is no longer a central element of transportation, and the saddle maker no longer occupies as important a place in the transport industry. Thus, to the extent the choice was made in light of knowledge of these consequences, it remains valid nonetheless. But the consequences, especially the economic consequences, are significant.

Still, the most contentious issue of the role of international and transnational issues in law school is the difficulty of arriving at agreement about the definition of the relevant terms and the methods for measuring their impact. International and transnational law are notorious for their ambiguity, as they can encompass more than one field, traditionally defined as such within American academia.[109] That is both the strength and weakness of a powerful yet dynamic and immature area of law. The issue is made more complicated by an increasingly powerful set of suggestions that the current traditional fields of law, and the courses defined around them, ought to be due for a substantial overhaul, even in their domestic context.[110] Some sort of working definition, and methods for "finding" evidence of its impact among stakeholders, is critical for assessing the value of expending resources on its integration into the programs of a law school.

---

[108] For a sense of this, *see*, e.g., Michael P. Scharf, *Internationalizing the Study of Law*, 20 Penn St. Intl. L. Rev. 29 (2001).

[109] *See*, e.g., Larry Catá Backer, *General Principles of Academic Specialization By Means of Certificate or Concentration Programs: Creating a Certificate Program in International, Comparative and Foreign Law at Penn State*, 20 Penn. St. Intl. L. Rev. 67, 85–101 (2001).

[110] *See*, e.g., Thomas D. Morgan, Educating Lawyers for the Future of the Legal Profession, *The George Washington University Law School Public Law and Legal Theory Working Paper No. 189* (2005), available at http://ssrn.com/abstract=881846 (last accessed Feb. 11, 2007).

These discussions, and the framework issues they invoke, are undertaken outside of the foundational issues touched on in *Educating Lawyers*. The very terms from which the issues are extracted suggest that this is something special, different and apart. It is something that must consciously be interwoven into existing legal education. And it is something that, because not yet critically necessary, can be treated as optional rather than as a critical and inseparability component of American legal education. Yet it is also clear that these discussions are integral to the methodological framework of *Educating Lawyers*. It is difficult to implement the integrative approach that serves as the foundation of *Educating Lawyers*, within a pedagogical framework that posits that integration (doctrine, practice and ethics) is indispensable except when teaching cross border law and legal issues.

As such, like the discussion about capabilities, the discussion about mission ignores the conceptual framework of *Educating Lawyers*. Indeed, the framework of that discussion might well tend to reinforce the academically oriented focus of legal education. Still, no discussion of an assessment of the necessity or form of incorporation of an international and transnational element in law school teaching and research avoids conflict over the law school mission. Law schools, like most other institutions, are notoriously reticent about articulating their mission in other than the most general terms. Mission statements are usually broad enough to accommodate virtually any form of legal education. This is not a criticism, but a reminder that the mission of law school is often apparent more from its practice than from its statements. The reality of mission, rather than its formal articulation, must be the basis for assessment. That, in turn, is a function of a variety of factors.

First, Internal Institutional Preferences are Important: The long-term preferences of stakeholders are a basic component of purpose. But, as the preceding discussion suggests, it is the most difficult component to assess fairly. Still, an assessment must be made, in order to successfully mediate among the various perspectives and provides a means of modification as preferences and outlook change. Provision ought to be made for the production of information that facilitates such a perspective shift. It would be fatal to any analysis of stakeholder preference to overlook its positive as well as its descriptive aspect. Law schools shape stakeholder preferences by modifying their behavior to change the character of their stakeholders.

Increasing student diversity, or LSAT scores, can significantly affect stakeholder preference going forward. Changing the composition of faculty can do the same. Evolving employer tastes have the same effect, but so does changing the law school's employer base. A law school must accept its past, and live in its present, but also has some power to shape its future by changing the inputs that produce the preferences (and character) of its stakeholders. In some schools, success in this respect has been accomplished on a fairly modest budget.[111] Even so, "there was some initial resistance to the proposal" to internationalize the traditional domestic law curriculum.[112]

Second, Abilities of the Faculty will Necessarily Reduce Options for Incorporation: The aptitude of faculty, over the long term, and their willingness to conform to changes in the values of the production of certain kinds of knowledge, will substantially affect the ability of a law school to incorporate changes, including but not limited to the addition of the international and transnational element, to the curriculum and research. Faculty committed to a particular world view, even one that is belied by the reality around them to which they may remain oblivious, or for which they have constructed a ready and plausible rationalization, may be a faculty unready to adopt change, even necessary change, with any degree of success. In such cases, either the aggregate composition of faculty will have to change or the matter put off. Reeducation is possible, but costly in terms of time and resources. Such faculty might be forced to conform, but conformity will yield mediocre results. Realism in assessment on this score is essential, no matter what the surrounding reality may be. Not every law school can serve as an industry leader.

Third, Without Consensus a Successful Incorporation is Unlikely: An institution led unwillingly to follow any course of action acts at its own peril. Consensus-building involves more than the accumulation of *diktaten*, commands reflecting the sometimes vindictive will of eager administrators, or a similar accumulation of silences cravenly translated as acceptance. It is always useful to recall King Canute's experience with the tides;[113] for us, the lesson is as valuable for those who would command the tides as for those who believe that the rising and falling of the tides is somehow an indication of volition. While such actions have the appearance of forward movement, they produce no deep impression and no solid foundation on which to build lasting institutional cultural change. The hard work of consensus-building, of building a desire to participate based on fair assessments of future realities, present capabilities and resources, and the benefits of success (a success that must be shared fairly among institutional actors), is critical

---

[111] *See*, e.g., Michael P. Scharf, *Internationalizing the Study of Law*, 20 Penn St. Intl. L. Rev. 29 (2001). Professor Scharf described the success of a program which, in 1999, offered faculty at the New England School of Law a stipend of $1,000 "if they would design and incorporate an international law teaching unit into their domestic law courses to ensure that students are exposed to international law issues in required and highly recommended courses throughout the curriculum." Id. at 31–32.

[112] Id. at 32. Ironically, some resistance came from those concerned that wide internationalization of the curriculum would adversely affect enrollment in the international specialty courses. Id. at 33.

[113] Canute sat at the seashore and unsuccessfully ordered back the tides to prove that kingly power has its limits (available at http://www.inspirationalstories.com/0/91.html) (last accessed Jan. 30, 2007).

in any program of change. Where consensus goes missing, failure, however packaged and veiled, will surely follow.

Consensus-building, however, can be accomplished in a variety of ways. At Harvard Law School, for example, consensus is expressed in the number of faculty actually embracing a particular method of teaching and researching.[114] At New York University Law School, consensus about the value of the international and transnational element in legal education, and its centrality to legal education, was solidified through the establishment of NYU's Hauser Global Law School Program.[115] But even New York University Law School started with a small number of faculty committed to internationalizing the curriculum.[116] Thus, the reality that consensus is an ongoing project is no proof of its failure. Alternatively, a broad consensus among faculty might be required before proceeding. Alternatively, a faculty and its administration may choose to "make facts" by a deliberate program of faculty hiring that effectively changes the basis of consensus within that body. The choice will likely depend on faculty or institutional culture. It may also depend on administrative choices—a willingness to take risks and follow through may dictate the basis for moving forward to achieve a necessary minimum consensus. But a minimum consensus is necessary.

Fourth, Available Resources are Critical: Change is not cost free. The allocation of resources directly impacts all faculty and law school programs. Resource allocation affects power relationships within a faculty. It also affects morale. Morale affects the ability of law schools to produce happy (and contributing) faculty and perhaps even contribute to the length of decanal tenure. A law school without the ability or will to commit the necessary resources to affect successfully the introduction of the transnational element into its teaching and research culture ought not to engage in the

---

[114] *See* discussion at text at notes 128–129, *supra*.

[115] *See* New York University, Hauser Global Law School Program, *About Us*, available at http://www.nyulawglobal.org/aboutus/aboutus.htm (last accessed Feb. 7, 2007) ("Since its inception in 1994, the HGLSP has overseen a radical change in the structure of NYU Law faculty and curriculum, the composition of the student body, and the range of extracurricular opportunities. The goal has been to transform legal education and make NYU Law a 'global' rather than merely a national law school.") Id.

[116] John Sexton relates how:

> [b]eginning in the late 1990s, "we asked for a single volunteer, subject neutral, from among the first year doctrinal faculty members. We have four first year sections. We asked for a volunteer from each of these four sections who would commit himself or herself to integrating global perspectives into his or her course. . . .After running that drill for one year we then asked for s second volunteer in each of the sections. So now we have global elements and perspectives being introduced in up to two of the five core courses. This is an intermediate step to a new and radical curriculum that we are going to be developing."

John E. Sexton, *Curricular Responses to Globalization*, 20 Penn St. Intl. L. Rev. 15, 17–18 (2001).

exercise. Law schools can remain true to their specific culture and objectives, that is, consciously elect to avoid a significant incorporation of the transnational element, without compromising on their ability to produce lawyers to serve specific market segments for legal services. In this context, it is important to remember that resource allocation and availability may take many forms, not all of which are financial. The issue of resources is thus intimately tied to the issue of consensus and institutional capacity. Resources, however, are not limited to economic resources. Stakeholder resources are also important. At least a critical number of faculty members must be willing to commit the time and energy to making a change of this kind possible. It might be possible to hire around resource shortfalls; but again, that option is sometimes not available to law schools with significant pressing obligations in other areas. Lastly, students must be willing to invest in the revamped curriculum. Even the most brilliant and foresighted reinvention of a faculty and its curriculum will serve no purpose if students fail to take advantage of it, and if employers fail to hire students thus trained.

Fifth, Realistic Expectations Define the Parameters of Successful Incorporation: The realities of the hierarchies of the legal academy, and the rigorously enforced behavioral expectations that flow from that hierarchy, are not easily changed. Well-resourced institutions at the top of the reputation pyramid can not only expend resources more accurately to divine the future, they can also expend resources to facilitate consensus and fund its attainment. That sort of facility is more difficult for less well-resourced law schools, which tend to be placed further down the reputation ladder. For law schools at the bottom of the reputation hierarchy, no such facility may be realistically available. This reality, usually avoided by the leveling rhetoric of academic self-assessments, is avoided at a law school's peril. Dreams sometimes may not be realized. A realistic self-assessment of the possibilities permitted a law school given its resources and place within the American academic reputation hierarchy is a necessary primary step in any consideration of moving to affect programs undertaken by reputation and resource leaders in the industry.

The last point of the preceding discussion ought to lead to a focus on the third great leg of analysis: a realistic assessment of capability. Capability provides the baseline for a number of decisions: the cost of embracing a program of international and transnational legal education, the form that program may or must take, the cost of amassing sufficient capability to make any such program viable, the likelihood of success for the program to be implemented, and the consequences, especially in terms of resource allocation, of embracing any such program.

Assessments of this type require the taking of an institutional inventory.[117] These sorts of inventories present difficulties beyond the need to

---

[117] Such an inventory must take into account a number of things. Among the most important might be the following: (1) Current course coverage; (2) Potential course coverage given faculty ability and preferences; (3) Current programs in place; (4) Potential

control for institutional or personal self-delusion. It is, for example, not always easy to determine who among the faculty already has an interest or engages in teaching of material that meets the programmatic needs of an international and transnational regime. There also may be a gap between identification of the willing and willingness to change old teaching and coverage habits. It is also not always easy to manage faculty education.[118] Suppose, for example, that a determination is made to add a "transnational" component to existing courses. Either existing single jurisdiction faculty will have to be retrained (a sensitive enough issue) or additional faculty resources will have to be deployed (by bringing in guest lecturers). Both generate costs.

Moreover, it is easy to overlook emerging institutional arrangements for accessing an international and transnational component in legal education. Among the easiest to ignore are programs of association with foreign law schools, systems of networked education that are becoming increasingly important.[119] Georgetown University, for example, is in the process of developing its Global Law School in collaboration with a number of foreign law schools. This endeavor is to be based in London.[120] In tight fiscal environments, leveraging through associations with foreign law schools may provide a viable alternative. Still, this is an alternative with its own costs.[121]

It is also not easy to determine the minimal course and program requirements. Such requirements may be substantially affected by objectives.[122]

---

programs that might be implemented; (5) Necessary course coverage to meet the objectives of adding the international and transnational dimension in legal education; (6) Necessary programs to meet the objectives of adding the international and transnational dimension in legal education; (7) Necessary faculty additions to meet coverage, research and other programmatic needs; and (8) Necessary administrative support necessary to support the programs.

[118] Thus, for example, this may affect matters like post tenure review processes, faculty support levels, teaching loads and the like. Essentially, incorporation in any of its aspects might change the set of fundamental contract and network relationships on which the field of legal production at the law school level has been organized for nearly a century. Those changes, to the extent they are fundamental enough, could require a great deal of attention, time and money. They will certainly pose significant institutional issues to the extent that its effects and obligations are meant to be spread widely among the faculty, or otherwise draw substantial resources away from traditionally privileged areas of funding.

[119] *See*, e.g., Chang-fa Lo, *International Conference on Legal Education Reform: Reflections and Perspectives*, 24 Wis. Intl. L. J. 1 (2006).

[120] For a discussion, *see* text at note 160, *infra*.

[121] *See* discussion, below, at text and notes 122, *infra*.

[122] This question involves both a consideration of the relationship between program content and student (what does one want the students to get out of the program), program content and faculty (what does one want to suggest about the relationship of law faculty to the fields of law to which they are devoting their professional careers), and program content to outside stakeholders—the bench and bar, prospective students, alumni, the local community and community of global peers (how does one want to *brand* the efforts). Branding is a particularly sensitive issue and one that affects both the internal and external relations of law schools as institutions

Planning involves shooting at a moving target on multiple levels. That reality affects the resources that would be realistically necessary to commit to the program. It may thus affect the form that any program of naturalizing the international and transnational element within a particular law school may take.

5.3.2 *Traditional Framework Structures for Incorporating the International and Transnational Element in Law School Curricula, Research and Service*

There are three traditional models for incorporating the international and transnational element into law school curricula: the *integration, aggregation* and *segregation* models. Each seeks to modify existing resources and teaching/research models to incorporate a transnational element into the curriculum. Each model offers a number of benefits but also has some detriments. The models are sketched in "pure" form. Of course, no law school has committed to any single model; most law schools have sought to incorporate some aspect of each of the models. The mix chosen will depend on the resources available at a law school, as well as its sense of itself, its mission and its determination of the centrality of transnational law orientation for the future of the professions (law and legal academic).

1. *Integration Model*: The first is the most comprehensive and "deep" form of integration, one that parallels the integration of "national" law in law school curricula, research and service at the start of the 20th century. This is an approach being attempted by a few institutions, most of which consider themselves (or might be considered by others) at the higher reputation levels of the legal academy. It is marked, at least in theory, by an attempt to refocus the educational and research hub of the law school from

---

within the hierarchy of institutions in the field. Thus, for example, branding within a field not recognized by rating groups (e.g. U.S. News & World Report) (U.S. News & World Report, Guide to Law Schools, Rankings, available at http://grad-schools.usnews.rankingsandreviews.com/usnews/edu/grad/rankings/law/lawindex_brief.php (accessed Aug. 27, 2007)) or even the Leiter Reports (*see* Brian Leiter's Law School Reports, available at http://leiterlawschool.typepad.com/ (last accessed Sept. 1, 2007)) may yield costs in excess of institutional advantages. The lack of institutional advantages invariably translates, in some respects, to the individual. For example, the U.S. News and World Report Rankings rank specialties in (1) clinical training, (2) dispute resolution, (3) environmental law, (4) healthcare law, (5) intellectual property law, (6) international law, (7) legal writing, (8) tax law, and (9) trial advocacy (Id. at http://grad-schools.usnews.rankingsandreviews.com/usnews/edu/grad/rankings-/law/lawindex_brief.php (last accessed Aug. 29, 2007)) but not in other fields.

the national to the transnational to the greatest extent feasible. The object is to produce generalists.[123]

For example, Yale Law School, through its dean, Harold Koh, "has made globalization a priority. Under his leadership. . . .The Law School's long-standing international tradition occupies a central place in its intellectual life, and many legal issues are approached from a global perspective. The devotion of its faculty and students to its myriad international projects has made Yale a first-class global law school."[124] Yale appears to have accomplished this by larding its general offerings with a host of programs and centers each dealing with some aspect or other of law that crosses borders.[125] Yale law students are offered a large number of "international law" courses and are told that "many domestic law courses contain international components."[126] Yale law students are also able to apply for "Graduate Certificates of Concentration in the following areas: International Development Studies, International Security Studies, African Studies, European Studies, Latin American Studies, Modern Middle East Studies."[127]

Harvard Law School offers a similar level of integration of the transnational element within the framework of J.D. education program. "At HLS an international perspective is foundational, rather than peripheral, to legal inquiry. And this forms the basis for scholarship and action that have tangible impact in the world."[128] This orientation requires a substantial institutional commitment from stakeholders. "More than half of the Harvard Law faculty incorporate international and comparative perspectives in their teaching, scholarship, and public service in a significant way. This year, they offer more than 65 HLS courses and reading groups focusing on international, foreign or comparative law."[129]

Georgetown University Law School offers a glimpse at a related form of implementation of the model. Georgetown's web site states a commitment "to preparing all of its students for a legal career in this increasingly globalized society. The array of course and seminar offerings at the Law

---

[123] *See*, e.g., Sebastien Lebel-Grenier, *What is a Transnational Legal Education*, 56 J. Leg. Educ. 190, 195–196 (2006).

[124] Yale Law School, International Law, available at http://www.law.yale.edu/internationalla-w.htm (accessed on or before Mar. 30, 2008).

[125] *See* Yale University website, *International Law Programs at Yale University*, available at http://www.law.yale.edu/academics/internationallawyaleuprograms.htm

[126] Yale Law School, International Law, Courses, available at http://www.law.yale.edu/acade-mics/internationallawcourses.asp (accessed on or before Mar. 30, 2008).

[127] Id.

[128] Harvard Law School, International Legal Studies at Harvard Law School, available at http://www.law.harvard.edu/ils/ (last accessed Feb. 4, 2007).

[129] Id. ("The scores of visitors and scholars from abroad, and some 4,000 alumni who live outside the United States, help make HLS truly international. Our research centers host hundreds of talks, workshops, and conferences with an international focus. And all of this activity draws on the world's foremost academic law library.") Id.

Center dealing with transnational, international, and comparative law in many forms is the most comprehensive in the country. Numbering about 100 in the 2005–2006 academic year."[130] This sort of program requires not only international and transnational law specialists, but critically, a willingness of other faculty "who have broadened the scope of their scholarship and teaching to encompass transnational, international and comparative aspects of their fields."[131] The job of the law school is made easier by its ability to exploit its location, offering opportunities to expand curricular and research possibilities at smaller marginal cost than would be the case at a similarly situated institution in a more remote location. The teaching focus of international and transnational issues is a one-week program of classes offered to first-year law students after the end of their first semester, which are meant to expose them to the transnational dimension of the domestic law to which they will be exposed.[132]

The University of the Pacific offers another variation on this approach.[133] The Law School web site explains that "The Pacific McGeorge initiative to globalize the curriculum took major steps forward this summer with the publication of more books in the Global Issues series by Thomson-West. The law school is at the forefront of a movement to prepare 21st Century students to practice in a legal world that has become increasingly global. The philosophy behind this initiative may be best summarized by Justice Stephen G. Breyer's statement that 'This world we live in is a world where it is out of date to teach foreign law in a course called Foreign Law.' "[134]

Other faculties across the United States have tried similar approaches on a more *ad hoc* basis.[135] It is possible, in fact, to move into an integration approach slowly—starting with just a few courses and working one's way to a fuller integration over time. Thus, for example, several years ago American University's Washington School of Law, "made revisions to the

[130] Georgetown Law School, International and Transnational Law Programs, available at https://www.law.georgetown.edu/oitp/ (last accessed Feb. 19, 2008).

[131] Id.

[132] *See* Id.

[133] University of the Pacific, *Globalizing the Curriculum*, available at http://www.mcgeorge.-edu/international/global/global_business/initiative.htm (accessed on or before Mar. 30, 2008).

[134] Id.

[135] *See*, e.g., Neil S. Siegel, *Some Modest Use of Transnational Legal Perspectives in First Year Constitutional Law*, 56 J. Leg. Educ. 201 (2006) (but cautioning that the transnational element remains "a relatively minor part of my overall course" Id. at 215); Rosalie Jukier, *Transnationalizing the Legal Curriculum: How to Teach What We Live*, 56 J. Leg. Educ. 172 (2006) (citing Roth Gordon, *Teaching the CISG in Contracts: The Challenges of Adding the International to First Year Contracts, in* 2006 AALS Conference Workshop Materials 141–144 (Jan. 2006)).

first year curriculum to incorporate international issues into traditional first year 'domestic' law courses."[136]

This more or less comprehensive approach is complicated and requires a large institutional commitment in terms of resources and a willingness to change traditional academic culture.[137] At its limit, this approach requires all faculty to change their approach to teaching and perhaps even to research. Just as the focus of research at elite institutions shifted from state to national issues and from technical to theoretical discourse, the focus of research under this new approach may require a shift from the national to the trans- or multi-jurisdictional. "The pull to follow the currently conventional thinking of the judiciary, and the inertia exerted by the traditional division of subjects within a law school curriculum, all tend to create barriers to any change in the current approach."[138] Thus, the integration model requires a certain amount of education of stakeholders and a willingness to develop programs for the long-term. In the absence of this sort of comprehensive and long-term commitment, this form of international law programming is unlikely to prove successful.

2. *Aggregation Model*: The second, and most popular, model of integration, is based on the "field of law" or aggregation model, by which international and transnational issues are segregated and privileged as one among several equal areas of the study of law, such as labor, corporate or tax law. The strength of this approach lies in its ability to leverage conventional approaches to legal education. The great danger of this approach is that it will reinforce the conventional framework that privileges a strictly delimited territorial approach to legal education.

Under this model, international and transnational law (however understood) is consolidated in a number of courses, the extent and number of which will vary with the tastes of a faculty, their resources, capacities and the perceived interests of their local markets. This method involves virtually no changes in the structure of a law school's programs. It reduces the issue to one of resource allocation. A number of courses are identified. These courses are developed and faculty found to teach them. Perhaps additional programs, ad hoc or more institutionalized in nature, are established, and students are encouraged to take advantage of the "value added" of such programs in the same way that they would be encouraged to take advantage of other institutional resources that might be good for them.

---

136 *See* Caludio Grossman's chapter in this volume.

137 As noted in an earlier work, "[t]here exist several significant impediments to any movement in this direction. The addition of international and comparative themes to existing courses, and especially existing first year courses, may present fatal obstacles." Larry Catá Backer, *Human Rights and Legal Education in the Western Hemisphere: Legal Parochialism and Hollow Universalism*, 21 Penn St. Intl. L. Rev. 115, 151 (2002).

138 Id. at 152.

At its most imposing, this method permits a law school to provide a structure for the study of law as it relates to jurisdictions outside the United States. The University of Michigan Law School has adopted such an approach. There, a single first year course now serves, like contracts and property and torts for their fields, as the organizing course for further study of issues that touch on matters beyond the territorial limits of the United States. "The Transnational Law course will not replace advanced courses in public international law, conflicts of law or international litigation, but will provide a common foundation, liberating teachers of the advanced courses to give deeper coverage of the respective materials."[139]

At its least imposing, this approach is informal, easily integrated with other similar programs, and reducing any possibility of privileging the international and transnational element of law. At the Pennsylvania State University Law School, for example, the faculty adopted changes in the mandatory curriculum creating a requirement for a first year law student elective. Among the elective courses offered is entitled "Transnational Law and Legal Issues."[140] Much more effective, perhaps, are short course consolidating programs such as that offered at Georgetown University through its Global Practice Exercise. "Each semester will begin with an intensive, multi-day exercise in transnational and/or comparative law, built around an important and timely issue. The exercise will provide an opportunity for the Center's diverse students and faculty to work together on a common legal problem."[141]

These sorts of aggregation or add-on programs run the risk of furthering the appearance of movement towards the incorporation of a lively international and transnational component to legal education without actually incorporating such instruction in fact. It can suggest that transnational law neither presents systemic issues of education nor requires a change in the way law is understood. International law becomes an add-on course.

---

[139] *See* Atik and Soubboth, at note 27, *supra*. The authors also note that "In making the Transnational Law course mandatory, the Michigan faculty 'conveys the important message that the international dimensions of law have become so pervasive that (as [their] alumni tell [them]) their study is not an option but a necessity. Michigan is meeting challenges in staffing four sections of the course and in preparing appropriate teaching materials. There is considerable interest in the Michigan model (at least among international law teachers) across the country.' " Id.

[140] One version of this course was created by this author. Its description can be found at http://www.personal.psu.edu/lcb11/trans_law.htm

[141] Georgetown University Law Center, Courses Offered Both Semesters, Global Practice Exercise, available at http://www.law.georgetown.edu/ctls/courses/both.html #GlobalPracticeE-xercise (last accessed Feb. 19, 2008). For an example of the program for the Spring 2008 academic year, *see* Georgetown University Law Center, Week One: Law in a Global Context, An Intensive Program Integrating Transnational Legal Perspectives into the First Year Curriculum, January 7–11, 2008, available at http://www.law.georgetown.edu/documents/weekone2008.pdf (last accessed Feb. 18, 2008).

It diverts resources but otherwise affects no fundamental change in the way the business of legal education is conducted. For many schools, especially those with very limited resources, this may be enough.[142]

3. *Segregation Model*: The third model is the segregation model. There are two basic approaches under this model. The usual approach is nicely illustrated by the University of Pittsburgh's Center for International Legal Education ("CILE") founded in the late 1990s "to provide a home for international and comparative law programs at the School of Law and to administer Pitt's LL.M. Program for Foreign Law Graduates, the Center has become a significant provider of legal education programs throughout the world. That process continues with the inauguration this year of the CILE Studies."[143] Another version is elaborated within the Cornell Law School.[144] Under this approach, a law school creates an administrative device that serves as the institutional base from which all international and transnational programs can be developed, offered and assessed, all to serve the education and research mission of the law school. This method is powerful. It can avoid the issue of systemic integration and the training of faculty across disciplines. It respects more or less traditional disciplinary boundaries within the conventional law school. It can provide an easy way to monitor resource allocation and the performance of the programs, now gathered together within a single sub-unit. It can also be combined with certificate or other specialized programs in legal education offered to willing law students.[145]

On the other hand, such a model can serve as a gateway to greater integration. That might be a good way of understanding the development of New York University's Hauser Global Law School Program, through which the Law School has been able to pace the naturalization of the transnational element in its program of instruction.[146] The success of the program

---

[142] Many law schools still face the situation described in 1997 with respect to academic course inventory for legal education. *See*, e.g., John A. Barrett, Jr., *International Legal Education in U.S. Law Schools: Plenty of Offerings but Too Few Students*, 31 Intl. Law. 845 (1997).

[143] Id. available at http://www.law.pitt.edu/academics/programs/cile-uncitral2005.php (accessed on or before Mar. 30, 2008).

[144] *See* Cornell University Law School, International, The Clarke Center for International and Comparative Legal Studies, available at http://www.lawschool.cornell.edu/international/ (last accessed Feb. 15, 2008). Endowed in 2001, the "Clarke Center provides an administrative infrastructure for faculty and student initiatives, and Clarke funds support international alumni activities and enhancement of the law library's international and comparative collections." Id.

[145] Thus, for example, Santa Clara University School of Law requires enrollment in one of its summer programs of study abroad as a requirement for receipt of a certificate in international law. *See* Santa Clara University, School of Law, Center for Global Law and Policy, International Law Certificate, available at http://www.scu.edu/law/international/international_ce-rtificate.html (last accessed Feb. 11, 2007).

[146] New York University, Hauser Global Law School Program, About Us, available at http://www.nyulawglobal.org/aboutus/aboutus.htm (last accessed Feb. 7, 2007).

has depended on the ability of New York University to attract a constant stream of foreign faculty for short visits to the New York University home campus.[147] Thus, rather than sending its students out into the world, it attempts to bring knowledge of the world to its students, and in the process appears to deepen the home faculty commitment to the program. There are great benefits for students having the "authentic" foreign element brought to them in New York City. But the resources required for this sort of program may be beyond the reach of all but a few schools.

5.3.3 Emerging Framework Structures: An Immersion Model for Incorporating the International and Transnational Element in Law School Curriculum, Research and Service

Two emerging framework structures stand out among the less traditional approaches to the incorporation of transnational elements in legal education. The first, the immersion model, applies the lessons of economic globalization to the business of legal education. Its success depends on the ability of a law school to forge effective networks with law schools in other states. Together, these networks of law schools could, by each offering little more than their own parochial law as the basis of instruction, provide students willing to travel among them the opportunity to acquire a strong grounding in law across jurisdictions. The second, the multi-disciplinary departmental model, is based on the idea that the transnational element in law is distinct enough to merit a substantial treatment in its own right. Grounded in the traditional segregation model, it extracts all international and transnational legal studies—teaching and research—from the undifferentiated law school curriculum and places it within associated or affiliated departments

---

"At New York University School of Law, globalization is…a fundamental organizing principle. The Hauser Global Law School Program (HGLSP) reflects the Law School's conviction that the practice of law has escaped the bounds of any particular jurisdiction and that legal education can no longer ignore the interpenetration of legal systems." Id.

[147] The Law School describes this for outsiders:

> Approximately 80 new courses have been taught by members of the Global Law Faculty, and approximately 50 courses have been co-taught with full-time NYU Law professors. These courses touch every part of the curriculum, including business law, criminal law, family law, international and comparative law, labor law, legal philosophy, property law, international taxation and trade regulation. The global faculty teach these courses to all Law School students, not merely to those who anticipate careers as international lawyers.

New York University School of Law, Hauser Global Law Studies Program, Courses, available at http://www.nyulawglobal.org/courses/globalcourses.htm (last accessed Feb. 8, 2007).

of international law or international affairs that is not just a separate law department but a focus of multi-disciplinary study built around the study of rule systems across borders.

1. *Immersion Model*: It is possible to construct out of the very recent developments in legal education, the skeleton of a possible alternative model that is identified here as the immersion model. This model suggests the disingenuousness of American academic retooling for the purposes of conveying the law of other places. It also places little value on the current form of delivering such education to American law students abroad—principally through summer and semester programs in which American students remain segregated for the most part in foreign places, taught for the most part by American faculty and from American case books or American materials—in English. The focus of this approach is to acknowledge that Americans are best at their own national law systems, and that others, likewise, are best at theirs. There is a shared knowledge with respect to cross-border law and international law perhaps, but even there, the perspective will be different.

The immersion method starts from the idea that law of other jurisdictions is best learned in those jurisdictions, with their students and in their language. It suggests that international and transnational law may require a sensitivity to context that makes collaborative efforts essential to understand all sides of any transaction involving the application of the law of multiple jurisdictions. As a consequence, a truly transnational program requires the participation of educational institutions in multiple jurisdictions. It requires the ability to learn in the language in which law is written—whether it be French, German, Mandarin or Thai, unless the institution is willing to limit exposure to English-only programs abroad. It accepts that beyond some level of generality, the transnational element of legal education must always be partial. Students must choose language, system and perspective. There can be no such thing, at a level of specificity necessary for practice, of the possibility of an acquisition of a generalist's knowledge. The object of such education, in the most developed case, ought to be licensing in the multiple jurisdictions studied. In less developed cases, the object might be to cultivate a level of expertise sufficient to be a careful observer of the law of the "foreign" jurisdiction. In this sense, the immersion perspective can be understood as classical comparative law applied. Where a program is satisfied with the cultivation of a more general knowledge—in foreign and domestic environments but grounded in conflicts of laws and international law and legal systems—the immersion program can be understood as closer to a classical education as a private or public international law education, though one ultimately based in a single domestic jurisdiction. It is possible to seek to produce generalists, even under an immersion approach.

In either case, the bulk of law school resources would not be used on "retooling" or otherwise requiring faculty trained in the municipal law of the state in which they might be licensed to learn something else. No incorporation of the "international", "transnational" or "comparative" element of law would be required. That education would come *in situ* abroad, to the extent that it is otherwise not attainable within the domestic institution. The greatest expenditure would be focused on the cultivation and maintenance of webs of relationships with other institutions in other states. This would require arrangements that would permit American students to study in other places, with reciprocal rights in the students of the host institution. American legal academic institutions already have a certain experience with more or less ad hoc relationships of this sort. But most of these relationships are flexible and informal, even in the context of formal institutionalizing relationships. Thus, for example, the North American Consortium on Legal Education (NACLE) has been operating for a number of years as a vehicle for the promotion of student and faculty exchanges among law schools in Canada, Mexico and the United States.[148] These sort of cooperative arrangements have been encouraged by authoritative institutions and personalities within legal academia.[149]

Still, institutionalizing these relationships and rationalizing them to provide a consistent and measurable cumulative educational experience would be more difficult. This is especially so where the object is not merely exchange but the attainment of an educational experience sufficiently detailed to merit the awarding of a degree. The difficulty is thus compounded by limitations of time and the requirements of licensing jurisdictions. Yet, there are institutions that have already begun to forge these networks. For example, Michigan State University College of Law has formally institutionalized a joint degree program with the law faculty of the University of Ottawa.[150]

---

[148] For a description, *see* Nancy B. Rapoport, *When Local IS Global: Using a Consortium of Law Schools to Encourage Global Thinking*, 20 Penn St. Intl. L. Rev. 19 (2001). The NACLE website suggests that "Laws emanate from legal cultures that are rooted in the history, culture, language, traditions and music of a society. By participating in a NACLE student exchange program, you will be gain a cultural experience that is as important as the learning experience of studying codes and judicial decisions. And you will take a journey that you will never forget." NACLE, Home Campuses, available at http://www.nacle.org/content.asp?secnu-m=17 (last accessed Feb. 9, 2007).

[149] *See*, e.g., Carl C. Monk, *Working Together: Developing Cooperation in International Legal Exchange*, 20 Penn St. Intl. L. Rev. 23 (2001).

[150] The description on the Michigan State University web site states:

> Graduates of the Joint J.D.–LL.B. Degree Program are ready to practice law transnationally. One of the most exciting programs at MSU College of Law and the University of Ottawa Faculty of Law, Common Law Section is their joint-degree program, where students earn both the American J.D. degree and the Canadian LL.B. degree. Earning both a U.S. and Canadian law degree will prepare students for the economic and social consequences of international integration and globalization, making graduates quite marketable on either side of the border.

The program permits students to choose where they begin their education. They are obliged to fulfill all of the mandatory course requirements at each institution but can earn their degrees by residence at each for two years.[151] Students must meet the entrance requirements of both institutions.[152] Other schools have similar single programs, including the University of Southern California,[153] Harvard Law School,[154] New York University Law School[155] and the University of Detroit Mercy School of Law.[156]

Some law schools have begun to develop more complex networks of joint degree programs. Columbia University Law School, for example, has instituted multiple joint degree programs among which a student may

The description of the program is available at http://www.law.msu.edu/academics/ac-multi-llb.html (last accessed Feb. 6, 2007).

151 Id.

152 Id.

153 The University of Southern California School of Law has established a joint degree program with the London School of Economics. *See* University of Southern California School of Law, Graduate and International Programs, available at http://lawgip.usc.edu/studyabroad/jdl-seinfo.cfm (last accessed Feb. 5, 2007). "The program, which began last year, currently includes three LSE students, who are studying at USC Law, while four USC Law students are studying abroad. LSE students participating in the program earn their J.D./LL.B. after completing two years of law study at LSE, followed by two years at USC Law." University of Southern California School of Law, News and Events, Semester Ends for Law Students in London, Dec. 1, 2006. USC also hosts a semester exchange program with the University of Hong Kong. *See* University of Southern California School of Law, Graduate and International Programs, available at http://lawgip.usc.edu/studyabroad/jdhkuinf-o.cfm (last accessed Feb. 5, 2007).

154 Harvard Law School offers a joint J.D. LL.M. degree program with Cambridge University in England. "This program offers Harvard JD candidates the opportunity to earn a Cambridge LLM and a Harvard JD in a total of three and a half years. Each year up to six Harvard 2Ls will be selected to spend their 3L year reading for the LLM degree in Cambridge, England. Following the LLM year, they return to HLS for their final JD semester." Harvard Law School, Joint Degree Programs, available at http://www.law.harvard.edu/academics/special_programs/jo-int.php#jdllm (last accessed Feb. 4, 2007).

155 New York University School of Law, NYU@NUS, The NYU School of Law and NUS Dual Degree Program, available at http://www.nyulawglobal.org/graduateadmissions/singapor-e/index.htm (last accessed Feb. 7, 2007). "New York University School of Law and National University of Singapore (NUS) are pleased to announce an exciting new dual degree program to be offered in Singapore at NUS. The inaugural class will begin in May 2007. Students enrolled in the NYU School of Law and NUS Dual Degree Program (NYU@NUS) will earn an LL.M. in Law and the Global Economy from NYU and an LL.M. from NUS. Courses will be taught by NYU and NUS faculty." Id.

156 *See*, e.g., the joint J.D. LL.B. program between the University of Windsor Faculty of Law and the University of Detroit Mercy School of Law, available at http://www.uwindsor.ca/jdllb (last accessed Feb. 1, 2007). The program suggests the value of this degree in the following terms: "In a competitive global economy, a key success factor is the ability to provide a service that your competitor cannot match. A joint degree can be the first step to advancing your competitive edge." Id.

choose.[157] What makes the Columbia program particularly interesting is that it is one of the few joint degree programs that are not tied to English language instruction. The Vermont Law School offers a similar dual degree program with universities in France that permit the student, upon completion of the program, to sit for licensing exams in both France and the United States.[158] The barrier of language, especially for American law students, may become a great impediment to the growth of these programs beyond a small group of universities.

However alluring this method might be, and for the purists there is some allure, it is difficult, at the moment, to gauge the willingness of American academics to put the bulk of their resources for international and transnational training in efforts that require a substantial investment in new faculty and new locations. Moreover, it is not clear that leveraging the "domestic" component of a network of globally placed law schools will provide any education in the transnational element of law. On the other hand, it requires much more administrative resources than academic resources. Law faculties continue to do what they have done in the way they have done it; administrators manage the network and their subordinates coordinate and implement the program through the movement of students. In a sense, this approach adapts the framework on which the E.U.'s highly successful Erasmus and Socrates Programs are grounded.[159] It does suggest that a

---

[157] This is described in its literature:

> In 1994, Columbia was the first U.S. Law School to establish a double degree program providing its participants with both a U.S. Juris Doctor and a foreign law degree, in this instance the French Maitrise en Droit. Recently, Columbia has expanded its foreign double degree programs to include a four-year JD/LLB from Columbia and the University of London, and a three-year JD/LL.M., also with the University of London, and a three-year JD/DESS with the Institut d'etudes politiques ("Sciences-Po") and the Universite de Paris I – Pantheon Sorbonne.

Columbia Law School, Double Degree Program, Foreign Dual Degree, available at http://www.law.columbia.edu/center_program/intl_progs/Double_degrees (last accessed Feb. 3, 2007).

[158] *See* Vermont Law School, Academic Program & Calendar: International & Comparative Law Programs: Program Options: Dual Degree Program, available at http://www.vermontlaw.edu/academic/index.cfm?doc_id=990 (last accessed Feb. 12, 2007) "Participating students spend two years of study at Vermont Law School and two years in France. The program is unique in two respects: it involves study at two French universities—the University of Cergy-Pontoise and the University of Montpellier—and it involves two internships at French law firms. . . .Graduates will be able to sit for the bar examination in each country, according to each country's requirements." Id.

[159] *See* generally Louis F. Del Duca, *Cooperation in Internationalizing Legal Education in Europe—Emerging New Players*, 20 Penn St. Intl. L. Rev. 7 (2001). The European Union describes the Socrates Program "Socrates is Europe's education programme and involves around 30 European countries. Its main objective is precisely to build up a Europe of knowledge and thus provide a better response to the major challenges of this new century. . . .Socrates advocates European cooperation in all areas

method of incorporating the transnational element might be on the basis of the creation of a network of relationships with other institutions worldwide, and moving students around such a network.

Perhaps the most ambitious version of an immersion model is being developed now by the Georgetown University Law Center. Starting in the 2008–09 academic year, the Law Center will "open a first-of-its-kind Center for Transnational Legal Studies in the heart of London's legal quarter. The program will bring together faculty and students from several of the world's top law schools to study transnational legal issues in a multicultural and transnational setting."[160] The program is organized as a joint venture with a network of international law school partners, including the University of Fribourg (in Switzerland), the Hebrew University of Jerusalem, King's College London, the University of Melbourne, the National University of Singapore and the University of Toronto.[161] Each of the participating law schools will send faculty and students to the Program. The object is to foster cross-jurisdictional communication and learning. Each student and faculty member brings to the program his or her own expertise which is then blended with those of the other participants to provide a multi-jurisdictional experience not only for the students but for faculty as well.[162]

The program will develop its own curriculum. "The program will also include a core course focused on transnational legal theory, a weekly workshop featuring some of the world's leading scholars and practitioners of international, transnational, and comparative law, and a participatory exercise to introduce students to each other and to the different perspectives that they bring to the Center." Interestingly, the

---

of education. This cooperation takes different forms: mobility (moving around Europe), organising joint projects, setting up European networks (disseminating ideas and good practice), and conducting studies and comparative analyses." Socrates, European Community action programme in the field of education (2000–2006), Gateway to education, available at http://ec.europa.eu/education/programmes/socrates/socra-tes_en.html (last accessed Jan. 31, 2007). Erasmus is the higher education portion of the Socrates II program; it "seeks to enhance the quality and reinforce the European dimension of higher education by encouraging transnational cooperation between universities, boosting European mobility and improving the transparency and full academic recognition of studies and qualifications throughout the Union." European Commission, Education and Training, Socrates-Erasmus: The European Community Programme in the Field of Higher Education, available at http://ec.europa.eu/education/programmes/socrates/erasmus/erasmus_en.html (last accessed Jan. 31, 2007).

160 Georgetown University Law Center, New Center for Transnational Legal Studies, available at http://www.law.georgetown.edu/ctls/info/index.html#Newctrtranslegal (last accessed Feb. 16, 2008).

161 Id.

162 "Students at the Center for Transnational Legal Studies will gain new perspectives and understandings through a concentrated program of international, transnational, and comparative law in a truly multicultural setting, with students and faculty from many other legal systems." Id.

curriculum, like the program, is a communal project, at least to some extent. It is intended to be "developed under the direction of an Academic Council comprised of leading faculty from all the founding schools, and coordinated by Georgetown."[163]

Even so, as with all internationalization of curriculum programs, there is a certain tension in the elaboration of this program. The descriptive materials, for example, remind students of the potential difficulties of searching for jobs while abroad during the heart of the traditional domestic job search season.[164] There is also a bit of the usual sort of gaming built into the program. "Students studying at the Center for Transnational Legal Studies will receive credit for each approved course for which they receive a passing grade. Individual courses and credits taken and the grades will appear on the Georgetown transcript, but the grades will not be factored into the Georgetown GPA."[165] Moreover, the necessities of the academic regime make it less possible to engage in more applied learning during the semester abroad.[166]

Most importantly, perhaps, are a number of structural limitations on programs of this kind built into domestically grounded rules for the delivery of legal education in the United States. In one respect, and for all of its ingenuity, the program is essentially a semester abroad program. The program is run by a consortium of law schools and the curriculum is a joint effort of these partners, but the framework is still limited by the residence and accreditation requirements of American legal education.[167] Additionally, the program is substantially tied to the home institution in critical ways. Most importantly, the program is not degree granting. Students receive a Certificate of Completion of Academic Study at the end of the semester and will offer degree credit.[168] In this respect, the program resembles a certificate

---

163 Id.

164 "Spending a semester abroad can be very beneficial to your overall career goals. However, it may also have implications for the timing of your job search. For example, the application and interview process for many judicial clerkships, government honor programs, and public interest fellowships occur during the fall of the final year of law school." Id.

165 Id.

166 "Students are discouraged from pursuing employment opportunities during the semester, but might consider a London or other overseas summer job preceding or following their semester at the Center." Id.

167 *See* ABA Standards for Approval of Law Schools, Standard 307, available at http://www.abanet.org/legaled/standards/standards.html (last accessed Feb. 19, 2008). For a discussion of the standards for the approval of foreign law study, *see* American Bar Association, Section on Legal Education and Admissions to the Bar, Foreign Study, available at http://www.abanet.org/legaled/studyabroad/foreignstudyhome.html (last accessed Feb. 19, 2008).

168 *See* Georgetown University Law Center, New Center for Transnational Legal Studies, available at http://www.law.georgetown.edu/ctls/info/index.html#Newctrtranslegal (last accessed Feb. 16, 2008).

program well developed within the American legal academy.[169] This is a particularly important issue because the program is available to Georgetown law students who have already completed their course of study leading to the J.D.[170] The ability to constitute a program capable of providing graduates with an advanced degree, perhaps by extending study over two semesters, would substantially enhance the value of this program beyond its origins as a certificate program and its semester abroad methodologies.

2. *Multi-Disciplinary Departmental Model*: Law schools have begun to consider the value of establishing schools or departments of international transactions or international affairs (a "DIA"). In a sense, it could be said to take the essence of the New York University model, based on the development of a self-contained but porous unit of the law school devoted to a particular focus of law related education,[171] and use that as a basis for the reconstruction of law school pedagogy. Alternatively, the department could be kept free of direct law school faculty participation or affiliation and serve merely as an organizing focus for the interdisciplinary teaching of the international and transnational elements of law.

It might be suggested that these new departments enrich the legal curriculum by offering courses of instruction designed to prepare individuals for positions of leadership in organizations that will bring global solutions to global problems. Such an approach would permit a law school not only to segregate international and transnational legal education within its institutional matrix, but also to use the segregation as a means of focusing on building bridges to related disciplines that would enrich any study of legal issues across borders. Thus, a DIA can serve as an institutional site for substantial, yet focused, efforts to build interdisciplinary elements into legal education. For schools where adherence to a traditional municipal (local, state or national) law focus is difficult to overcome, this may serve as a means of preserving the traditional core focus of the institution while creating an open-ended framework for the expansion of non-traditional approaches to the study of new legal issues.

A DIA can also serve as a space within which all of the international and transnational energies of a law school can be focused. This approach is essentially the conceptual opposite of the immersion model. Instead of incorporating the transnational element within the curriculum and research/service of a substantial portion of the faculty, the multi-disciplinary department model starts with the assumption that the most efficient means of bringing the transnational element of law into law schools is to segregate

---

[169] *See* Larry Catá Backer, *General Principles of Academic Specialization By Means of Certificate or Concentration Programs: Creating a Certificate Program in International, Comparative and Foreign Law at Penn State*, 20 Penn. St. Int. L. Rev. 67 (2001).

[170] "Georgetown students are also invited to apply to attend the Center for a semester following graduation." Id.

[171] *See* discussion, *supra*, at text and notes 146–147.

the efforts. Once segregated, the transnational elements can be extracted and privileged within an environment in which it can be amplified by other related disciplines—international relations, politics, economics and business, for example. This extraction and recombination points to the great synergies possible with this approach, putting together lawyers and academics from related fields working together in an increasingly unified and powerful academic discipline with many sub-disciplines (international law, international relations, comparative law, political theory, etc.).[172] It provides efficiency and convenience, making international and transnational issues easy to place, maintain and resource.

On the other hand, there can be significant difficulties with this approach. For example, at its worst, it can serve as little more than a vehicle for empire building by deans and others eager to create something else to brag about without directly affecting the operation of the law school as such. Related to that is the issue of connectivity. Such a program runs a real risk of relating to law in name only. Unmoored from traditional programs, they might become orphans to be ultimately abandoned or perhaps merged with international studies or other graduate departments. This approach also runs the risk of isolating faculty from its creation and operation. DIA programs can be effectuated outside of the law school environment. Law school faculty could have little to say about its structure, operations and most important, relationship to the law school itself. To the extent that a DIA would be operated independently of the law school, it would run the risk of losing core law school support.

There are two substantially different methods of incorporating a DIA. The first would be to affiliate a non-law DIA into the official structure of a law school as an autonomous department. Such a department would house the multi-disciplinary elements of transnational legal education. Its personnel could include faculty from other schools in a university, serving on a joint appointment basis. Alternatively, the law school could serve as the tenure home for a small core of faculty whose primary emphasis is not on law but who work in law-related areas of their respective fields—everything from law and economics to politics, business and international relations. The department would then serve as the focus through which an integrated system of law and law-related courses emphasizing the transnational element could be developed and offered. It also serves as a place where other activities—conferences, workshops, grants, and other programs—can be housed.

---

[172] This model suggests the Canadian approach of teaching civil and common law within one faculty, but the division is along distinct functional lines. For a discussion of the approach at McGill, *see* Peter L. Strauss, *Transsystemia—Are We Approaching a New Langdellian Moment? Is McGill Leading the Way?* 56 J. Leg. Educ. 161 (2006); Rosalie Jukier, *Transnationalizing the Legal Curriculum: How to Teach What We Live*, 56 J. Leg. Educ. 172 (2006).

Alternatively, it might be possible to move all law school faculty with primary international and transnational research or teaching interests to an affiliated DIA. They, along with non-law faculty, could together constitute an autonomous and internally complete department within the law school. Courses offered by these faculty (along with those offered by the members of that School) would be cross-listed as law school courses, and all research and programmatic issues associated with the international and transnational element of law could be funneled through the department of International Affairs. An associate dean of international law programs at the law school could also serve as an associate dean of academic affairs at the Department of International Affairs. Under this approach, the law school would have created a vehicle through which it could separate the domestic from the transnational elements of legal education. The principal benefit would be to avoid disruption in the way law schools operate. Rather than force or induce change within a law school, a DIA model would serve as an addition (albeit an extremely significant one) to the body of the law school and its mission. It would change the fundamental orientation of a law school from strictly legal to effectively multi-disciplinary. It moves law schools away from a strict professional school model to one that might appear to reclaim its place within the traditional university, but without affecting the primary mission to train lawyers.

Despite its severe limitations (from the perspective of running an integrated law program), this model has yet to be successfully implemented in the United States,[173] but it has certain possibilities that may be worth exploring in more detail. The section that follows suggests some of the issues that may arise in the creation and implementation of a DIA model within (or affiliated with) a law school. It proposes a possible approach to the implementation of such a program. It focuses on the addition of non-law related elements to the DIA and assumes that these elements will serve to supplement the inclusion of all of the non-domestic (international, comparative, foreign and transnational) law elements (and faculty) from the law school. In some cases, law schools might even consider creating an integrated but freestanding degree-granting department. Such a DIA would not only serve as an institutional space for the transnational resources of a law school, but also provide graduate level education in the related areas of international affairs. It is that model that serves as a basis for the discussion that follows.

---

[173] In 2007, the board of trustees of the Pennsylvania State University approved the creation of a School of International Affairs to be affiliated with the Penn State Law School. It is far too early to tell, however, how the model will actually be incorporated within that university structure and more specifically the development of its relationship and integration into the operations of the law school there. *See* University to Establish School of International Affairs (Feb. 1, 2007), available at http://www.giveto.psu.edu/news/003866/default.aspx (last accessed Feb. 9, 2007).

A DIA affiliated with a law school should differ in significant ways from a typical school or department of international or foreign affairs. A DIA with strong connection to the work of a law school should concentrate on the law aspects of all areas of international affairs. The DIA might then serve not only law students but also graduate students with an interest in international affairs from other university departments. In this form, such a department could serve as the focal point of a J.D. program as well as a department autonomous enough to make available its own graduate degree (a master's degree and ultimately perhaps even doctoral programs).[174] Recipients of post-graduate degrees in international affairs or international transactions would be prepared to become highly effective participants in the formulation, analysis, advocacy, implementation and monitoring of policy in governmental or private organizations. This section considers the contours of such a freestanding but affiliated department.

i. *Rationale and Objectives*: DIA will be most effective if it can avoid two great pitfalls. The first would be to duplicate substantive study in fields already offering graduate degrees at the university. DIA would then merely repeat what already exists. The second pitfall would be to repeat what already exists in the law school by creating another focused legal postgraduate degree—a dressed up LL.M. To differentiate itself a DIA program would have to offer something unlike anything already offered. A good DIA program should advance a new and distinct mode of analysis. This mode of analysis should provide the basis for transforming the substantive knowledge from the other academic units of a university into policy, and from policy into action.

DIA could create an environment in which to focus on all aspects of challenges that transcend national boundaries. Today, these challenges can be global, regional or bi-lateral. Challenges touch on all aspects of human

---

[174] Indeed, it might be possible to use the DIA not only as a place within which to develop multi-disciplinary degree programs (masters and doctoral programs) but also an essential resource in the building of post J.D. law programs that focus on transnational aspects of law (from an LL.M. to S.J.D. programs). And significantly, such an association might be useful as a means of providing degrees that are recognized in other jurisdictions. As an example, the Bologna Process states that it is "an intergovernmental initiative which aims to create a European Higher Education Area (EHEA) by 2010 and to promote the European system of higher education worldwide. It now has 45 signatory countries and it is conducted outside the formal decision-making framework of the European Union. Decision-making within the Process rests on the consent of all the participating countries." Europe Unit UK, The Bologna Process, available at http://www.europeunit.ac.uk/bologna_process/index.cfm (last accessed Feb. 1, 2007). For a description of the Bologna Process for degree recognition, *see*, e.g., The U.K. HE Europe Unit, *Guide to the Bologna Process*, available at http://www.europeunit.ac.uk/resources/Guide%20to%20the%20Bologna%20Process%20booklet.pdf (last accessed Feb. 1, 2007). For a discussion of its application in the context of American legal education, *see* Laurel S. Terry, *The Bologna Process and Its Implications for U.S. Legal Education*, 57(2) J. Legal Educ. 237 (2007).

interaction; they can range from migration, to communicable diseases, to trade barriers, to corruption, to access to education, food and economic opportunity. Actors meeting those challenges are no longer just governmental: policy is now an integral part of the operation of a great constellation of nongovernmental actors, ranging from organizations formed to further specific policy goals, to global religious organizations, to large multi-national corporations. DIA could focus on the major transnational policy actors affecting and affected by law, actual current policy issues, the language and recognized approaches to contemporary policy analysis and the methodologies of implementation and monitoring of policy "as applied."

Based on this focus on the policy actors, contemporary policy problems, forms of policy analysis and methodologies of implementation of solutions to problems with global effect, DIA could offer a course of study. The principal aim of this course of study would be to provide students with comprehensive and rigorous training sufficient to enable them to function effectively in international affairs, from the conceptualization and formulation of policy to its implementation and monitoring.

The DIA approach presents issues of separation, as in the case of accreditation. The establishment of a department of international affairs within a law school has certain implications for accreditation, but none for certification or licensure. Accreditation may be obtained through a professional organization—the Association of Professional Schools of International Affairs ("APDIA"). APDIA "comprises 29 member schools in the United States, Asia and Europe dedicated to the improvement of professional education in international affairs and the advancement thereby of international understanding, prosperity, peace, and security. APDIA members work to promote excellence in professional, international affairs education worldwide by sharing information and ideas among member schools and with other higher education institutions, the international affairs community, and the general public."[175] Membership in APDIA need not be required for the DIA to commence operation, but is highly desirable that this should be the ultimate goal.

Membership in APDIA requires conformity to a number of requirements.[176] These criteria can be demonstrated in a variety of ways.[177] In addition, the law school would have to be sensitive to accreditation issues

---

[175] For information on APDIA, *see* their website at http://www.apDIA.org/apDIA/index.php

[176] These include the following: (a) an educational program of high academic quality; (b) a substantial and demonstrated commitment to the study of international affairs; (c) a basic commitment to graduate professional training; and (d) significant autonomy within a major university, e.g., as one would expect to find with a law school or graduate business school. *See* APDIA membership qualifications available at http://www.apDIA.org/apDIA/membership/membership.php (accessed on or before Mar. 30, 2008).

[177] The APDIA describes these as follows:

under ABA[178] and AALS[179] rules. These would require a showing that the additional programs would not substantially detract from the traditional J.D. program.

ii. *Formalizing the DIA: Vision and Mission Statements*: Mission and vision statements can provide a useful method for the articulation of well tailored objectives for a DIA meant to be centered on law. Though usually largely general, they can provide the boundaries for the implementation of any program. These statements may be a critical means of keeping the law school effectively tied to the development of any DIA.

A vision statement ought to provide a general framework within which a law related program of international affairs could be constructed and against which such a program could be measured.[180] The mission statement ought to provide the department with the opportunity to focus its

---

> The existence of these qualifications may be demonstrated by the following: (a) significant programs of research and publications in international affairs; (b) an integrated curriculum comprised of courses for the most part, if not exclusively, developed and located in the professional international affairs school; (c) an integrated curriculum which combines professional training, the study of geographical regions, and the analytical tools of specialized disciplines; (d) a record of educating graduates for and in cooperation with distinctive clienteles, including international affairs agencies, international business and financial corporations, international organizations, and the communications and academic professions; (e) a substantial, if not exclusive, commitment to professionally oriented graduate education; (f) a faculty for the most part integral to or designated for the professional school; (g) a relationship to the parent university characterized by substantial autonomy as is usual to a professional school within higher education; (h) programs abroad, including exchange and affiliation arrangements.

See APDIA Membership Qualifications, available at http://www.apDIA.org/apDIA/membership/membership.php (accessed on or before Mar. 30, 2008).

178 On law school accreditation, *see*, e.g., The Princeton Review, What You Should Know About Law School Accreditation, available at http://www.princetonreview.com/law/research/ar-ticles/find/accreditation.asp (last accessed Aug. 12, 2007). It is possible that separation may detract from accreditation since it might be viewed as drawing resources away from law teaching in a manner to goes against the policies of the accreditation standards.

179 On the rules of the Association of American Law Schools, *see* American Association of Law Schools, Bylaws and Executive Regulations Pertaining to the Requirements of Membership (Aug. 2005), available at http://www.aals.org/about_handbook_requirements.php (last accessed Aug. 30, 2007).

180 A vision statement for a department of international affairs intimately tied to a law school should include a reference to its focus (for example, to be a leading institution for defining and strengthening the field of international affairs (IA) in the academic community worldwide). It should describe the going forward basis of its connection with programs of traditional legal education (for example, provide the foundation for the implementation of DIA's unique mission). It could also point to the general nature of the connection between international affairs and law in the planned courses of study (for example, to be known for conducting boundary-pushing, multi- and inter-disciplinary research focused on the integration of the key constructs of international or cross border affairs—key public and private institutional actors developing, advocating, implementing

objectives.[181] It should memorialize a commitment to the teaching of international and transnational legal issues by indicating the nature of its commitment to the training of students[182] and should indicate the nature of the department's focus on research and service.[183] The mission statement might also indicate the sort of training the department will impart.[184] In addition, it might be worth considering the ways in which the DIA could leverage the particular strengths of the law school to which it is affiliated. These might include strengths in local or regional law, faculty or programmatic strengths in interdisciplinary collaboration, policy, analysis, or collaborations across the university, a particular emphasis on collaborative learning and especially learning through the use of on-line and in-class technologies as well as cutting-edge pedagogies such as problem-based learning models of teaching and learning, or facility in the use of information technology to increase accessibility to the curricula through programs of sharing alone and in partnership with other related academic enterprises.

In considering the mission or vision statements, there should be a significant consideration of the ways the department could be built as an organization that insists on respect for individual and intellectual diversity that defines the interdisciplinary vision demands from the faculty, staff, and students. The process of developing either a mission or vision statement could also serve as the point in the planning and implementation process in which the organizers can think through how the department could be used to create a broad-based set of curricula that shares a commitment to the global perspectives of education, especially to the extent they might draw on existing strengths and curricular elements already in place in the institution. The importance of additional programs—such as conferences,

---

and monitoring policy—that crosses disciplinary boundaries and links theory with application).

[181] For example, it might provide that the department will serve as the academic unit where the knowledge derived from the substantive fields of study at a research university is cast into policy terms, transformed into rules, and applied by institutional and other actors into action that directly affect the lives of people and institutions.

[182] For example, a mission statement might provide that the department is committed to prepare individuals for positions of leadership in organizations that will bring global solutions to global problems.

[183] For example, the mission statement might suggest generally the ways in which department will seek to improve the lives of people through high quality teaching and learning, internationally recognized research and outreach, and associations with leading IA global institutions.

[184] The mission statement, for example, can state that DIA degree holders will be prepared to become highly effective participants in the formulation, analysis, advocacy, implementation and monitoring of policy in governmental or private organizations. DIA will offer a rigorous program of professional education founded on a multi-disciplinary approach to the training of its students. And the DIA will train students in the application of theory and substantive analysis to practical issues in international affairs.

joint research projects, partnerships with business, industry, government, and other educational institutions, student joint educational programs, and faculty sabbatical placements (inbound and outbound)—ought to be developed as well.

iii. *An Example of a Possible Core Curriculum*: The DIA curriculum could be built upon the realities of the actual "business" of law-based international affairs in the contemporary world. That focus, for example, could be divided into four areas of study: actors,[185] policy,[186] tools[187] and realization.[188]

---

[185] International affairs are not conducted in a vacuum. Since 1945, the business of international affairs, and especially in its expression through law, has been institutionalized within a complex matrix of public and private institutions. The number of forms of public institutions has expanded significantly in the last century. Global political organization has moved from a loose set of interactions among nation-state to systems of national interdependence in which a number of new forms of other public international actors play increasingly important roles. These new actors range from loose global associations, centered on the United Nations, to overlapping bi-lateral and regional systems of economic, human rights and criminal regulation. But the greatest change in governance since 1945 has occurred in the private sector. The end of the twentieth century has witnessed the institutionalization of what is now recognized as international civil society. This is made up of countless groups organized in a variety of different ways to further all forms of policy objectives. These groups now play an increasingly important role in shaping policy. They play an even more important role in monitoring the implementation of policy. Thus, a basic understanding of the actors involved in the discourse of issues that require multi-national responses is essential for individuals involved in international affairs.

[186] The expression of international affairs in law are understood in policy terms. Policy expresses the substance of international affairs. Policy is an elastic concept embracing laws, rules, actions, plans and behaviors, as well as their social and legislative ramifications. It can be expressed as the things public entities choose to do (e.g., to build a dam to generate power) or not do (e.g., not to build a dam to preserve the environment). It can also be understood as a product of the collective effect of the conscious choices of private entities (e.g., to standardize scientific terminology). And it can include rules or understandings resulting from the action or lack of action of individual private actors (e.g., standardization of letters of credit). Policy is given life through the actions of actors through which it is formulated, implemented, and monitored. It is the language of substantive discourse of actors in the international affairs field.

[187] Policy does not appear unbidden. Policy does not sell itself to actors in international the public and private spheres of institutional society. Policy must be conceived, formulated, explained, justified, defended and advanced. Each of these functions requires certain analytic tools. These tools are drawn from a variety of disciplines: economics, sociology, politics, philosophy, psychology, mathematics, linguistics, quantitative analysis and empirical methods (e.g., econometrics), law, and business. Each provides a means of systematically evaluating alternative means of conceiving, developing, and achieving social goals. These tools supply a common language for policy choices among actors; they supply a mechanics for valuing choices among policy options. An ability to understand and use analytic tools is essential to the development of policy and the steering of policy to implementation.

[188] The object of policy is implementation. The rules of that implementation touch on issues of law and other disciplines. Policies unrealized are goals unrealized and good

The interdisciplinary and cooperative potential of DIA could be realized beyond the core curriculum. The objective would be to combine this core training with a specialized study in one or more areas. The curriculum also might draw upon regional or cultural subspecialties and language training. The emphasis, of course, would be on leveraging resources. For example, it might be possible to develop a set of curricular offerings to enable candidates for the Master's degree to select an area of concentration (AC). ACs could be designed to reflect the evolving emphases of policy makers and the interests of the students. Most could be identified as the substance of an evolving core course *Introduction to Current Policy Challenges*.

For programs of this kind, leveraging resources will be a critical factor in its success. For example, a DIA would have to rely on a large number of cross-listed courses. The mechanics of cross listing within large institutions, however, can also eat resources—the time and effort required to comply with multi-departmental and university rules for consultation, approval and cost sharing. This model would tend to favor larger capacity general purpose institutions over smaller and more focused institutions. Or it would require the expenditure of large sums to create courses where none existed before. Still, depending on the resources of the institution considering this alternative, the DIA model could offer its students the opportunity to choose an emphasis that could meet virtually any interest—from geography, to information technology, to agriculture, law, journalism, the social sciences, education, mathematics, the hard sciences or any other substantive field.[189]

The specific courses suggested for completing each of these concentrations would have to be developed at every institution. Once developed, students will also be encouraged to develop their own specialization based on their needs and desires. Programs of concentration will be adopted in close cooperation with DIA core and affiliate faculty, who will act as program of study advisors to DIA-Master's students.

---

undone. Taking policy from conceptualization to adoption represents one of the great tasks and serves as one of the great rewards of policy actors. Realization of policy does not happen by itself. It requires navigating complex, multi-state and multi-level systems of governance. It may require action among private actors as well as more formal action in the public sphere. There are systems, and systematic approaches, to policy realization. It requires an understanding of systems and politics, of law and psychology. Moreover, approaches to implementation may differ substantially from approaches to monitoring implemented policy, or seeking policy change. Approaches could also differ depending on the place of the actor within the systems of public and private actors involved in policy decision-making. A critical understanding of these complexities is essential to those who intend to further policy objectives.

[189] Areas of concentration, then, could emphasize the relative strengths of a particular institution. In this sense, DIA offers the potential for internal leveraging of capacity and deepening a branding of the institution within its fields of demonstrated competence. For some institutions that might mean a focus on dispute resolution, of others business transactions or finance, and for others human rights elements.

The development of concentrations also poses risks for law affiliated programs. Programs leading to their own degrees may well take on a life of their own. Moreover, interdisciplinary studies programs have a way of moving toward one or another of their component parts. If the focus is to privilege law, then it becomes critical to structure programs so that the emphasis on the legal aspects of the matters studied remains clear. But this may be difficult to the extent that the DIA program becomes autonomous, or more closely affiliated to other schools or fields of study. The great danger of segregation, even in an association context, such as that contemplated with a DIA model, is to avoid the likelihood of separation. It may be difficult to avoid the metamorphosis of such department from a law-based program to just another graduate program in the social sciences. As the authors of *Educating Lawyers* noted with some alarm, the pull of the university model is very strong.[190] The institutional structure of DIA programs may well pose the most significant threat to its own project of building international and transnational capacity for legal education.

5.4 Globalization of Education Models and the Principles of Educating Lawyers

Educating Lawyers had added a new and important wrinkle to the evaluation of the suitability of the forms used to integrate a global law element in American legal education. So too does the move toward the internationalization of the curriculum. Like the philosophy underlying *Educating Lawyers*, the normative basis supporting curricular internationalization is meant to serve the bar as a principal stakeholder in the industry producing lawyers and judges. Both also suggest the underlying difficulties of satisfying stakeholders in a multi-stakeholder industry in which institutional dynamics tend to favor one stakeholder class over others. That complexity might perhaps explain why the Carnegie Foundation appears as oblivious to the problem of curricular internationalization as those who have been working on internationalization have been to the important issues raised in *Educating Lawyers*.

Of course, not every law school is oblivious to the need to fold into its internationalization pedagogy the doctrinal-professional-ethical pedagogical standard of *Educating Lawyers*. The rhetoric of change usually includes some reference to the international curriculum. Georgetown's Global Practice Exercise is meant to "introduce students to the process of tackling real-world legal problems that transcend national boundaries."[191]

---

[190] *Educating Lawyers, supra* note 14, at 4, and discussion, *supra* notes 165–174.

[191] *See* Georgetown University Law Center, Courses Offered Both Semesters, Global Practice Exercise, available at http://www.law.georgetown.edu/ctls/courses/both.html #GlobalPracticeE-xercise (last accessed Feb. 19, 2008).

5.4.1 *Should Internationalization Be Sensitive to the Principles of Educating Lawyers?*

The argument presented here has taken it as given that there ought to be some integration between the domestic and international programs of study developed in law schools. For that reason alone it appears that to the extent that *Educating Lawyers* represents an important change in the pedagogy of legal education in its domestic law aspects, those changes ought to carry over to the issue of curricular internationalization as well. Still, this is a presumption worth considering a little further.

Consider the possibility that *Educating Lawyers* has nothing to do with the internationalization of the American law school curriculum. This argument can take several forms: First, there is a substantial difference between domestic and international law courses. Second, law schools have little capacity for teaching the practical and ethical aspects of law not tied to jurisdictions of licensure and practice. Third, the traditional pedagogy that forms part of the internationalizing curriculum itself rejects the *Educating Lawyers* approach. Fourth, the object of internationalization is not really to teach law in the same way as domestic law is taught. Fifth, the thrust of legal harmonization efforts renders *Educating Lawyers* substantially irrelevant.

First, the argument that there is a substantial difference between domestic and international law courses, though strong on its surface, is ultimately unsatisfying. It might be possible to suggest that domestic law and foreign or international law are substantially different in force, effect and consequence.[192] What applies to the teaching of domestic law might thus be irrelevant to the teaching of non-domestic regulatory regimes. This might be especially true since states rarely, if ever, test to international or foreign law. Since the practical and ethical element is more closely tied to those courses with respect to which there is an expectation of knowledge of such a framework (as in those areas tested to the bar), non-domestic courses need not address these issues. One could argue, for example, that forcing the teaching of non-domestic courses in an "American" context would denature that law and distort its transmission to the point that the thing taught bears no essential relation to its nominal origins. Comparative law scholars have sometimes taken something like this position with respect to

---

[192] But this confuses arguments with respect to field of legal study versus the methodology appropriate to that of that study. For an argument with respect to the distinctiveness of international litigation (but not necessarily to the need to teach it differently), *see*, e.g., Samuel P. Baumgartner, *Is Transnational Litigation Different?*, 25 U. Pa. J. Intl. Econ. L. 1297 (2004).

legal transplantations and interpretation.[193] Others have suggested a more positive perspective.[194]

> Many legal problems are conceptually the same wherever they arise. Jurists confront the same problem, for example, whenever a legal system protects private property, but allows the owner's rights to yield in cases of necessity. . . .We want our property law to protect owners but also people in urgent need. . . .Reconciling these norms is difficult, and solutions are often imperfect. But the problems are the same wherever they are encountered.[195]

This is a point strongly echoed in *Educating Lawyers*. A principal object of the pedagogical discussion was to drive home the point that teaching, to be effective, may require something more than what the traditional academic pedagogy requires. Transmission is a critical component of education. A signature pedagogy is thus both critical to any successful methodology and to the socialization process involved in the transmission of domestic and other law.[196] There is little reason to suggest merely because international training is different from domestic law training that this allows for a different socialization process. In any case, much of what passes for non-domestic law is hardly that. With the exception of foreign law, much of what passes for international and transnational law is actually domestic law, at least in the sense that it is incorporated into the American legal landscape in one way or another. There is nothing foreign or magical about the law of treaties, the law of human rights and humanitarian law, or customary international law. There are precise relationships between domestic law and these instruments or regulatory mechanisms, but there is hardly a cultural barrier cutting them off from domestic law.

Second, that law schools have little capacity for teaching the practical and ethical aspects of law not tied to jurisdictions of licensure and practice, while true enough in many cases, is irrelevant to the issue of the method of instruction and the value of that instructional methodology for students. This is particularly true with respect to foreign and comparative law. American law schools, for example, are not equipped to train students for the practice of the law of the European Union. The civil law method, or Shari'a, requires a precisely acquired expertise that may be difficult to pick up. This point touches most strongly on the practical education portion of *Educating Lawyers*. Without a connection to the licensing jurisdiction, it may be difficult to adequately incorporate the practice element. This

---

[193] *See*, e.g., William Ewald, *Comparative Jurisprudence (I): What Was It Like to Try a Rat?*, 143 U. Pa. L. Rev. 1889, 1896 (1995); Pierre Legrand, *On the Singularity of Law*, 47 Harv. Intl. L. J. 517, 522–525 (2006).

[194] *See*, e.g., Alan Watson, Legal Transplants: An Approach to Comparative Law (2nd ed. 1993) (1974).

[195] James Gordley, *Comparative Legal Research: Its Function in the Development of Harmonized Law*, 43 Am. J. Comp. L. 555, 560 (1995).

[196] *Educating Lawyers, supra*, note 14, at 4.

might be felt most acutely in the area of foreign law, and least acutely in areas such as international business transactions, commercial law or international arbitration classes. Consequently, with respect to these aspects of law, incorporation may be demanding.

Resource incapacity also touches on another important aspect of both incorporation of non-domestic law into the American law school curriculum and, more generally, on the changes proposed in *Educating Lawyers*. One of the great difficulties of teaching any subject beyond domestic law is the lack of resources. The accrediting agencies have been most sensitive to the resource issue in examining the allocation of resources within a law school. It is likely that the accrediting bodies will tend to expect that, all things being equal, that the marginal dollar of resources available should be expended to strengthen the domestic, rather than to expand the international aspects of legal education.[197] That insight is much more likely to govern the assessment of a law school's expansion of its course offerings and other educational programs beyond those necessary for preparation for local bar examinations among those law schools with less elevated reputations. Ironically, then, more modest forms of incorporation are more likely to pass muster with lower-ranked law schools than with law schools with more celebrated reputations.

As a general rule, lower-ranked schools are assumed to have fewer resources available to devote to teaching practice areas not tested on the bar examination. As a consequence, accreditation and reputational realities will tend to exacerbate a resource gap between lower and higher ranked law schools. It would follow that lower ranked law schools will be less able to incorporate non-domestic law into their curriculum than higher ranked schools. Still, the fact that lower ranked schools will be less likely to provide the same offerings as higher ranked (or better financially endowed) schools, does not touch on the key issue of *Educating Lawyers*—the form that these offerings should take. Merely because offerings will be more modest does not necessarily mean that the form of those offerings will be purely doctrinal. Moreover, there are a number of ways of overcoming the lack of resources. For example, it may be possible to combine a foreign post-graduate law degree program with an incorporation program in a way that makes it possible for a resource-modest law school to provide a richer level of offerings. Thus, targeted masters (LLM) students might be given tuition breaks in return for teaching practicum or applied foreign or transnational law segments of courses offered under the supervision of resident faculty. Capacity, then, is a relative matter, and might be susceptible to some flexibility with an appropriate use of resident talent.

---

[197] *See* ABA Standards for Approval of Law Schools, Standard 307, available at http://www.abanet.org/legaled/standards/standards.html (last accessed Feb. 19, 2008).

Third, though the traditional pedagogy of international and especially foreign law itself rejects the *Educating Lawyers* approach, that alone ought not to suggest a values maximizing pedagogy within American law schools. The pedagogy of foreign law schools has been an object of much discussion.[198] In a sense this argument would turn the thrust of *Educating Lawyers* against itself. It embraces the assumption that legal education involves a strong element of socialization. But because the socialization is targeted to non-domestic law, it ought to be taught the same way in America that it is overseas Ironically, many foreign law faculties have looked to the American law school as a model precisely because it is able to meld doctrine, practice and ethics to an extent impossible under traditional civil law regimes.[199] Moreover, the fact that foreign legal education follows its own dynamic does not necessarily require mindless mimicry in this country. There is a tendency, especially in those law schools that have imported foreign law school educational talent, to incorporate the mores of that faculty within the borders of the subject taught by that faculty. There is nothing easier than to allow the foreign faculty member to have her way in connection with the teaching of the foreign, comparative or international law that is the subject of their expertise. But the comfort of the traditions of a home jurisdiction and the methods of law training abroad may not translate well into an American educational environment. Indeed, one of the great insights of comparative law is the difficulty of transposition from one legal system to another.[200] The same terms may have very different meanings in different legal traditions.[201] Thus, the fact that law is taught in a particular way at the University of London, or that a faculty member taught in a particular way at the University of Bruges, for example, ought not to have much weight in determining how courses should be structured at an American law school.

Fourth, the object of internationalization is not really to teach law in the same way that domestic law is taught. The argument might go something

---

[198] *See*, e.g., Martin F. Bohmer, *Sobre la inexistencia del derecho de interés público en Argentina*, 3 Revista Jurídica de la Universidad de Palermo 131, 139 (Apr. 1998) and discussion at Larry Catá Backer, *Human Rights and Legal Education in the Western Hemisphere: Legal Parochialism and Hollow Universalism*, 21 Penn St. Intl. L. Rev. 115, 147–149 (2002).

[199] *See*, e.g., Larry Catá Backer, *Human Rights and Legal Education in the Western Hemisphere: Legal Parochialism and Hollow Universalism*, 21 Penn St. Intl. L. Rev. 115 (2002).

[200] On the difficulties of legal transpositions, *see*, e.g., Peter de Cruz, Comparative Law in a Changing World 510–517 (London: Routledge-Cavendish, 3rd ed., 2007); Bernhard Grossfeld, Core Questions of Comparative Law 97–99, 239–242 (Vivian Grosswald Curran, trans., Durham, NC: Carolina Academic Press, 2005).

[201] *See*, e.g., Juenger, *Listening to Law Professors Talk About Good Faith: Some Afterthoughts*, 69 Tulane L. Rev. 1255 (1995); Nicholas Kasirer, *Lex-Icographie Mercatoria*, 47 Am. J. Comp. L. 653 (1999).

like this: American law schools are constructed to do only one thing well—to train law students in the study and practice of the law which they might actually practice under license from the relevant licensing agency. Legal education must reflect the connection between doctrine and practice. No such connection exists between non-domestic law and practice. Yet this argument fails for a couple of reasons. First, there is nothing exotic about much of what passes for non-domestic law. International substantive law incorporated into law in this country is domestic law.[202] International (or transnational) arbitration systems are also domestic law in the sense that such systems are available to American clients and may be enforced in American courts.[203] Although they do have a logic and a social context of their own, that context is domestic in the sense that it is also part of the arsenal of an American lawyer's tools. What the argument reduces itself to, at best, is its comparative and foreign law components—the law of foreign states has a culture and logic of its own that ought to be respected if it is to be transmitted appropriately.[204] While it is true enough that American law schools are ill-equipped to teach the law of any foreign state, they are as capable as anyone else to teach the law of supra-national and international organizations. Indeed, to the extent that American lawyers already practice before agencies and institutions of such organizations, American law faculty already have a responsibility to train their students to work in those arenas. Indeed, as part of the local practice, transnational lawyering is local lawyering. International arbitration, the regulatory aspects of supra-national organizations, cross border contracts, financial transactions, or litigation, the rights of parties under bilateral investment treaties and the like all suggest the same sort of training imperatives as the law of domestic property that served as the basis of *Educating Lawyers*.

Fifth, the fact that legal harmonization in other parts of the globe might work against the suggested pedagogy developed in *Educating Lawyers* does not render it substantially irrelevant to efforts to incorporate non-domestic law into courses at American Law schools. Among the most interesting arguments that might be raised against the need to integrate the insights of *Educating Lawyers* into efforts to incorporate non-domestic law in American law schools is its value in the global market for competence. Just as domestic law-based American legal education is necessarily tied to state bar examinations, so non-domestic law must be tied to international standardization for degree recognition. Among the most important movements toward the harmonization of degree requirements has been the Bologna

---

202 This includes everything from the Foreign Tort Claims Act, 28 U.S.C. §1346 (2000), to the United Nations Convention for the International Sale of goods. *See infra* note 208.

203 *See infra*, note 207.

204 For the argument from the comparative law perspective, *see* Vivian G. Curran, *Cultural Immersion, Difference and Categories in U.S. Comparative Law*, 46 Am. J. Comp. L. 43, 71–73 (1998).

process instituted through the European Union.[205] That effort is not so much concerned with practice or ethics. It is much more focused on doctrine and a necessary aggregation of like content courses for mutual recognition of degrees.[206] On the other hand, harmonization for the purpose of degree recognition does not necessarily suggest inconsistency with the pedagogical thrust of *Educating Lawyers*. While it might suggest a need to devote greater resources to meet the requirements of both, there is nothing in current harmonization efforts that suggests a hostility to practice and ethics.

It appears, then, that a number of arguments against the application of *Educating Lawyers* are not particularly preclusive. What they suggest is that non-domestic law has traditionally been taught differently, that it requires a particular expertise, that its value maximization for students (and institutions) may be judged by standards that ignore the focus of *Educating Layers*, and that it is different from domestic law. But none of these objections are necessarily fatal to the introduction of the integrative pedagogy of *Educating Lawyers*. Still, the arguments do have a certain underlying power that it would be foolish to ignore. At a minimum, these arguments suggest that the integrative approach might be applied differently to the non-domestic law parts of the curriculum. That portion of the curriculum is not as deeply tied as others to the core areas of practice and licensure examination in American jurisdictions. Also, the methodologies of practice and ethics may differ from those applicable to domestic law. For example, lawyering domestic disputes or counseling on domestic matters requires a knowledge base and a set of ethics and risk matrices that would be quite different in the context of a cross-border matter or one involving supra national dispute resolution systems[207] or substantive law.[208] Lastly, expertise in the practical aspects of non-domestic law may require the retention of personnel from other jurisdictions to an extent that may be beyond the means of many law schools.

---

[205] *See* Laurel Terry, *The Bologna Process and Its Implications for U.S. Legal Education*, 57(2) J. Legal Educ. 237 (2007).

[206] *See* Id.

[207] An example might be arbitration under a foreign based arbitration system or ICSID. "ICSID is an autonomous international institution established under the Convention on the Settlement of Investment Disputes between States and Nationals of Other States with over one hundred and forty member States." International Centre for Settlement of Investment Disputes, available at http://icsid.worldbank.org/ICSID/Index.jsp (last accessed Feb. 14, 2008).

[208] The most commonly encountered example might be contracts subject to the United Nations Convention for the International Sale of Goods (CISG). United Nations Convention on Contracts for the International Sale of Goods, Vienna, 11 April 1980, S.Treaty Document Number 98–99 (1984), UN Document Number A/CONF 97/19, 1489 UNTS 3, available at http://www.uncitral.org/uncitral/en/uncitral_texts/sale_goods/1980CISG.html (last accessed Feb. 12, 2008).

Moreover, aspects of international legal education may not need the academy to the extent that might commonly be supposed. There are any number of non-law school academic programs rising to meet these needs, targeted to serve the needs of global civil society. For example, Streetlaw, Inc.:[209]

> has formed partnerships with local educators, legal practitioners and human rights organizations to design programs, curricula and training that will enable them to conduct their own programs. Our international partners have benefited from Street Law's existing curricula in law, human rights, democracy, crime prevention and conflict resolution. Through its philosophy and programs, Street Law embraces entire communities around the world as classrooms for effective citizenship.[210]

These programs represents hybrids of sorts—where outside organizations work to put together a framework of doctrine-practice-ethics targeted to the needs of particular sets of stakeholder. For this purpose the law school plays a role, but is hardly central to the efforts. Law schools have not always played the central role that they do today in the education of lawyers, and it may not always be necessary that they do so. To the extent that important stakeholders find the internal logic of law schools within their university academic setting increasingly incompatible with their own needs, the probability rises that alternatives will emerge.

5.4.2 *Suggestions for Integration*

For all of the difficulties, then, there is a certain logic to seeking an integration of internationalization models within the conceptual framework of *Educating Lawyers*. At one end, one might embrace this approach because the authors of *Educating Lawyers* are right. At the other end of the spectrum, one can reject the validity of the arguments but concede its power with a large stakeholder group—the bar (and through them the accrediting agencies). One approach would seek to integrate international and foreign law into the curriculum for the benefits of integration in and of themselves. The other would seek at least the forms of integration necessary to satisfy powerful constituencies. Either way, it might well make sense

---

[209] "Street Law is practical, participatory education about law, democracy, and human rights. A unique blend of content and methodology, Street Law uses techniques that promote cooperative learning, critical thinking, and the ability to participate in a democratic society. For 30 years, Street Law, Inc.'s programs and curricula have promoted knowledge of legal rights and responsibilities, engagement in the democratic process, and belief in the rule of law, among both youth and adults." Streelaw, Inc., Who Are We?, available at http://www.streetlaw.org/conte-nt.asp?ContentId=130 (last accessed Feb. 17, 2008).

[210] Streetlaw, Inc., International Programs, available at http://www.streetlaw.org/world.html (last accessed Feb. 17, 2008).

to accommodate the thrust of *Educating Lawyers* into systems integrating internationalizing programs within law school curricula.

Still, desire and capacity are not the same. It may not be possible to amalgamate the efforts to incorporate non-domestic law with efforts to integrate doctrine practice and ethics into legal education. *Educating Lawyers* reminds us that lawyers must be taught to be social regulators,[211] as well as social actors, functioning within the legal system.[212] Those functions are reflected in the parallels within legal reasoning itself—at once a complex and artificially constrained body of reasoning, and a web of categories and rules that constrain individual aspirations and manage conflict.[213] These forces tend to pull lawyers in two directions—toward technical proficiency without any moral constraint, but also toward normatively sound positions without technical precision. All of these vectors must be satisfied in the socialization of lawyers into their profession. The same ought to apply to the incorporation of non-domestic law into the American law school curriculum. Perhaps the reality of American legal education points to a realistic solution that is limited to merely outward or "empty" compliance with the form of these suggestions. Even so, that alone might represent an important benefit for the education of students. The American approach to changes in pedagogy has been to mimic the form and hope for an eventual acculturation to the normative basis from which the form derives.

Putting this together, it is not enough to train students in the techniques of non-domestic law; it is equally important to expose students to the practice and moral elements of the legal systems to which the law student is exposed. Successful incorporation of non-domestic law might profit from its integration into the curriculum as something that is not "special" or "different." Such integration deepens the incorporation of these courses within the instructional culture of an institution. "The desired integration, like competent practice, requires constant mutual adjustment among the emphases of the three parts, so that conceptual analysis is not only taught in doctrinal classrooms, nor is professional purpose and identity taught only in courses identified as such."[214] To some extent, this is possible even within a modest program. It is possible to achieve this objective even in those institutions that have little intention of embracing a belief in the value of the integrative approach. This section suggests possible approaches in the context of the different forms of integration currently being elaborated in American law schools.

---

[211] *Educating Lawyers, supra* note 14, at 82 ("in principle, lawyers have an obligation to see to the proper functioning of the institutions of the law" Id.).

[212] Id. This is most often understood as part of the advocacy function of lawyers on behalf of their clients. Id.

[213] Id. at 83.

[214] Id. at 125.

The first element of integration focuses on the signature pedagogy highlighted in *Educating Lawyers*.[215] The integration model is probably most suited to this approach. All of the incorporation models are heavily focused on doctrine. That is the easy part of the task. The difficulty lies in the appropriate pedagogy for instruction. The integration model privileges the expertise and focus on the domestic aspect of whatever course is serving as the nexus of integration. In that respect it offers the least satisfying way of incorporating doctrine, unless the faculty member is adroit enough to manage two disciplines. Even so, where the focus is on domestic law—civil procedure, corporations, constitutional law, or the like—the result will be the tendency to marginalize the non-domestic element of the material. In this sense doctrine might suffer. It might suffer even more where the faculty have been brought into this regime reluctantly or are unsure of their ability to fold non-domestic law into their teaching. Aggregation, segregation and immersion models are much more likely to serve as a basis for the construction of the sort of signature pedagogy that would function as the base for instruction in doctrine without marginalizing the material within domestic law driven courses.

As to the pedagogy itself, it seems here that the limitations of the case dialogue method, so well discussed in *Educating Lawyers*[216], can be most powerfully felt. Though possible, it is not clear that the case dialogue method is most suitable for conveying the essence of European Union law, though its insights might to some extent translate. The case dialogue method itself, as signature pedagogy, becomes more problematic when applied to instruction in civil law. Yet even there the reality of changes in civil law suggest a place for case dialogue instruction as a lens through which the codes are understood. On the other hand, problems as a lens through which to understand the workings of a code might be suitable. Certainly, among American faculties there are some who have already adopted this sort of approach in teaching heavily code-based domestic law courses such as corporations and commercial law.[217] The important lesson, though, is that international and foreign law can be taught using American pedagogical instruments without losing the power of instruction.

The second element of integration is a sensitivity to practice issues.[218] On the one hand, the practice aspects of foreign and international law to which the United States does not subscribe present serious difficulties. Clearly, the immersion model might appear to be best suited to drawing out the practice aspects of non-domestic law, especially where the education

---

[215] *Educating Lawyers, supra* note 14, at 47–86.

[216] *See Educating Lawyers, supra* note 14 at 75–78.

[217] "While simulated practice can be an important site for developing skills and understanding essential for practice, it can also provide the setting for teaching the ethical demands of practice." Id. at 158.

[218] *Educating Lawyers, supra* note 14, at 87–125.

occurs outside the United States. Internships, discussions with local practitioners and the local bar, for example, all add a significant dimension to the usual doctrinal education that serves as the core of any pedagogical program. With respect to those aspects of incorporation attempted within American law schools, the segregation and immersion models might be suited best to translate practice into the pedagogy. That can be done either by importing faculty to the home institution or exporting students to host sites. The importation of faculty can be folded into the usual recruitment process. Alternatively, recruiting temporary or short-term staff might serve to bring in the necessary practice expertise. On the other hand, for international and transnational courses, native expertise is sufficient to build into the curriculum a practice aspect. In this respect, internationally-oriented faculty are in substantially the same position as domestic law faculty.

The third element of integration is the values dimension of a legal education.[219] Here incorporation presents an interesting dimension. On the one hand, international (that is non-domestic) courses ought to deepen the moral values instruction of American law for the construction of ethical lawyers—a great objective of *Educating Lawyers*. On the other hand, non-domestic law is as bound up as American law within the ethical and moral framework from which it arises. Doctrinal education, and even practice, may necessarily be bundled up with a cultural understanding of the law studied. This insight, of course, is far more powerful with respect to foreign law, than it might be with international law. For international law in which the United States participates, there is a great incentive to teach them through the moral lens of American law, with a nod to the comparative aspects of the cultural understandings of the other parties to these instruments. With respect to global law—commercial law, investment and the like—such comparative cultural understanding may be essential. Yet this creates a difficulty—the greater the need for inter-cultural/ethical sensitivity, the greater the problem of expertise. Such difficulties raise the resource issues in a way that significantly impacts the ability of schools with modest means, or even schools more reasonably endowed, to adequately provide for incorporation.

In this connection a word on the multi-departmental approach may be useful. The DIA approach is an ambitious program, but one with great weaknesses. The DIA approach may develop incentives that make it harder rather than easier for the alternative to keep its focus on law. As a response to the problem of transnational legal education that is effectively untried and little developed, DIA is unique. For that reason, I have devoted substantial space to developing a "best case" set of arguments for a DIA approach to internationalizing the law school curriculum. Still, there is much to be said for an expansion of law school programs outside the traditional model of

[219] *Educating Lawyers, supra* note 14, at 126–161.

legal education, especially where it concerns an expansion of legal training beyond the confines for which traditional law schools were created.

Still, the DIA model ought to raise serious concerns. Among the most serious are "as applied" criticisms. For example, construction of such programs can serve more as monument building than as something useful "on the ground." The DIA model is most useful for large multipurpose research institutions that are seeking to add to their collection of offerings. That sort of environment increases the risk that programs will remain more impressive on paper than in reality. They may become a vehicle for churning students. It is possible, for example, for administrators to see in such a program a means of increasing student residence at the university by recruiting law students (and perhaps others) to an additional program requiring the payment of additional fees. The value, of course, is in the collection of an additional degree. But it might have been possible to integrate the programs into existing institutional contexts rather than to separate out its elements. This is especially problematical where the bulk of courses for a DIA is drawn from a series of "cross listed" offerings. In such a case, there is very little value added for students, but a greater administrative value added. I am not sure how easy it may be for administrators to avoid this temptation.

Moreover, at a personal level, the DIA serves as little more than a vehicle for empire building by deans and others eager to control larger budgets and more personnel without directly affecting the operation of the law school as such. Connectivity could be sacrificed to institutional imperatives that might draw the DIA away from, rather than closer to, the law school. In large research universities, the creation of entities such as a DIA may subject them to the realities of department politics in a way that has unintended but very real consequences. That additional funding can be quite valuable at the margin if the number of new faculty and new offerings can be kept to a minimum through the system of cross listings. It can also serve as another means of rewarding or punishing personnel. But the same sorts of temptations face participating faculty. Institutional discipline, and an eye on remaining true to the institutional vision, is always a difficult task. In creating a new enterprise, that task grows more difficult.

Equally important are a number of connectivity issues. The further isolated the internationalization efforts become from the traditional structures and pedagogy of the law school, the less likely such a program will have an influence on legal education. This is not an approach to integration. It serves principally as an escape from the legal academy, but escape here leaves legal education substantially untouched. Thus, the very success of the DIA will be the basis for its failure in changing legal education except perhaps at the margin. Such programs run a real risk of relating to law in name only—and becoming just another graduate department populating large research universities. Unmoored to traditional programs, DIA programs might become either orphans (and ultimately abandoned) or become merged with international studies or other graduate departments where they might better belong. To the extent that DIA is operated independently of the law school (other than at the administrative level) DIA runs the risk of losing core law school support.

In a sense then, the isolation that provides the key benefit to DIA, also poses its greatest sets of risk. At its most independent, DIA can easily become unmoored from the American law school. It becomes something else—perhaps an institution with greater affinity to its European counterparts than to its American roots. Isolating international, comparative and foreign law faculty, separating and isolating international, foreign and comparative law programs tends to reduce rather than to increase the visibility and availability of these aspects of legal training to the average student. It also draws faculty into ever tighter field-bound groups, reducing interfield communication among law faculty. The field becomes independent of the law school experience—something as different as the business school. Lastly, DIA could lose touch with the essential teaching mission of the law school—the training of lawyers. The more closely that DIA comes to resemble traditional graduate programs, the less useful it might appear to a professional school. In addition, there are fine graduate programs in the fields of international affairs that do much of what DIA attempts, perhaps more successfully so.

It should be remembered that a DIA model is expensive. It draws a tremendous amount of resources. It may be beyond the capacity of all but the largest institutions. The institutional resources necessary to ensure that a DIA remains tethered to the law school are probably large—in terms of labor resources and attention to changes in their respective evolution. To that extent, at least, the DIA model can serve only a very limited role in the incorporation of transnational elements into legal education. A DIA should not be undertaken lightly, and might well have to be supervised heavily. At its core, DIA may be hopelessly incompatible with the form or substance, and certainly inimical to the insights, of *Educating Lawyers*.

5.5 Conclusion, on the Value of Crossing These Parallel Tracks

Resources and capacity, then, should serve as the foundation for the discussion of the incorporation of foreign and international law into the law school curriculum. The additional focus on practice and ethics in *Educating Lawyers* tends to raise the costs of providing a high level of instruction. Two consequences are likely. The first is that law schools will have to scale back. That scaling back will more likely occur at the less wealthy and less well-known institutions. This will exacerbate the rising "class system" among American law schools. Thus, it may come to pass that the ability to afford the sort of incorporation of non-domestic law in the context of the three part integrative approach of *Educating Lawyers* will serve as another status marker among law schools. The second is that costs encourage form over substance. Even with respect to incorporation of the ideals of *Educating Lawyers*, this tendency is apparent.

Reading carefully through the heart of the Carnegie Report, it becomes clear that the integrative approach encourages the development of a larger and better-respected class of clinical and writing faculty,[220] with greater emphasis on professional responsibility and legal ethics.[221] This might value form over the intention of the authors,[222] but it represents a path left open, if only for the short-term.[223] In either case, it appears that not every method of internationalization will prove useful in incorporating the integrative model advanced in *Educating Lawyers*. The integration model, may in fact be the least promising vehicle for incorporating the pedagogical framework of *Educating Lawyers* successfully. The aggregation model offers a compromise, but might lack enough resources to bring in ethics and practice elements. Although both approaches would be likely to require substantially more resources, the segregation and immersion models may be better alternatives. In this respect the difficulties of incorporation parallel the problems of adopting the integrative model of *Educating Lawyers* within the domestic law curriculum.[224]

Internationalization of the legal curriculum is inevitable. So is the connection between legal education and the needs of the bench and bar. As the Georgetown University Law Center web site notes:

> Although much of international legal practice may involve corporate or transactional work, litigators, too, are finding that their practices are more and more "transnational" in the sense that their cases involve events and evidence from, or the law of, another country. Litigation is also increasingly "international" in that cases may be tried before international tribunals or panels of arbitrators or may be decided under international law.[225]

---

220 *Educating Lawyers, supra* note 14 at 104–111, 120–122.

221 Id. at 132–138, 148–151.

222 "The problem demands their careful rethinking of both the existing curriculum and the pedagogies that law schools amply to produce a more coherent and integrated initiation into the life of the law." Id. at 147.

223 "However, in all movements for innovation, champions and leaders are essential factors in determining whether or not a possibility becomes realized. Here the developing network of faculty and deans concerned with improving legal education is a key resource waiting to be developed further and put to good use." Id. at 202.

224 "However, as we have seen, there are major obstacles such a development will have to overcome. A trade-off between higher costs and greater educational effectiveness is one. Resistance to change in a largely successful and comfortable academic enterprise is another." Id.

225 Georgetown University Law Center, Global Law Scholars, Our Raison d'Être, available at http://www.law.georgetown.edu/gls/ (last accessed Feb. 15, 2008).

Many law schools have already begun to respond to this change in the environment in which lawyers must be trained. On the academic side, research that remains tied to a particular locale will be marginalized as increasingly parochial in the coming decades. Likewise, law schools that ignore the needs of the practicing bar will find themselves cut off from the profession. There are several possible responses to the need to integrate legal internationalization and the interests of the practicing bar within law schools.

Whatever model is chosen, whatever choice is made, it is clear that at some level, the character of American legal education is changing. Jonathan Cahn, a partner at Coudert Brothers at the time he wrote this, got it right when he suggested to legal academics:

> Your challenge, as educators, is to learn enough about the global legal organization and the cross border disciplines they rely upon, to design courses that are relevant, that give your students mobility within the culture of those organizations. Obviously, this task places an emphasis on both transferable disciplines and a capacity with comparative law that enables the lawyer to transfer these competencies (and individual experiences) across national borders from one legal system to another.[226]

Cahn identifies the core of the transnational element in law that many law schools have attempted to capture. These efforts have developed several different models for preparing students to meet the challenges of legal problems that cross borders and jurisdictions. Whatever model is preferred will be likely to face some resistance from those whose current practices will be upset by a more "globalized" curriculum. But change cannot be avoided. The Carnegie Report on Educating Lawyers suggests a method for evaluating different approaches to internationalizing the curriculum, in the light of the needs of the practicing bar. If law school is to be relevant to lawyers, it would be wise for law schools to be sensitive to the Carnegie framework in fashioning their approach to legal internationalization. Law schools should consider the application of the principles in *Educating Lawyers* because the Carnegie Report reflects the attitudes and desires of the bar, which law schools must respect, even as they seek to change and improve them.

---

[226] Jonathan D. Cahn, *The Global Legal Professional and the Challenges to Legal Education*, 20 Penn St. Intl. L. Rev. 55, 61 (2001) (emphasis in the original).

Chapter 6
Resolving Multicultural Legal Cases: A Bottom Up Perspective on the Internationalization of Law

Wibo M. van Rossum

6.1 Introduction

Why are jurists and especially jurists in the international and transnational field of law, interested in internationalization, and what do they mean by it? When a word ends with "–ization" it is clear that we are talking about a process. To speak of "internationalization" of law implies that some new type of law is becoming more important. Does that mean that "international" law is becoming more important to the detriment of "domestic" law? Or is it the nature of domestic law itself that is changing? One view might be that the scope of law is simply expanding, through the *juridification* of social norms that were previously outside the legal realm.

Apart from being viewed as a legal process, the internationalization of law should be seen as connected to a *social* process of globalization in and of society and the world at large. Globalization refers to the increasing migration of people with its cultural assimilation and concomitant multiculturalization, the growing international flow of capital and economic exchange, and the increasing interdependence of states, social groups and networks of people and organizations. Lawyers and legal academicians are interested in this social process because it influences the law and legal order in multiple and divergent ways. Lawyers today cannot restrict themselves to studying black letter law, because globalization has created an abundance of other norm systems that also regulate human behavior.[1]

The social process of globalization leads not only to an expansion of norm systems and to the internationalization of law, but also to a

W.M. van Rossum (✉)
Department of Socio-legal Studies, Utrecht University School of Law, Utrecht, The Netherlands
e-mail: w.m.vanrossum@uu.nl

[1] Martti Koskenniemi, *Fragmentation of International Law: Difficulties Arising from the Diversification and Expansion of International Law*, Report of the Study Group of the International Law Commission. (2007); Paul Schiff Berman, *A Pluralist Approach to International Law*, 32 Yale J. Int'l L., 301–29 (2007).

J. Klabbers, M. Sellers (eds.), *The Internationalization of Law and Legal Education*, Ius Gentium: Comparative Perspectives on Law and Justice 2,
DOI 10.1007/978-1-4020-9494-1_6,

contextualization of these systems. Contextualization means that legal decisions cannot just follow from legal rules on a one to one basis. This has always been the case, but now there is a growing awareness not only of the fact that rules do not predict legal outcomes, but also that in some cases this *should* be so. As a consequence, legal decisions are only predictable when all circumstances of a situation or case are known.[2]

Law could once be systematized, unified, internally harmonized, and considered and studied as a coherent system. Today that situation is different even though academic lawyers still focus most of their efforts on doctrine. A study group in Norway has aptly characterized the present state of affairs:

> Governmental authority is horizontally and vertically dispersed. The legal situation of individuals and private entities is no longer solely dependent on municipal law. States have accepted treaty regimes whereby international authorities exercise regulatory power that interferes with domestic authority. New dispute-settling bodies proliferate on the international plane, and we are increasingly aware of the considerable influence exercised by the private sector on international decision-making processes. Polycentric decision-making structures and fragmented spheres of law, in short, constitute today's international law. This has risen to the level of what can properly be termed a 'new international law' emerging as a patch-work of norms, institutions and actors on various overlapping levels.[3]

Although this quotation refers to international law, its observations are equally true of domestic law. There has been a multiplication of sources of law and a concomitant decline in certainty, hierarchy and coherence.

6.2 A Neo-Modern Attitude Toward Law

A "post-modern" lawyer might embrace the emergence of "polycentric decision-making structures and fragmented spheres of law". He or she would add the word 'plural' to all the 'old words' and would define social and legal problems as a challenge. So indeed, a postmodernist might say that we have plural systems, plural forms of coherence, plural orders, plural legalities, and plural hierarchies.[4]

Many lawyers and academic jurists worry that globalization will diminish the importance of law and legal norms. Other factors seem to be gaining

---

[2] Agnes T.M. Schreiner, *European Star Laws. An Essay on the Europeanisation of Private Law*, Global Jurist Topics, Issue 2 (2003).

[3] Ivar Alvik, et al., The New International Law, *Polycentric decision-making structures and fragmented spheres of law: What implications for the new generation of international legal discourse*? Download from http://www.jus.uio.no/forskning/grupper/intrel/nil-conference/ (Last visited Sept. 1, 2007) (2007).

[4] Andreas Fischer-Lescano & Gunther Teubner, *Regime-Collisions: The Vain Search for Legal Unity in the Fragmentation of Global Law*, 25 Mich. J. Int'l L. 999–1046 (2004).

influence over power and international relations. Law is internationalizing and universalizing, but also becoming fragmented, contextualizing and localizing. Lawyers must consider how to understand and maintain the system of law in the midst of all the other influential rule systems. The sociology and anthropology of law can help to situate law in this "neo-modern" world order. Neo-modern is a more accurate description of the current situation than "post-modern", because "post-modern" implies relativsm and playful eclecticism. The term "neo-modern" distances itself from the European-dominated conceptions of modernism, without abandoning the optimistic aim of controlling state power and creating a more just society.[5]

The neo-modern situation of law and the attitude of lawyers who exemplify it is not a "middle road" between modern and post-modern attitudes. The neo-modern approach to law should be understood as containing *both* contrasting attitudes at the same time, within the same person. Lawyers have to play out both approaches, not fixing them but *exchanging* them. In the neo-modern approach to law, the old figure of the "Janus head" returns.[6] Law should not only be its own fervent advocate but also its most serious critic.

Mireille Delmas-Marty has a somewhat more modernist attitude. This is not only apparent from the first sentence of her book *Towards a Truly Common Law*: "An orderly landscape. That is what we want."[7] We can also deduce her position from her lecture "The imaginative forces of law," in which her goal is to dig up the "universal" from among the great variety of legal systems. She wants to find "a common grammar" in order to harmonize or hybridize. She wants a pluralist but systemic diversity: plurality in *one* system or in other words "ordered pluralism."[8] Inherent in her lecture is an almost naïve faith in law: "Global problems will be solved as soon as we have our problems with law resolved". Then there's hope for the future. This mind-set pictures one side of today's necessary attitudes toward law.

The other side of the coin is relativism, contextualization, and localization. It requires realizing that law no longer hovers "above" society, but is an integral part of society (in the same way as religion, cultural norms, routine, local expectations, and time and place dependant peculiarities).

---

[5] Neo-modernism applied to legal studies is quite new. The term is sometimes used in architectural studies and in art. Central to the idea of neo-modernism is that post-modernism went too far in its critique on modernism, but that some of it nevertheless stuck.

[6] G. Teubner, *The Two Faces of Janus: Rethinking Legal Pluralism*, 13 Cardozo L. Rev., 1443–6 (1992).

[7] Mireille Delmas-Marty, *Towards a Truly Common Law. Europe as a Laboratory for Legal Pluralism. Cambridge*, (Cambridge University Press) (2007).

[8] Mireille Delmas-Marty, *The Imaginative Forces of Law*, Chinese Journal of International Law, 623–27 (2003).

This mind-set also must be present in the jurist, whether lawyer, judge or academician. It is subjectivist, relativist, and very pragmatic. Andreas Paulus has expressed this neo-modern way of looking at things:

> If the lawyer stops pretending that the outcome of her analysis is the result of a purely objective analysis, if she admits and demonstrates the element of (conscious) choice and individual commitment, the legal enterprise wins much credibility and loses little of its normativity, understood not as a simple conformity of life to general rules but as the quest for public accountability of the exercise of all sorts of power over human beings.[9]

This Janus-faced conception of law has distinct qualities compared to religious, economic, and other rule systems. Neo-modern law has a commitment to universalism, but also an eye for practical solutions. Neo-modern law has the virtue of justice in concrete instances, while at the same time maintaining general rules of a fair procedure. Not to forget the principle of equal treatment and other human rights, which can be seen as an important export product from the west. These distinct qualities of the law need to be put up front, not only by legal scholars, but also by legal professionals on the shop floor of the law. If we want to retain law as a rule system that has certain advantages over other rule systems and has some distinct virtues, lawyers should have more of a "sellers attitude" in the marketplace of rule systems. This "sellers attitude" needs to be learned, and seems to be absent in today's legal practice. This attitude of the seller is particularly important in multicultural cases. In these kinds of cases "western law" may be challenged by other forms of "law", such as religious "law". Migration confronts many modern western states with the challenge of cultural pluralization, including a pluralization of legal systems. Instead of one national legal system, neatly codified and with occasional customary norms, the Netherlands now has diversity of written and unwritten religiously based legal systems. Whatever we might think of the concept of legal pluralism, this factual presence of western and Islamic law within one nation surely is legal pluralism, and it is here to stay.[10]

The theoretical explanation given above of the fragmented, plural, patchy nature of neo-modern law can be supplemented with more empirical evidence. How do lawyers and judges in the Netherlands do their ordinary day-to-day work? How do they argue their positions? Which arguments are socially accepted, and how much of the actual decision-making process

---

[9] Andreas L. Paulus, *International Law After Postmodernism: Towards Renewal or Decline of International Law*? 14 Leiden J. Int'l L., 727–55 (2001).

[10] Brian Z.Tamanaha, *The Folly of the 'Social Scientific' Concept of Legal Pluralism*, 20 J. L. Soc'y, Issue 2, 192–212 (1993).

Sally Falk Moore, *Certainties Undone: Fifty Turbulent Years of Legal Anthropology 1949–1999*, 7 Journal of the Royal Anthropological Institute (N.S.), 95–116 (2001).

comes into the open and becomes known to the parties? In other words, what actually happens at the shop floor of the law in the Netherlands?[11]

6.3 A Look at Empirical Material: Multicultural Legal Cases

This paragraph will draw on my empirical research in multicultural legal cases: Cases in which (legal) cultures clash. New interpretations of Dutch legal rules or legal concepts sometimes arise out of this clash, but most of the time there seems to be a "standard Dutch approach" of lawyers and judges, even though in theory – as is clear from my interviews – they are willing to find room for what can be called a multiculturalization of law. One interesting example is a case of multiculturalization that came before the Dutch Supreme Court in 1983. The parties, a Dutch/Chinese employer and employee, quarrelled over whether there was a labour contract between them or not. The legal rule says that people are bound to a contract when they agree. How do people know that they agree? Normally, they have to show the signs of "agreement." People show the signs of agreement when the other party may reasonably infer agreement from their behavior. This is a two-way process. The issue in this case was: "Is it possible that this process of reasonably inferring agreement from behavior, is different among two Dutch/Chinese people?" The lower court said 'no', the Supreme Court said 'yes'. Which means 'agreeing on a contract' in the Netherlands is culturally specific.[12]

The main part of the report "Gelet op de cultuur" consists of an extensive reconstruction of five actual legal cases (three family law cases, two labor law cases).[13] The cases were selected after a time-consuming search of lawyers' offices and a local lower court in one of the larger cities in the Netherlands. During 2005 about twenty lawyers who regularly deal with legal cases involving parties from ethnic minorities were extensively interviewed about their own experiences in multicultural cases. Most of them were further interviewed by telephone every month about their experiences in the past month. They were asked specifically for actual cases (preferably not yet "closed") with a potential for bringing distinct cultural institutions, concepts or practices to bear on the legal decision-making process. Did the

---

[11] Empirical research of course cannot say anything on 'the' law, but can only give a glimpse on the practice of some parts of the legal field. The focus in this research is mainly on the process of decision making of judges and lawyers in non-criminal cases.

[12] J.H. Nieuwenhuis, Aan de rand van de krater. Multiculturele rechtsvinding in het burgerlijk recht; realiteiten en perspectieven, In P.B. Cliteur en V. Van Den Eeckhout (red.) *Multiculturalisme, cultuurrelativisme en sociale cohesie*, Leiden, Den Haag: E.M. Meijers Instituut, Boom Juridische Uitgevers, 333–4 (2001).

[13] The report 'Paying Attention to Culture' was published in 2007 and was funded by the Raad voor de rechtspraak, the Council for the Judiciary.

lawyers come across new cases in which they had the idea that cultural issues regarding their client might come to play a role? How did they assess that role, and in which way might culture be juridically relevant? Did they hear of cases from other lawyers that were somehow "culture related"? Some lawyers were willing to make available all the previous year's files, and be interviewed about them. In addition to lawyers' offices, cases were collected at a local court in the family section and the "kantonrechter" section.[14] In this latter section all the completed files covering the first half of 2005 were analyzed, and when relevant the deciding judge was contacted for an interview. All judges in the family section were interviewed in a round table, during which several cases came to the fore. The files of these cases were analyzed and the judges who took the decisions in these cases were extensively interviewed about the relevancy of cultural issues for the decision.

Several cases could be reconstructed by in-depth interviewing of the party or parties, the lawyers, judge and other officials, and occasionally agencies such as the Child Care and Protection Board. I could also make use of data from several discussion sessions with judges and prosecutors about the interpretation and legal relevancy of cultural issues. Many official judgments of Dutch courts are available as well, as are many state-of-the-art reviews from the last 5 or 6 years regarding the direction in which multiculturality is developing in Dutch law. Taken together the five cases in the report reflect the typical attitude of Dutch legal professionals towards multicultural legal problems.

Summaries of two cases in the report will help to illustrate my central argument that the legal professionals on the shop floor should do much more to re-fashion the law as an attractive rule system. Ordinary legal professionals today only seem to act locally, that is they unreflectively adapt to local circumstances, the Dutch legal culture at hand and the standard interpretations available. They should make themselves more aware of the intuitive choices they make and be more clear and open about their argumentation of specific decisions. "Cultural clashes" in legal cases almost "ask" for such an approach. Legal professionals should realize that today the legal system requires their stronger support.

The first case concerns Rachida, a woman of Moroccan origin living in the Netherlands who after divorce wanted the custody over her children. The legal question concerned what would be in the best interests of the children. The second case concerns Hamid, a man of Turkish origin living in the Netherlands who after divorce was facing accusations of "honor related violence" by his ex-wife. He suspected that she strategically accused him

[14] A kantonrechter is a single judge allowed to decide i.a. on all labour law cases, and on cases in which the amound of money the plaintiff asks for does not exceed € 5000.

because she wanted custody over their children. The judge went along with her arguments. According to Hamid, there was no "fair hearing."

6.3.1 *Rachida and the Possibility of an Islamic Based "Interest of the Child"*

In the Netherlands there is recent debate about the abduction of children to the country of origin by Islamic fathers. There was a celebrated case of the children Sara and Ammar, who were abducted from the Netherlands to Syria by their biological father in 2004. Overall, the mother came across as having been a little naive and having had too much faith for too long in the good intentions of the father, who promised again and again during the strenuous marriage to "better his life" and be good to her. After divorce the children lived with her, while the father saw his children regularly. One day, pretending he was taking them off for a holiday to Disneyworld Paris, the father abducted Sara and Ammar and took them to Syria. After the abduction, the Dutch mother visited her children every few months, but she could not persuade her ex-husband to let the children go. He said that he acted in the best interests of the children by having them grow up in proper surroundings, and that this conformed with Islamic-based Syrian law. Islamic law says that after divorce custody (wilaya) will stay with the father, assigning him the responsibility of ensuring a proper upbringing. The right to raise and care for the child (hadana) remains with the mother. Syria, like all Islamic countries, did not sign the 1980 Hague Convention on International Child Abduction. Islamic countries oppose the equality principle concerning men and women in the custody of children after divorce. After two years the children Sara and Ammar were able to flee to the Dutch embassy, and after much diplomacy, negotiation and mediation were allowed to go back to the Netherlands.

This case and similar cases attract a lot of media attention. They set up an image of a "typical Islamic abduction" that has something to do with the "Islamic upbringing" of the children. This image consists of men who secretly prepare and make plans for abduction while women are submissive or know nothing. This image goes hand in hand with the picture of women who under Islamic law seem to be treated as second class humans. When it comes to important financial decisions concerning their children or to choosing the right education, the father has the only and final say. Women are only allowed "to do the household work and take daily care of their children." This has been the stereotype.

The discussion on abduction of children to Islamic countries came to a sort of legal crescendo in 2004, when a judge, Van der Reijt, wrote in the Dutch *Journal for the Judiciary* about his taking part in "the first Arab-European conference of judges on child abduction." He concluded: "It is highly irresponsible for a juvenile judge to order a mother after divorce to let the young child visit the father regularly if the father is of Arab and Islamic origin, the mother isn't, and the child is living in her place."[15] The implication was that there should be no parental access to Muslim men. (Abduction by men to Islamic countries attracts the most attention, even though women by far outnumber men when it comes to abduction, and abduction to "treaty countries" outnumbers by far abduction to "non-treaty countries.")[16]

I have selected Rachida's case from my empirical research because it helps us to focus on the issue of the "interest of the child" in cases awarding custody to only one parent in relation to the issue of abduction by Islamic men.

Rachida is a woman of Moroccan origin who married when she was 17. She married Aziz, then 30 years old and an illegal immigrant, in the Netherlands. Rachida's parents had selected Aziz as a wedding candidate and strongly advised Rachida to accept. Three children were born of the marriage: two girls and one boy.

After 12 years of marriage, Aziz fell in love with a young woman during a holiday in Morocco. He regularly visited her from then on. After two years the family again visited Morocco. Aziz however planned to leave his family there, to marry the young girl, and to take her to Holland. He took Rachida's passport away, and moved his three children to secret locations. He wanted Rachida to approve his second marriage.[17]

Rachida contacted her brother and parents in the Netherlands, who immediately traveled to Morocco. They pleaded, cajoled, contacted the police, and put pressure on Aziz, so that finally Rachida could get her passport back. She was able to return to Holland with her two daughters. But she could not find the boy. Aziz apparently considered his son to be better off with his family in Morocco.

Back in Holland, Rachida sought a divorce and a court order saying that her children could stay and live with her. The Child Care and Protection Board issued a report (a judge is legally obliged to ask for such a report in these kind of cases) which endorsed this result. The Board, however, also advised (without being asked) that Rachida should receive legal custody to

---

[15] F.A. van der Reijt, De eerste Arabisch-Europese rechtersconferentie over kinderontvoering, gehouden te Malta van 14 tot 17 maart 2004, Trema, 453–456 (2004).

[16] Centrum Internationale Kinderontvoering (2007) Jaarrapportage juni 2006–mei 2007.

[17] Aziz clearly had not oriented himself on the requirements of Dutch law concerning immigration. First, he should be divorced from Rachida in accordance with Dutch law before he could think of marrying in a legally valid way according to Dutch law. Second, there would have been all sorts of income and other requirements for the new wife to come to the Netherlands.

the exclusion of Aziz.[18] This advice was largely based on the opinion that Aziz "did not act in the best interest of his children." Aziz had refused to react to questions from the Child Care and Protection Board and to appointments for interviews and observations. The researchers of the Board came to the conclusion that Aziz had "abducted" his son, had "threatened to abduct" his two girls once back in Holland, and had tried to dump his wife in Morocco.[19]

Thus, in Rachida's case "abduction" played a leading role in the Board's advice and consequently in the court's legal decision. When professionals such as judges and researchers of the Board talk about child abduction in Islamic cases, typically the father is the abductor, the father acts on the basis of a secret plan, and the mother is submissive or "caught in a web of lies". Although the information and facts in Rachida's case could have led to a more nuanced opinion about what really happened in the "abduction", the judge and other professionals quickly endorsed this cliché version of abduction. For example, Rachida told me in the interviews that she knew what Aziz was up to because he told her about it and tried to win her over. Moreover, he packed the suitcases with clothes typically suited for wintertime, while they went on a summer holiday. Rachida admitted in the interview: "I knew what he wanted to do." Again at the Spanish-Moroccan border Aziz told Rachida that "of course she knew that he wanted her to stay in Morocco, because he was going to marry a second time." Rachida protested but went along anyway.[20]

The Board's researchers who wrote the report and advised the court, said in the interview that they vaguely knew what had actually happened: "They went for a holiday, and then he left them there, isn't that it?" Some time later in the interview, this possibility for nuance became lost in more clichéd terms: "He did not consult the mother, the child did not even have an opportunity to say goodbye and was suddenly pulled out of his familiar environment." The judge went along with the Board. In particular, the fact that the Board advised about custody without having been asked caught the attention of the judge. "That is very exceptional. I have never seen that before. When the Board advises like this without being asked, then I think

[18] The law in article 251 of Book 1 of the Dutch civil code provides legal custody to both parents after a divorce. The judge may deviate from this rule 'in the interest of the child'.
[19] Just that same year a report was issued on these kind of issues. See ACVZ (Adviescommissie voor Vreemdelingenzaken), *Tegen de wil achtergebleven*. (*Left behind*) Den Haag, ACVZ, 2005; See also C. Verwers, L.M. van der Knaap and L. Vervoorn, *Internationale kinderontvoering*, (*International Child Abduction*) Ministerie van Justitie, WODC, Cahier, 2006.
[20] From the interviews I held it is not clear why she went along; her lawyer did not know either. Maybe there was a lot of pressure from Aziz, maybe she was naive, maybe she wanted just to see what would happen or maybe she wanted it to happen to put her marriage to the test or something. The point is nobody knows, but the officials interpreted her behavior as submissive or unknowing.

there must be a very good reason for it, they must have been shocked by the father." The Board could not have been shocked, however, as we have seen, because they had never even met him. They themselves said they gave the premature advice because they knew that "the question was going to come up anyway, one day or another; besides it's completely up to the judge to decide what he does with our report and advice".

The Board advised the court to award custody exclusively to the mother. Here we can see that the assessment of "abduction" by Aziz coupled with his not showing up at the Board's request, leads to a certain legal outcome. Awarding custody to only one of the parents is allowed according to Dutch law if it is in "the interest of the child". The legal question thus is, what the meaning is of this open legal concept. According to many legal and semi-legal professionals, it goes without saying that affective harmony, radiating from a biological parent who is permanently available in a steady household, must be used as the criterion for the decision of custody and of which household to place the children in. In Rachida's case this could only lead to one decision, which was to award Rachida solely with the custody over her children.

Did the Board and the judge consider whether Aziz might have acted in the interests of his children? As we have seen, the Board found this possibly to be out of the question. In the interview they said: "This child is in Morocco. Other people are raising him. We don't know how well he is, we only know that he is not being raised by his father because the father is not in Morocco very often. And we think that a child has to be raised by a parent. That is the most important thing."[21] The act of abduction coupled with Aziz having his child raised by *others*, leads to a firm 'no' to the question whether it is in the interest of the child that Aziz have custody.

In her judgment the judge merely referred to the advice of the Board. In the interview she said:

> I have talked this over with the court clerk and we thought it important to keep the case in our hands, that is to decide this case even after the boy had been in Morocco for over a year, and to decide that Dutch law was applicable. We believed that it would be better for the child if we looked at the case from the perspective of Dutch law. Because we knew that if we were to apply Moroccan law, which also would have been possible according to private international law, the mother would have not had anything to say. My estimation is that most of my colleagues, in these kinds of issues, will do their best to apply Dutch law.

Interpretation in the case of Rachida was based on guess-work developed from preconceptions about abduction and the legal role of men and women in Islamic/Moroccan social relations. Combined with the unquestioned standard interpretation of what is in the interest of children, this type of legal reasoning and decision-making is forming a barrier to

---

[21] *See also* Article 9 of the Convention on the Rights of the Child.

multiculturalization and internationalization of the law. It hinders multiculturalization because it too easily assumes that the "filling in" of open legal concepts is culturally neutral instead of "colored by culture".[22] And it hinders internationalization because legal professionals do not grasp the opportunity to re-interpret national law in terms of human rights, do not make the values of modern law explicit (equal treatment of men and women), or possibly even search for and promote common values underlying Moroccan/Islamic and Dutch law.

What could have happened if these legal professionals had developed a "neo-modern attitude" towards the law? What should these legal professionals have done? They should have made their assumptions explicit. For example: The judge could have strongly asked Rachida in court about the how and when of the abduction. She also could have asked her what she saw as the benefit of exclusionary custody over her children. Did she really want that? Or did the request only arise because the Child Care and Protection Board mentioned it in its report? And why didn't the judge ask both parents whether and if so why they preferred Dutch to Moroccan law (or vice versa)? Why not critically question the Board about a possible "islamic-based interest of the child." Aziz must have had the interest of his children to some extent in his mind when he moved them to Morocco. He was, after all, according to Moroccan/Islamic family law, the custodian over his children, and had prime responsibility over their proper upbringing. All these questions would probably have complicated the case enormously, but that is no excuse for having evaded them. The answers would have provided the opportunity to discuss the meanings of the open legal norm "interest of the child," gender roles in Moroccan and Dutch culture, and preferences of child-rearing in different countries. It would also have given the parties the opportunity to argue whether Dutch law and its underlying principles of human rights actually provided the best solution to the case. (None of this necessarily implies that the decision of the Court should or would have been different.)

By overlooking the opportunity to promote Dutch law in the marketplace of rule systems, legal professionals weaken their ability to re-fashion an appealing and attractive system of law that is able to compete with those other norm systems.

6.3.2 Hamid and His "Unfair Hearing"

Hamid's case involves the divorce of a couple of Turkish origin, in which the contested points were the determination of custody over and place

---

[22] I do not mean to say that we *always* need a culturally coloured filling in of open legal concepts. My point is that the question whether we want it or not, doesn't even come up.

of residence of their two children. The wife, Meryem, had been living in the Netherlands for quite some time, the husband Hamid had come over from Turkey for the wedding (an arranged marriage). They had lived in the Netherlands for several years and the marriage went fairly well, but after six years when her second baby was born, Meryem became depressed, the couple started to argue, and finally she left their mutual home for an unknown destination. The report of the Child Care and Protection Board stated that Meryem wanted to "integrate in Dutch culture" while the husband wanted her to "stay true to Turkish culture." The wife was absent for one and a half years, during which time the children lived with a sister of Hamid and, for over a year, with his parents in Turkey. Hamid started a divorce procedure, Dutch law was applicable, and he obtained the divorce in due course. Meanwhile Meryem sought custody of the children and requested that the children live permanently with her rather than the father or his family. Both ex-spouses at the time of the legal decision over custody had found a new life partner: Hamid a young woman from Turkey, Meryem a Dutch man of Turkish origin.

Regarding the matter of custody and place of residence, the judge ordered the Child Care and Protection Board to produce a report on the situation to evaluate how to serve the interests of the children best. The report said that Hamid had "mainly looked after his own interests and had neglected the interest of his children," because he had not taken care of his children himself. The Board attributed Hamid's conflict with his wife to his Turkish cultural background in which "his honor had been damaged." This damage to Hamid's honor was also the reason, according to the report, for violent threats made by Hamid against his wife (there were no police reports on this, however). Hamid also had once written a nasty letter to his wife, after her new friend had phoned Hamid's family in Turkey and demanded that they release the children. Meryem reported to the Board's officers that she was scared. Moreover, from the behavior of the children when on the Board's premises, the reporting officer "had the feeling" that the young children related very well to their mother (notwithstanding the fact that they had not seen her for years, and that the younger child did not even know his mother) and that they were somehow fearful of their father. There was very little evidence to corroborate this view, since Hamid had never personally taken the children to the Board. Nevertheless, this interpretation of "damaged honor" and consequent "possible violent revenge" and even "abduction of the children" stuck. The judge adopted the Board's interpretation and followed their advice to hold separate hearings for the mother and the father, to avoid a possibly violent outburst from the father. The judge said in an interview: "I know of honor related violence among Turks, and since Hamid is of Turkish origin I have to take warnings more seriously compared to an ordinary Dutch couple. This case could indeed have lead to violence."

The Board's suggestion caused Hamid to be heard separately from his ex-wife in a special session of the court. Meryem was heard in the morning without Hamid knowing this. When he came to court, his lawyer told him of the hearing that morning. He became angry, saying it wasn't fair because he did not get the same opportunities as his ex-wife. He felt that all his actions were always viewed in an unfavorable light and that Meryem constantly got the benefit of the doubt. In his interview with me Hamid complained that the judge viewed him in the context of unfair stereotypes, making it very difficult for him to present himself favorably. The only way that he thought he could have countered the false image painted by his wife would have been to confront her directly with the absurdity of her accusations. In Hamid's view, which seems to have been colored by his culture, it is essential to deal face to face when discussing important issues. With paperwork you cannot really get to the truth; 'paper can lie'. When persons lie or are dishonest in person, however, everybody notices. It is common sense in Turkey that you need personal contact in order to gain trust and to be able to assess untrustworthiness. Business contracts are seldom executed in Turkey without first having a number of conversations and several social meetings. In other words: not being able to attend the session with his ex-wife was a violation of Hamid's cultural standards. This however, went unnoticed by all legal professionals.

The judge said in the interview she took the decision to hear both parties in separate sessions, because the Board advised her to do so. The judge thought that it would be better to "stay on the safe side" of a possible outbreak of violence, and besides that "it would be much better in this case to let each party speak in complete freedom, and without interference."

Is having separate sessions legally allowed? Dutch law states in article 19 of the Civil Code of Procedure that "parties must each have the opportunity to bring their arguments forward and to comment on the points of view and documents of the opposing party that have come to the knowledge of the judge".[23] Article 6 of the European Convention on Human Rights requires that there be a "fair hearing." This normally requires that "everyone who is a party to . . . proceedings shall have a reasonable opportunity of presenting his case to the Court under conditions which do not place him at substantial disadvantage vis-à-vis his opponent."[24] Standard interpretation of the principle of a fair hearing is further that "[t]he right to an adversarial trial

---

[23] In full: De rechter stelt partijen over en weer in de gelegenheid hun standpunten naar voren te brengen en toe te lichten en zich uit te laten over elkaars standpunten en over alle bescheiden en andere gegevens die in de procedure ter kennis van de rechter zijn gebracht, een en ander tenzij uit de wet anders voortvloeit. Bij zijn beslissing baseert de rechter zijn oordeel, ten nadele van een der partijen, niet op bescheiden of andere gegevens waarover die partij zich niet voldoende heeft kunnen uitlaten.

[24] Kaufman v. Belgium, 50 D.R. 98 (1986).

means the opportunity for the parties to have knowledge of and comment on the observations filed or evidence adduced by the other party."[25]

It is clear that the standard interpretation of article 6 leaves some room for discussion. Was Hamid put at a "*substantial* disadvantage" vis-a-vis Meryem? Is his being able to *comment later that day* on "what the judge said his former wife said earlier that morning", sufficiently adversarial? We don't know, but probably there was no violation. Even if we know that it is common (and scientific) sense that communication consists for the most part of non-verbal signs. This is why courtroom hearings are required. A courtroom hearing seems even more important when it is necessary, as in this case, critically to examine the worth or value of statements. To see and interpret how parties react to each other's statements may be invaluable for getting to the heart of the matter. Judges should at least keep this in mind when deciding on issues such as who must be present in court when others are heard. This, however, is not the most important conclusion.

The more important implication in this case is that legal professionals did not discuss the issue in the light of article 6. The issue of a fair hearing was never even raised.

Hamid's lawyer observed in the formal arguments before the court:

> It seems to me that the court believes the story of the mother: That my client is a brute and very dangerous. Now if that were so, then the court would have been right by have planned separate sessions. If not, we need wisdom, wisdom with the court. Because if the court takes decisions based only on the fear that violence *might* happen, we are far from justice. And let me be clear: There is hardly any evidence of a violent attitude on the part of my client. I must therefore conclude that I see fear with the court. And fear is a bad legal advisor.

The lawyer in the interview:

> This court really felt threatened by my arguments. The judge defended her decision for separate sessions fiercely. She argued that "this court has no fear, but what should we do when we get a telephone call advising...? Well, then we take the measures we think are necessary. But this does not mean this has consequences for our final decision!"

Neither the lawyer nor the judge argued on the basis of formal legal rules and neither referred to the principle of a fair hearing. The arguments concentrated on the right interpretation of the behavior of Hamid and the plausibility of the accusations made by Meryem. Perhaps mentioning the "fair trial" principle was regarded as a heavy weapon, not to be used lightly. Dutch legal culture is one of pragmatic arguments and compromise, always seeking the middle ground.[26]

Had the legal professionals in Hamid's case taken a reflective, articulated and explicit or in other words neo-modern attitude towards the issue, the

---

[25] *See also* Ruiz-Mateos v. Spain, 16 ECrtHR 505 (1993).

[26] Fred J. Bruinsma, Dutch Law in Action. Nijmegen: Ars Aequi Libri, (2003).

culture clash would have become more visible: A clash between the preference for orality in face-to-face contact in Turkish culture and the dominance of the written word in Dutch legal culture. Thus a clash between Hamid's Turkish culturally fueled notion of the principle of a fair hearing versus the standard interpretation that it is sufficient when you have the opportunity to "comment on what the judge says your opponent said". The consequence of this is that an important possibility for the "internationalization of law" in the sense of "selling" the value of a "fair trial" in the Dutch legal system is left fallow. I think that it would have been much better if more questions had been asked. Why did Meryem run away from home without her children? If Hamid used violence at the time, why doesn't anybody know? Why did it take the divorce action from Hamid before she laid a claim for custody? Why did Hamid threaten his wife in a letter? Why should the court believe that he is not really a violent man? How does he relate his "damaged honor" to what we in the Netherlands know about honor-related violence? Again, all these questions would probably have complicated the case enormously, but that is not sufficient reason to evade them. Instead, they would have provided the opportunity to discuss and make clear to the parties how and why certain decisions were taken, and if and in what sense their Turkish cultural background was playing a legally relevant role. The "Janus face" of neo-modern law means that lawyers and judges also be advocates of the devil. Their decisions would be more effective in the long run if they made their implicit arguments and preconceptions more visible.

6.4 Conclusion

Sally Merry has made the important observation that often "Human rights activists have little resonance at the grass roots."[27] Merry has identified a gap between the "human rights activists", who are part of an academic, international elite committed to the universality of human rights, and the lawyers and other professionals working at the level of ordinary, daily practice, who must cope with the fragmentation and plural condition of law among other rule systems, seeking justice in concrete instances.[28] My research confirms this observation: Legal professionals in the daily practice of local low-level courts do not automatically consider the requirements of formal human rights. They should be encouraged to do so. Difficult questions about abduction, the Moroccan way of raising children, the relevancy of being Turkish in relation to honor-related violence, and of being Turkish in relation to what might constitute a fair hearing, deserve to be addressed.

[27] Sally Engle Merry, *Human Rights and Gender Violence: Translating International Law into Local Justice*, Chicago Series in Law and Society (2006) at 164.
[28] Id.

Such questions would pave the way for a more open courtroom discussion under the supervision of an impartial judge, who could defend the basic principles of modern law while keeping eyes and ears open for practical solutions.

The neo-modern attitude to law would not be without some undesirable consequences. If implicit interpretations and assumptions were made more open, and if lawyers always openly put forward the advantages but also the limits of modern law and its principles, there might be greater conflict in society. As we all know, it is not possible nor desirable that everybody in every situation always speaks out openly about their assumptions and implicit value judgments. Social rules, often in the form of routines, stereotypes and assumptions about what is normal behavior, are the oil in the social machine.[29] Lawyers would probably have to proceed forward slowly, gradually working to change the culture of legal practice. This shift in legal culture is necessary not only because of changed social circumstances, but also because of the pretensions of the law. Doesn't the law present itself as the ultimate arbiter of disputes? If you can't find a solution yourself, the law is there to help you and to offer due process. The legal sphere is and should be different from other social spheres. The courtroom in particular is a place in which everything can and should be said. In my research I did not come across the neo-modern lawyer very often. The ordinary lawyer is much more common, such as the one who said in an interview that:

> In court I will never use the argument that the Islamic upbringing of a child – including not eating pig's meat, reading the Koran, regularly visiting to the mosque, wearing a scarf – is in the child's interest. Not even when my client is convinced that it is. Because if I were to say so, I would not serve the interests of my client. We would have to close the file, and my client would lose the opportunity [of having] his child live with him. So I try to convince my clients right here in my office, probably in several sessions that take quite some time, that his argument makes no sense. It may make sense from his point of view, fine, but there's this other person at the other table thinking that the best situation for the children is to grow up differently.
>
> Secondly, we are dealing with a judge from the Netherlands, in the Dutch legal system, and in Dutch society. Whether someone is Dutch or Islamic, is not that relevant, because the children need to grow up in the Netherlands. And that's the starting point for every argument.

I wonder what the clients of lawyers such as this one think of Dutch law and of Dutch society. My guess would be that their belief in modern law and their confidence that the law also serves their interests is very small. And that would be bad for modern law in the era of globalization.

---

[29] Harold Garfinkel, Studies in Ethnomethodology, Englewood Cliffs, (N.J., Prentice-Hall Inc.) (1967).

Chapter 7
Maternity Leave Laws in the United States in the Light of European Legislation

Candace Saari Kovacic-Fleischer

A comparison of maternity (and paternity) leave laws in the United States and the European Union could be stated in two phrases: United States, not much; European Union, a lot. Countries in the European Union and in much of the world provide lengthy paid maternity leaves and some paternity leaves. Although many companies in the United States provide their workers with paid family leaves, many do not. United States law does not require or fund paid family leaves. This makes it difficult for workers in the United States to balance family concerns with work.

The difference between how the United States and the countries in the European Union provide family leave benefits raises questions in the context of "internationalization." Internationalization suggests information-sharing across borders. With increased information, countries and companies acquire new ideas, or learn more about "foreign" ideas. "Good" ideas can be borrowed from one country and adapted to fit the needs of another. Internationalization also suggests increased interaction between countries. Because there is such a discrepancy between the United States and the countries of the European Union (and other parts of the world) in how the governments handle social needs, one wonders why the U.S. stands alone and whether its policies affect international interactions, including trade, between the United States and the European Union.

Perhaps the United States will not continue to stand alone. During the first half of the twentieth century, the United States Supreme Court shifted from striking down laws that regulate workers' wages and hours, to upholding them. In opinions reflecting more concern for workers, it occasionally looked to European laws already in place. Although considerable resistance remains in the United States to laws that regulate the workplace, the United States has slowly enacted laws to provide some social benefits and to prohibit discrimination in the workplace. In recent years the Supreme Court

C.S. Kovacic-Fleischer (✉)
American University Washington College of Law, Washington, DC, USA
e-mail: kovacic@wcl.american.edu

J. Klabbers, M. Sellers (eds.), *The Internationalization of Law and Legal Education*, Ius Gentium: Comparative Perspectives on Law and Justice 2,
DOI 10.1007/978-1-4020-9494-1_7,

has upheld these laws, although not without dissent. Perhaps this trend will continue. Perhaps the United States will look to the European Union, and internationalization will have a role in softening United States resistance to governmentally required or provided paid family benefits for workers. On the other hand, that resistance is deeply entrenched.

One can see the competing values invoked by United States proponents and opponents of laws that regulate the workplace by looking at Supreme Court cases that strike down or uphold those laws. Since the Supreme Court has the power to invalidate acts of Congress on the ground that they violate the Constitution,[1] much social legislation in the United States gets challenged in the Supreme Court. This discussion will describe the difficulty that the United States has had in passing social legislation by viewing it through the eyes of the United States Supreme Court during five different eras in the twentieth century: Laissez-faire economics and wage and hour legislation, 1905–1941; President Franklin D. Roosevelt's "New Deal" Social Security Act, 1935–1937; World War II and employment legislation, 1940–1948; the Civil Rights and Women's movements and employment legislation, 1963–1978; and, the Family and Medical Leave Act of 1993. This study will conclude with questions raised by viewing domestic United States policy in the context of "internationalization" as described by the other chapters in this volume. This comparison guides the author's conclusions, which were influenced by this discussion.

7.1 Laissez-Faire Economics and Wage and Hour Legislation, 1905–1941

In the early twentieth century when the United States Supreme Court was striking down laws that regulate hours and wages of workers, at least some European countries already had those laws in place. As the Supreme Court began to change its view about such legislation, it gave an occasional glance toward European laws. Before that change, however, the divergence in attitudes about social legislation was illustrated by *Lochner v. New York*,[2] one of the early cases dealing with governmental regulation of working conditions that reached the United States Supreme Court.

In *Lochner* the State of New York had passed a law preventing bakery owners from requiring employees to work for more than 10 hours a day or 60 hours a week. It was enacted after studies had shown serious danger, and more danger than in most occupations, to workers from long hours in bakeries. A bakery owner in New York who had been indicted for having violated New York's law argued that it violated the Due Process clause of

[1] *See* Marbury v. Madison, 5 U.S. 137 (1803).
[2] Lochner v. New York, 198 U.S. 45 (1905).

the Fourteenth Amendment to the U.S. Constitution. That clause prohibits states from depriving "any person of life, liberty, or property without due process of law."

Although the New York courts agreed with the state's legislators that the law was valid,[3] the Supreme Court disagreed, having reviewed the case because the bakery owners' challenge to the law was under the United States Constitution. The Court said that a state's police power to protect its citizens was not unlimited. The Court, applying its "common understanding" of the workplace, asserted that "the trade of a baker has never been regarded as an unhealthy one."[4] Perhaps reflecting the "rugged individualism" often associated with United States' policies, the Court invoked "the right of the individual to his personal liberty interest,"[5] holding that an employee had the freedom to contract with an employer to work as many hours as he wanted to support his family. Almost as an aside, the Court noted that, "Of course the liberty of contract relating to labor includes both parties to it. The one has as much right to purchase as the other to sell labor,"[6] thus dispensing with the suggestion that workers, needing jobs and having little leverage, require protection from employers. Again emphasizing individuality, the Court said,

> There is no contention that bakers as a class are not equal in intelligence and capacity to men in other trades or manual occupations, or that they are not able to assert their rights and care for themselves without the protecting arm of the State, interfering with their independence of judgment and of action.[7]

Justice Harlan, dissenting in *Lochner* viewed the case differently. In contrast to the Court's view of the equal relationship between employee and employer, he said,

> It may be that the statute had its origin, in part, in the belief that employers and employes [*sic*] in such establishments were not upon an equal footing, and that the necessities of the latter often compelled them to submit to such exactions as unduly taxed their strength. Be this as it may, the statute must be taken as expressing the belief of the people of New York that, as a general rule, and in the case of the average man, labor in excess of sixty hours during a week in such establishments may endanger the health of those who thus labor.[8]

He then asserted that the Court should not be "concerned with the wisdom or policy of legislation"[9] as long as the law had a substantial relationship to a lawful purpose, in New York's case, to protect health. His view

---

[3] Id. at 57.
[4] Id. at 59.
[5] Id. at 56.
[6] Id.
[7] Id. at 57.
[8] Id. at 69.
[9] Id.

did not prevail. Thus, in 1905, rugged individualism triumphed over state protection.

State protection triumphed three years later, but only for women. Oregon had passed a law that prohibited employers in a "mechanical establishment, or factory, or laundry" from employing women for more than 10 hours a day. The owner of a laundry was convicted of having violated the law. He challenged its constitutionality in a case that reached the U.S Supreme Court, *Muller v. Oregon*.[10] The Court distinguished *Lochner* on the ground that women were different from men, frail and in need of protection. The unanimous Court explained,

> That woman's physical structure and the performance of maternal functions place her at a disadvantage in the struggle for subsistence is obvious. This is especially true when the burdens of motherhood are upon her. Even when they are not, by abundant testimony of the medical fraternity continuance for a long time on her feet at work, repeating this from day to day, tends to injurious effects upon the body, and as healthy mothers are essential to vigorous offspring, the physical well-being of woman becomes an object of public interest and care in order to preserve the strength and vigor of the race.
>
> Still again, history discloses the fact that woman has always been dependent upon man. He established his control at the outset by superior physical strength, and this control in various forms, with diminishing intensity, has continued to the present...Education was long denied her, and while now the doors of the school room are opened and her opportunities for acquiring knowledge are great, yet even with that and the consequent increase of capacity for business affairs it is still true that in the struggle for subsistence she is not an equal competitor with her brother..... [S]he is properly placed in a class by herself, and legislation designed for her protection may be sustained, even when like legislation is not necessary for men and could not be sustained....The limitations which this statute places upon her contractual powers, upon her right to agree with her employer as to the time she shall labor, are not imposed solely for her benefit, but also largely for the benefit of all.[11]

While initially hailed as a progressive decision allowing states to begin to regulate sweatshop working conditions, it backfired on women, making them less desirable and valuable employees because they could not work as long as men could. In addition, the Court's demeaning language justified the view that women were inferior workers.

Muller led to a debate that continues to the present, whether laws that are written only for women can ever be advantageous to them, even when those laws deal with conditions biologically and indisputably unique to them, such as pregnancy and breastfeeding. The competing views in the debate are known as "equal treatment" versus "special treatment" or "equal opportunity." Whether one chooses the "special treatment" or "equal opportunity" title at times dictates the outcome of the debate: "equal

---

[10] Muller v. Oregon, 208 U.S. 412, 417 (1908).
[11] Id. at 421–422.

opportunity" being preferred by its proponents, equality having special place in United States law and policy.[12]

Having upheld maximum hour laws for women in *Muller*, the Court upheld that protection for men nine years later. In 1917 *Bunting v. Oregon*[13] upheld a maximum hour law for both men and women. In upholding the law, the Court never mentioned *Lochner*'s freedom-of-contract-due-process analysis although the lawyer representing Bunting, who had been convicted for having violated the law, relied upon it. Apparently the arguments of future Justice Felix Frankfurter, representing Oregon, convinced the Justices to ignore *Lochner*. Frankfurter argued in *Bunting* that *Lochner*'s reasoning was outmoded as it had been based, not on "scientific scrutiny" or "authoritative interpretation of accredited facts" but on the Justices' "common understanding"[14] of working conditions. The Court in *Bunting* upheld the hours law, quoting with approval from the Oregon Supreme Court's opinion,

> "In view of the well-known fact that the custom in our industries does not sanction a longer service than 10 hours per day, it cannot be held, as a matter of law, that the legislative requirement is unreasonable or arbitrary as to hours of labor."

To add justification to its holding, the Court quoted further from the Oregon Supreme Court's opinion:

> "Statistics show that the average daily working time among working-men in different countries is, in Australia, 8 hours; in Great Britain, 9; in the United States, 9 3/4; in Denmark, 9 3/4; in Norway, 10; Sweden, France, and Switzerland, 10 1/2; Germany, 10 1/4; Belgium, Italy, and Austria, 11; and in Russia, 12 hours."[15]

For the first time in the Supreme Court's consideration of maximum hour laws, "internationalization" had a role.

Although in *Bunting* the Supreme Court had upheld laws regulating hours for both men and women, it continued to be leery of state legislation that interfered with employers' decisions. This was still a time of *laissez faire* economics in the U.S. Five years after *Bunting* was decided, the Court in *Adkins v. Children's Hospital*,[16] in 1923, struck down a law passed by Congress for the District of Columbia that required employers to pay at least a minimum wage to women and children.[17] Although fifteen years prior in *Muller* the Court had said that "it is still true that in the struggle for subsistence she is not an equal competitor with her brother," the Court in *Adkins* did not equate wage laws with health or, apparently, "subsistence." Rather, noting the passage of the Nineteenth Amendment,

---

[12] *See* Fourteenth Amendment to the United States Constitution ("nor shall any State . . . deny to any person . . . the equal protection of the laws"..).

[13] Bunting v. Oregon, 243 U.S. 426 (1917).

[14] *Bunting*, 243 U.S., at 432.

[15] Id. at 438–439.

[16] Adkins v. Children's Hospital, 261 U.S. 525 (1923).

[17] Congress was responsible for the District of Columbia, the capital of the United States.

which gave women in the United States the right to vote, the Court said that, except for physical differences, inequalities between men and women had "come almost, if not quite, to the vanishing point."[18]

Although the Court had not cited *Lochner* in its earlier decision in *Bunting*, in *Adkins* the Court revived *Lochner* and its freedom-of-contract-liberty-interest analysis, saying,

> [W]hile the physical differences [between men and women] must be recognized in appropriate cases, and legislation fixing hours or conditions of work may properly take them into account, we cannot accept the doctrine that women of mature age, *sui juris*, require or may be subjected to restrictions upon their liberty of contract which could not lawfully be imposed in the case of men under similar circumstances. To do so would be to ignore all the implications to be drawn from the present day trend of legislation, as well as that of common thought and usage, by which woman is accorded emancipation from the old doctrine that she must be given special protection or be subjected to special restraint in her contractual and civil relationships.[19]

The Court thus articulated, in the context of minimum wage legislation, part of the "equal treatment/special treatment" debate that had begun after *Muller* had upheld maximum hour legislation for women. In *Adkins* the Court chose the "equal treatment" side of the debate. Apparently limiting hours, and in doing so decreasing women's wages, was one thing, but increasing their wages was something else entirely.

Chief Justice Taft in his dissent in *Bunting* pointed out that the Court's reasoning disadvantaged women by creating unequal opportunities, for the legislators who enacted the minimum wage law for women might have assumed that "the class receiving least pay, are not upon a full level of equality of choice with their employer and in their necessitous circumstances are prone to accept pretty much anything that is offered."[20] Felix Frankfurter, who had been counsel to Oregon in *Bunting*, and was counsel for the District of Columbia in *Adkins*, had argued that Congress' findings from its hearings supported the law's rationality. Congress, he said,

> found that alarming public evils had resulted, and threatened in increasing measure, from the widespread existence of a deficit between the essential needs for decent life and the actual earnings of large numbers of women workers of the District. In the judgment of Congress, based upon unchallenged facts, these conditions impaired the health of this generation of women and thereby threatened the coming generation through undernourishment, demoralizing shelter and insufficient medical care....The purpose of the act was to provide for the deficit between the cost of women's labor, i.e., the means necessary to keep labor going – and any rate of women's pay below the minimum level for living, and thereby to eliminate all the evils attendant upon such deficit upon a large scale.[21]

---

[18] *Adkins*, 261 U.S., at 553.

[19] Id.

[20] Id. at 562, (Taft, C.J., dissenting).

[21] *Adkins*, 261 U.S., at 528–529.

Justice Oliver Wendell Holmes, in his dissent in *Adkins*, pointed to minimum wage laws in Great Britain, "Victoria" (Canada) and Australia as evidence of the reasonableness of such laws.[22] Thus, Justice Holmes used "internationalization" to dispute the reasoning of the majority. His arguments eventually prevailed when the Supreme Court, in *West Coast Hotel Co. v. Parrish*,[23] overruled *Adkins* and its reliance on *Lochner* fourteen years later in 1937.

West Coast Hotel applied the reasoning of *Muller*, which had upheld maximum hour legislation for women, to a minimum wage law for women that had been passed in the State of Washington. The Court held,

> What can be closer to the public interest than the health of women and their protection from unscrupulous and overreaching employers? And if the protection of women is a legitimate end of the exercise of state power, how can it be said that the requirement of the payment of a minimum wage fairly fixed in order to meet the very necessities of existence is not an admissible means to that end? The legislature of the State was clearly entitled to consider the situation of women in employment, the fact that they are in the class receiving the least pay, that their bargaining power is relatively weak, and that they are the ready victims of those who would take advantage of their necessitous circumstances. The legislature was entitled to adopt measures to reduce the evils of the "sweating system," the exploiting of workers at wages so low as to be insufficient to meet the bare cost of living, thus making their very helplessness the occasion of a most injurious competition.[24]

One year after the Court had decided *West Coast Hotel*, Congress passed the Fair Labor Standards Act, which prohibited employers in specified industries from employing child labor and required them to pay, to both men and women, a minimum wage and an extra wage for work over 40 hours per week.[25] This was the first time a wage and hour law was enacted by the federal government to govern employers in all of the states.

With Felix Frankfurter, who had successfully represented Oregon in *Bunting* and unsuccessfully represented the District of Columbia in *Adkins*, now on the Supreme Court, the Supreme Court upheld the constitutionality of the FLSA in 1941 in *United States v. Darby*.[26] In *Darby* a manufacturer of finished lumber was indicted for selling it across state lines without having paid his workers the minimum wage or extra wage for overtime work.[27] Most of the Court's unanimous opinion in *Darby* was devoted to explaining why the federal government had power under the Commerce Clause of the United States Constitution to regulate actions of state employers. The court addressed the issue, which had elicited so much discussion in prior years,

---

[22] Id. at 570–571, (Holmes, J., dissenting).

[23] West Coast Hotel Co. v. Parrish, 300 U.S. 379 (1937).

[24] Id. at 398–399.

[25] 29 U.S.C. §201 *et. seq*.

[26] United States v. Darby, 312 U.S. 100 (1941).

[27] Id. at 111.

whether the government could protect workers with wage and hour laws, in three sentences,

> Since our decision in *West Coast Hotel Co.* v. *Parrish*, 300 U.S. 379, it is no longer open to question that the fixing of a minimum wage is within the legislative power and that the bare fact of its exercise is not a denial of due process under the Fifth more than under the Fourteenth Amendment. Nor is it any longer open to question that it is within the legislative power to fix maximum hours. . . . *Muller* v. *Oregon*, 208 U.S. 412; *Bunting* v. *Oregon*, 243 U.S. 426. . . . Similarly the statute is not objectionable because applied alike to both men and women. Cf. *Bunting* v. *Oregon*, 243 U.S. 426.[28]

Lawyers from the United States commonly use the abbreviation "cf." ("confer") as a signal that the cited case does not stand exactly for the proposition for which it is being cited, but could be relevant. *Bunting*, "cfed" in this way by the Court, had upheld maximum hour laws for men and women, but had avoided the question whether minimum wage laws for men and women, previously upheld only for women in *West Coast Hotel*, would be constitutional. *Darby* decided that they were, with little comment.

As described above, the debate about the validity of wage and hour laws continued from 1905 until 1941. While wage and hour laws regulate employers' decisions about those matters, they do not provide governmental benefits directly to workers. Before the FLSA had been passed and the wage hour debate had ended, after Roosevelt had been elected and with the Great Depression worsening, the federal government passed the Social Security Act of 1935, which would involve the federal government in providing benefits directly to individuals.[29]

7.2 President Franklin D. Roosevelt's "New Deal" Social Security Act

The Social Security Act of 1935, a major federal program to deal with a major national depression, created a number of programs. It provided retirement benefits (Old Age Assistance) for working men and federal unemployment benefits to be funded by taxing employee wages. While the old age assistance would be administered entirely by the federal government, the unemployment benefits would be administered by the states under federal supervision. The Social Security Act also authorized the federal government to provide grant money from its general tax revenues to states so

---

[28] *Darby*, 312 U.S., at 125.

[29] Wilbur J. Cohen, *Symposium: The New Deal and its Legacy: The Development of the Social Security Act of 1935: Reflection Some Fifty Years Later*, 68 Minn. L. Rev 379, 382–383 (1983). Wilbur Cohen is regarded as among the principal architects of the Social Security Act.

that they could administer aid to needy dependent children and the needy elderly and blind.[30]

When the Social Security Act was passed in 1935, the Supreme Court had yet to decide *West Coast Hotel v. Parrish*, which would overturn *Adkins v. Children's Hospital*.[31] In *Adkins*, twelve years prior to the passage of the Social Security Act, the Supreme Court had invalidated the District of Columbia's minimum wage law for women and revived *Lochner*'s freedom-of-contract-as-liberty-interest under the Due Process Clause of the Constitution. Although the minimum wage act at issue in *Adkins* had been passed by Congress, the act was not a federal law in that it applied to the entire country; rather, it was an act passed pursuant to Congress's role of governing the District of Columbia, the capital of the United States. Thus, all the wage/hour cases up to that time had involved federal Constitutional challenges to state, or quasi-state in the case of the District of Columbia, laws. As described above, many of these state statutes had been struck down by the Supreme Court. Ironically, the Social Security Act was challenged in the courts on the ground that it violated the "state's rights" provision of the United States Constitution, the Tenth Amendment.

The Tenth Amendment was the last of the amendments that were added in 1791 to the Constitution, which had been ratified in 1789. It provided that "The powers not delegated to the United States by the Constitution, nor prohibited by it to the States, are reserved to the States respectively, or to the people." The challenges to the Social Security Act were heard in two cases: *Steward Machine Company v. Davis*[32] resolved the challenge to the unemployment benefits program of the Act, while *Helvering v. Davis*[33] resolved the challenge to the retirement benefits program. Because the programs were to be funded by wage reductions (taxes) from employees' pay, the suits were brought nominally against Davis, who was the Collector of Internal Revenue. In both cases the opinions were written by Justice Benjamin Cardozo and announced on the same day in May of 1937, only two months after the Court decided *West Coast Hotel v. Parrish*.

In *Steward Machine* and *Helvering*, Justice Cardozo rejected the Tenth Amendment challenges by describing the national nature of the Great Depression.

> [T]here is need to remind ourselves of facts as to the problem of unemployment that are now matters of common knowledge. *West Coast Hotel Co.* v. *Parrish*, 300 U.S. 379....During the years 1929 to 1936, when the country was passing through a cyclical depression, the number of the unemployed mounted to unprecedented heights. Often the average was more than 10 million; at times a peak was attained of 16 million or more. Disaster to the breadwinner meant disaster to dependents.

---

[30] Id.

[31] *Adkins*, 261 U.S. 525.

[32] Steward Machine Company v. Davis, 301 U.S. 548 (1937).

[33] Helvering v. Davis, 301 U.S. 619 (1937).

> Accordingly the roll of the unemployed, itself formidable enough, was only a partial roll of the destitute or needy. The fact developed quickly that the states were unable to give the requisite relief. The problem had become national in area and dimensions. There was need of help from the nation if the people were not to starve. . . .[34]

The Justices in dissent were outraged. Justices McReynolds said, "The doctrine thus announced and often repeated [the right of self-government, by the States], I had supposed was firmly established. . . .. Unfortunately, the decision just announced opens the way for practical annihilation of this theory. . . ."[35] Justice Sutherland, joined by Justice Van Devanter, said, "The threat implicit in the present encroachment upon the administrative functions of the states is that greater encroachments. . . .will follow."[36] Finally Justice Butler said, "The terms of the measure make it clear that the tax and credit device was intended to enable federal officers virtually to control the exertion of powers of the States in a field in which they alone have jurisdiction and from which the United States is by the Constitution excluded."[37]

In *Helvering* Justice Cardozo reiterated the theme of national calamity,

> Nor is the concept of the general welfare static. Needs that were narrow or parochial a century ago may be interwoven in our day with the well-being of the Nation. What is critical or urgent changes with the times.
>
> The purge of nation-wide calamity that began in 1929 has taught us many lessons. Not the least is the solidarity of interests that may once have seemed to be divided. Unemployment spreads from State to State, the hinterland now settled that in pioneer days gave an avenue of escape. . . .Spreading from State to State, unemployment is an ill not particular but general, which may be checked, if Congress so determines, by the resources of the Nation. If this can have been doubtful until now, our ruling today in the case of the *Steward Machine Co., supra*, has set the doubt at rest. But the ill is all one, or at least not greatly different, whether men are thrown out of work because there is no longer work to do or because the disabilities of age make them incapable of doing it. Rescue becomes necessary irrespective of the cause. The hope behind this statute is to save men and women from the rigors of the poor house as well as from the haunting fear that such a lot awaits them when journey's end is near.[38]

Considering the *laissez faire* economics that prevailed in American political thought in the early part of the twentieth century, and the Supreme Court's insistence that it was embedded in the Constitution, the adoption and judicial upholding of the both the Social Security and the Fair Labor Standards Acts were monumental changes. Many compromises were

---

[34] *Steward Machine*, 301 U.S., at 586–587.

[35] Id. at 599 (McReynolds, dissenting).

[36] Id. at 616 (Sutherland, dissenting).

[37] Id. at 618 (Butler, dissenting).

[38] *Helvering*, 301 U.S., at 641–644.

required to produce bills that could pass in Congress. As Professor Wilbur Cohen, who was one of the drafters of the Social Security Act and Secretary of Health, Education and Welfare (HEW) under President Johnson, said of the Social Security Act,

> Although the Act was viewed as a radical program by some conservatives and viewed as a conservative one by some liberals, many political figures looked upon it as a middle-of-the-road program designed to preserve the social and economic structure of the nation, struggling in the midst of the most severe economic depression the republic had ever encountered. Thus, some individuals vigorously opposed the program, most others welcomed it, and others, while critical of some aspects, acknowledged that it was probably the best compromise available at the time within the structure of a capitalistic, free market economy and a democratic, representative legislative system.[39]

One bill that had competed with the Social Security Act's unemployment provisions bears mentioning here because it would have provided maternity benefits. The Workers' Unemployment and Social Insurance Bill was modeled, at least in part, on European practices. As Professor Kenneth Casebeer describes, its "benefits were to be administered through European style workers' councils."[40] The Workers' Bill would have provided for "a system of unemployment and social insurance for the purpose of providing insurance for all workers and farmers unemployed through no fault of their own in amounts equal to average local wages" and for "the establishment of other forms of social insurance . . . for the purpose of paying workers and farmers insurance for loss of wages because of part-time work, sickness, accident, old age, or maternity."[41] Ahead of its time, the Workers' Bill also provided that it "shall be extended to workers and farmers without discrimination because of age, sex, race, or color, religious or political opinion, or affiliation, whether they be industrial, agricultural, domestic, or professional workers, for all time lost."[42]

At various hearings before and after the passage of the Social Security Act, Congress heard about the need for maternity benefits. Dr. Emily N. Pierson testified:

> There are in the United States 2,425,000 married women of child-bearing age (18–45 years) gainfully employed in the United States. One in every five workers is a woman, and of these, one in every four is married. . . . [There is] a very close relation between economic security and the maternal mortality rate. The other

---

[39] Cohen, *supra* n. 29, at 382–383 (1983).

[40] Kenneth M. Casebeer, *Unemployment Insurance: American Social Wage, Labor Organizaiton and Legal Ideology*, 35 B.C. L. Rev 259, 266 (1994).

[41] Workers' Unemployment and Social Insurance Bill *quoted in* Kenneth M. Casebeer, *Unemployment Insurance: American Social Wage, Labor Organizaiton and Legal Ideology*, 35 B.C. L. Rev 259, 296–297 (1994).

[42] Id.

causative factors, such as the quality and availability of medical care, do not alter this fact.[43]

Ella Bloor testified:

I think very few of us who are in the cities realize the poverty that the women are suffering, especially the young women in the farm districts, on account of not only the drought and the usual conditions there, but especially the fact of maternity in these isolated places....We found in the women's section of the unemployed congress which took place in Washington recently, when I met with those women two or three times, that they were especially interested in this part of the bill, about maternity...not only the farm women, but working women everywhere.[44]

Whether maternity benefits might have received consideration in another bill cannot be known. The fact that those benefits were included in a bill with a funding mechanism most likely viewed as radical at the time may not have helped. The Workers' Bill provided:

Funds for such insurance shall hereafter be provided at the expense of the Government and of employers, and...funds to be raised by the Government shall be secured by taxing inheritance and gifts, and by taxing individual and corporation incomes of $ 5,000 per year and over. No tax or contribution in any form shall be levied on workers for the purposes of this Act.[45]

No doubt this funding mechanism would have faced opposition, especially from those who still retained not only ardent states rights views, but also *Lochner*-type views of the employer-employee relationship. As Professor Cohen described, the funding mechanism of the Social Security Act was an important mechanism to maintain its political viability. Professor Cohen observed that,

Roosevelt was very concerned about the possible political change or repeal of the old age insurance program in the future. Thus, he supported and justified the use of contributory payroll taxes to finance the insurance programs as "the" method that would assure continuation and support of a statutory and political "right" of individuals to receive benefits without an income or "needs" test in time of financial constraints.

At the time he signed the Social Security Act into law, President Roosevelt explained his basic incremental approach when he said that the Social Security Act "represents a corner stone in a structure which is being built but is by no

---

[43] Social Insurance: Hearings on S. 3475 Before the Senate Comm. on Education and Labor, 74th Cong., 2d Sess., 56–57 (1936) (statement of Dr. Emily N. Pierson) *quoted in* Workers' Bill quoted in Kenneth M. Casebeer, *Unemployment Insurance: American Social Wage, Labor Organizaiton and Legal Ideology*, 35 B.C. L. Rev 259, 294 (1994).
[44] Unemployment, Old Age, and Social Insurance: Hearings on H.R. 2827 Before Subcomm. of the House Comm. on Labor, 74th Cong., 1st Sess., 129–30 (1935) (statement of Ella Reeve Bloor) *quoted in* Kenneth M. Casebeer, *Unemployment Insurance: American Social Wage, Labor Organizaiton and Legal Ideology*, 35 B.C. L. Rev 259, 294 (1994).
[45] Workers' Unemployment and Social Insurance Bill *quoted in* Kenneth M. Casebeer, *Unemployment Insurance: American Social Wage, Labor Organizaiton and Legal Ideology*, 35 B.C. L. Rev 259, 296–297 (1994).

means complete." The building of the program has been a continuing process which Roosevelt expected to go on until the program provided protection against all the major hazards of life "from the cradle to the grave."[46]

Although many countries in the European Union and elsewhere had and have "cradle to grave" protections for their people, Roosevelt's expectation of what would happen in the United States has not taken place. Little by little, however, the Social Security Act has expanded. In 1939 it was amended to add survivors' and old-age benefits for wives and widows of workers covered by Social Security and in 1950 to provide those benefits to husbands and widowers.[47] It was amended again in 1956 to include disability insurance and in 1965 to include Medicare, a medical insurance program for those of retirement age.[48] In 1977 the Supreme Court had occasion to review the 1939 amendment and said that "dependency, not need, [was] the criterion for inclusion" of wives and widows.[49] That the "old age" benefits were not to be based on need emphasizes the political exigency that required the Social Security Act, and its later amendments, to be an insurance based plan, not a "general welfare" plan.[50]

7.3 World War II and Employment Legislation, 1940–1948

Maternity benefits never became part of the Social Security Act, nor were they provided in federal legislation until more that 50 years later. As will be discussed below, the Family and Medical Leave Act, passed in 1993, was the first federal statute to provide parental leave and health related leaves, although they are unpaid, for no more than 12 weeks and are only required to be given by large employers. By this time European countries, and most of the countries in the world, provided paid, and usually lengthy, maternity leaves, frequently funded at least in part with general taxes, not taxes solely on workers' wages. Often those countries provide paternity leaves as well.

Although during the New Deal Congress passed much social legislation, the only legislation related to leaves from work involved veterans. Before the United States entered World War II at the end of 1941, Congress had passed the Selective Training and Service Act of 1940, which provided that private employers "shall restore" former employees, who were honorably

---

46 Cohen, *supra* n. 29, at 407.

47 Califano v. Goldfarb, 430 U.S. 199, 216 (1977).

48 Edward D. Berkowitz, Mr. Social Security: The Life of Wilbur J. Cohen (forward by Joseph A. Califano).

49 *Goldfarb*, 430 U.S. at 213 (holding that differential survival benefits for widows and widowers violated the Constitution).

50 While the Social Security Act did provide federal grants to the states for welfare for the needy, general funding for welfare has less political support than insurance-type benefits in the U.S. *See* Cohen, *supra* n. 29 at 406.

discharged, to their former "position or to a position of like seniority, status, and pay unless the employer's circumstances have so changed as to make it impossible or unreasonable to do so."[51] Congress has extended that Act many times. It is currently known as the Uniformed Services Employment and Reemployment Rights Act.[52] As with prior acts, it provides employment leaves for veterans for up to 5 years.[53] When veterans return they are entitled to receive the wages, benefits and seniority they would have had as if they not been in the service.[54] When there was a draft, the veterans' leave and benefits applied to those who volunteered as well as to those who were drafted.[55] For veterans returning from World War II Congress passed the "GI bill", which paid for veteran's post high school education. During World War II, not only were maternity benefits not legislated, but at least one state had passed legislation that excluded women from certain jobs. A law passed in Michigan in 1945 prohibited women from having jobs as bartenders unless they were the wife or daughter of a male owner. The law was challenged as violating the Equal Protection Clause of the Constitution.[56] The Supreme Court upheld it in *Goesaert v. Cleary*[57] although there were three dissenters. Apparently not taking the issue seriously, Justice Frankfurter in his majority opinion wrote, "Beguiling as the subject is, it need not detain us long. . . .We are, to be sure, dealing with a historic calling. We meet the alewife, sprightly and ribald, in Shakespeare, . . ."[58] The Court held that the distinction in the Michigan law was rational and concluded, "Since the line they [in Michigan] have drawn is not without a basis in reason, we cannot give ear to the suggestion that the real impulse behind this legislation was an unchivalrous desire of male bartenders to try to monopolize the calling."[59] As the case was decided in 1948, one might ask whether this lack of chivalry was related to the fact that men were returning from war.

---

[51] *See*, Accardi v. Pennsylvania Railroad Co., 383 U.S. 225 (1966), *quoting* the Selective Training and Service Act of 1940.

[52] 38 U.S.C. §4301, *et seq*.

[53] 38 U.S.C. § 4312.

[54] 38 U.S.C. §4316 (a) provides, "A person who is reemployed under this chapter is entitled to the seniority and other rights and benefits determined by seniority that the person had on the date of the commencement of service in the uniformed services plus the additional seniority and rights and benefits that such person would have attained if the person had remained continuously employed."

[55] Vietnam Era Veterans' Readjustment Assistance Act of 1974, 38 U.S.C. §2021 et seq., 38 U.S.C. §§2021, 2024. *See also* Schaller v. Board of Education of Elmwood Local School District, 449 F. Supp. 30 (W.D. Ohio 1978).

[56] The Equal Protection Clause of the Fourteenth Amendment to the U.S. Constitution provides "nor shall any State . . .deny to any person . . .the equal protection of the laws".

[57] Goesaert v. Cleary, 335 U.S. 464 (1948).

[58] Id. at 465.

[59] Id. at 467.

Historians differ as to the effect of World War on women's desire for work outside the home. Some view it as a time when women indicated a distaste for employment, illustrated by a popular, although mixed metaphor, that at the end of the war could be heard "the thundering herds of women stampeding back to the nest."[60] Others refer to the famous poster of "Rosie the Riveter" as ushering in a time when women realized that they were capable of handling work outside the home and enjoying it.[61] Such debates may not have been as pronounced in Europe as so many men had been lost during the war.

7.4 The Civil Rights and Women's Movements, Employment Legislation, 1963–1978

Very little, if any, federal legislation aided women who wanted or needed employment until the early 1960s. As a result of the Civil Rights and Women's movements, two important acts were passed. In 1963 Congress passed the Equal Pay Act, which amended the Fair Labor Standards Act to require employers to pay men and women the same rate for equal work of similar skill, effort and working conditions.[62] One year later Congress passed the Civil Rights Act of 1964, Title VII of which prohibited employers from discriminating against workers because of their race, religion, sex, national origin and color.[63] About a decade after Title VII was passed, the Supreme Court ruled in two cases that discrimination against pregnant women was not sex discrimination. *Geduldig v. Aiello*[64] involved a constitutional challenge to California's disability insurance program that covered all short term disabilities except pregnancy. The Court ruled that because there were women in both classes of pregnant and nonpregnant people, discrimination against pregnancy was not sex discrimination. *General Electric Co. v. Gilbert*,[65] involved a Civil Rights Act of 1964 Title VII challenge to an employer's plan similar to California's. The Court applied the same reasoning and also noted that the company was paying more in benefits to women than to men.

Congress, in response, amended Title VII with the Pregnancy Discrimination Act (PDA) of 1978, which provided:

---

[60] *See, e.g.*, EEOC v. Madison Community Unit School Dist., 818 F.2d 577, 582 (1982) (quoting Congressman Goodell, 109 Cong. Rec. 9208 (1963)).

[61] *See, e.g.*, Borelli v. Brusseau, 16 Cal. Rptr. 2d 16, 24 (Poche, J., dissenting).

[62] 29 U.S.C. § 206(d).

[63] 42 U.S.C. §2000e, *et seq*.

[64] Geduldig v. Aiello, 417 U.S. 484 (1974).

[65] General Electric Co. v. Gilbert, 429 U.S. 125 (1976).

> The terms "because of sex" or "on the basis of sex" include, but are not limited to, because of or on the basis of pregnancy, childbirth, or related medical conditions; and women affected by pregnancy, childbirth, or related medical conditions shall be treated the same for all employment-related purposes, including receipt of benefits under fringe benefit programs, as other persons not so affected but similar in their ability or inability to work[66]

Pregnancy issues challenge the concept of equality. If an employer provides no benefits except those for pregnant women, women may be viewed as less desirable workers than men, and may also be resented by their colleagues. If an employer provides no benefits to anyone, then women are not singled out. If they need time from work for pregnancy, however, they will lose their job while men who become fathers will not. Thus, there is no way to be "equal" because men and women's reproductive abilities are not the same. Of course an individual woman could decide not to become pregnant, but that would not be a beneficial resolution of the debate from a societal point of view.

The PDA can be read as having both equal opportunity and equal treatment clauses. The first clause defining discrimination, does not specify whether discrimination is equal treatment or opportunity. The second clause, in the context of offering benefits, uses explicit "treated the same" language in the context of pregnancy. The "equal treatment/special treatment or equal opportunity" debate surfaced during the wage and hour legislation debate. During that time, no matter how the debate was resolved, women were disadvantaged. The Court in *Muller*[67] allowed Oregon to provide women with "special treatment" by upholding a state's maximum hours legislation. As noted earlier, although that legislation was designed to end some of the sweatshop conditions, it backfired against women. Later in *Adkins*[68] the Court refused to let the District of Columbia provide women with the "special treatment" of a minimum wage for them. The Court invalidated the law on the ground that women should not be treated differently from men. After *Muller*, women received lower wages than men; after *Adkins*, women continued to receive lower wages.

Countries in the European Union generally do not adopt the "equal treatment" model of equality. Rather, their family leave laws frequently provide lengthier leave for women than for men. This disparity in leaves is criticized by some as perpetuating the distinction between men's and women's jobs, but praised by others as enabling mothers to both keep their jobs and have meaningful time with their newborns.

As in the 1910s, in the 1960s and 1970s some states passed their own employment laws. California passed a law requiring employers to provide women with up to four months of unpaid leave for disability caused by

66 42 U.S.C. §2000e(k).
67 Muller v. Oregon, 208 U.S. 412 (1908)
68 *Adkins*, 261 U.S. 525.

pregnancy. An employer challenged this law on the ground that it was preempted by Title VII, a federal statute which, under the Supremacy Clause of the Constitution, invalidates any state statute that interferes with it. In *California Federal Savings & Loan Assn. v. Guerra*,[69] the employer relied on the "treated the same" language of the PDA, arguing that because California did not require employers to provide up to four months of leave to "other persons not [affected by pregnancy] but similar in their ability or inability to work," the California law interfered with Title VII. Feminists filed *amicus curiae* briefs on both sides of the case. The "equal treatment" feminists sided with the bank, while the "equal opportunity" feminists sided with California, which was defending its statute.[70] The majority, in an opinion by Justice Thurgood Marshall, held in *CalFed* that "Congress intended the PDA to be 'a floor beneath which pregnancy disability benefits may not drop – not a ceiling above which they may not rise.' "[71] Sounding as if he were adopting the "equal opportunity" approach to Title VII, Justice Marshall also said, "By 'taking pregnancy into account,' California's pregnancy disability-leave statute allows women, as well as men, to have families without losing their jobs."[72] He did not say, however, that Title VII requires pregnancy-specific policies to be provided, no matter what programs an employer does or does not provide, to ensure that women do not have to choose between families and jobs. To have said that would have been difficult as the legislative history to the PDA contained specific statements that it did not require employers to provide benefits if they were not doing so.[73] The federal government's reluctance to tell employers what to do was still present.

Justice White, for the dissent in *CalFed*, quoted that legislative history, which was from the House Report, and noted that it did not change the antidiscrimination focus of Title VII and did not give women preferential treatment.

> It must be emphasized that this legislation, *operating as part of Title VII*, prohibits only discriminatory treatment. Therefore, it does not require employers to treat pregnant employees in any particular manner with respect to hiring, permitting them to continue working, providing sick leave, furnishing medical and hospital benefits, providing disability benefits, or any other matter. H. R. 6075 in no way requires the institution of any new programs where none currently exist. The bill would simply require that pregnant women be treated the same as other employees on the basis of their ability or inability to work.[74]

---

[69] California Federal Savings & Loan Assn. v. Guerra, 479 U.S. 272 (1987).
[70] Id. at 274. *See also* Candace S. Kovacic[-Fleischer], *Remedying Underinclusive Statutes*, 33 Wayne L. Rev. 39, 76–80 (1986).
[71] *CalFed*, at 285, *quoting from* the Ninth Circuit's opinion.
[72] Id. at 289.
[73] Id. at 286–287 and at 299 (White, J., dissenting).
[74] Id. at 299 (White, J. dissenting).

CalFed did not resolve the equal treatment/equal opportunity debate. It held only that states may provide pregnant women with extra benefits for physical disabilities from their unique condition. It did not say that those benefits *must* be provided if women are to achieve equality in the workplace.

One can see the ghost of *Lochner* in the way courts have interpreted the second clause of the PDA, the clause requiring pregnant women merely to be "treated the same. . . .as other persons not so affected but similar in their ability or inability to work." The ghost of *Lochner* is particularly evident in cases brought and lost by pregnant women because, as one court said, "employers can treat pregnant women as badly as they treat similarly affected but nonpregnant employees."[75] Treating employees badly would not seem to be good policy. It evokes visions of the sweatshops of the early 1900s. Treating pregnant women badly also would not seem to be good policy. Even treating employees well, but ignoring any possibility that pregnancy and childbirth might create needs, such as time off and breastfeeding, that do not occur with any other condition, disadvantages women. One can see in these cases that while *Lochner* may have been overruled, its "rugged individualism" and its reluctance to have government interfere with employer decisions still lingers.

7.5 The Family and Medical Leave Act of 1993

Although the FLSA, passed in 1938, imposed wage and hour affirmative obligations on employers and Title VII, passed in 1964, imposed prohibitions, neither of those statutes required employers to provide maternity, paternity or sick leaves, or health insurance. No statute required employers to accommodate just one group of employees. That changed in 1990. Congress passed, and President George H.W. Bush signed, the Americans with Disabilities Act (ADA).[76] The ADA requires employers to make affirmative accommodations, even those that cost money, for disabled workers so that they can work. The ghost of *Lochner* was not vanquished entirely by the passage of the ADA, however. Two days after President George H.W. Bush signed the ADA in June of 1990, he vetoed the Family and Medical Leave Act (FMLA). He vetoed it again two years later. It was not until

[75] Troupe v. May Dep't Stores Co., 20 F.3d 734, 738 (7th Cir.1994)(holding that a woman suffering from morning sickness was fired for tardiness, not pregnancy); *See also* Candace Saari Kovacic-Fleischer, *Litigating Against Employment Penalties for Pregnancy, Breastfeeding and Childcare*, 44 Vill. L. Rev. 355 (1999)(describing and critiquing many cases brought unsuccessfully under the PDA).

[76] 42 U.S.C. §12101, *et seq*.

after President Clinton was elected, that the FMLA was signed into law.[77] Perhaps the reason for President H.W. Bush's differing treatment of the two acts was that the ADA would enable those who are disabled to work and therefore, it would be hoped, stay off welfare and pay taxes, while the FMLA is about people on leave. Although those on leave are caring, without pay, for babies and the sick and elderly, they are not "working" for their employer. The Calvinistic "work ethic" of the United States' early settlers is an entrenched value as is the rugged individualist.

The FMLA was eventually enacted in 1993. It was the first act that President William Jefferson Clinton signed into law. It requires employers with 50 or more employees to provide up to 12 weeks of unpaid leave for the birth or adoption of a child, or to care for oneself or close family members with serious medical conditions.[78] These benefits may not seem like much to people from European Union countries, or from many other countries in the world, but as the history of social legislation in the United States illustrates, these benefits were a big step in the American context.

The policies of the FMLA received support from a surprising corner, the Supreme Court in an opinion written by the late Chief Justice Rehnquist, who is usually viewed as having been a conservative Justice. In *Nevada Department of Human Resources v. Hibbs*,[79] Chief Justice Rehnquist, writing for the Court, held that one purpose of the FMLA was to remedy sex discrimination caused by unequal family obligations.[80] Then he held that "state practices [which] continue to reinforce the stereotype of women as caregivers" such as denying men leaves comparable to those for women, discriminate on the basis of sex.[81] Finally he held that a statute that "simply mandated gender equality in the administration of leave benefits . . . would allow States to provide for no family leave at all. . . . such a policy would exclude far more women than men from the workplace . . ."[82] Thus he noted that an equal treatment policy, depending on the policy, can have unequal results. He did not need to address however, whether the FMLA can provide "special treatment" for women because that Act is written in gender neutral terms, with the hope that it will encourage men to seek family leaves.

---

[77] *See* Linda Hamilton Krieger, *Forward – Backlash Against the ADA: Interdisciplinary Perspectives and Implications for Social Justice Strategies*, 21 Berkeley J. Emp. & Labor L. 1 (2000).

[78] 29 U.S.C. §2601, *et. seq*.

[79] Nev. Dep't of Human Res. v. Hibbs, 538 U.S. 721 (2003).

[80] Id. at 729

[81] Id. at 738.

[82] Id.

7.6 Conclusion

Supreme Court decisions demonstrate some of the values that compete when the United States enacts legislation that regulates the workplace. I would like to see the United States enact more "family friendly" legislation, borrowing from examples in the European Union as so many workers struggle in the United States to fulfill their family obligations without losing their jobs. The history set forth in this paper helps to explain why the United States has developed such an unusually strong reluctance to fund maternity and other family leaves. Greater exposure to European practices and integration with European law may soften this tradition.

Tracing the history of social legislation from wage and hour laws to the Family and Medical Leave Act through the eyes of the United States Supreme Court, shows how the United States has expanded its view of the government's role in the private workplace over time, but expansion in Europe has occurred much more quickly. Americans have a long tradition of opposing government power, particularly Federal power. This tradition has made American legislatures and courts resistant to social engineering. Family leave policies might seem to benefit all family members, but they still imply government activism. There are many sociological explanations for American attitudes, many of which have little to do with the law. Europeans have been more comfortable with government intervention, but this too may be changing. Some in the European Union may be questioning whether generous benefits help or hurt their economies. Economists may seek to compare the impact of governmentally funded, mandated leaves of the European Union with the unfunded few mandates of the United States. Determining which system is "best", however, requires recognizing that leave policies are not the only difference between the European Union and the United States, and that "best" can be measured in many different ways.

This discussion has sought to identify and explain some of the origins of American exceptionalism, and the gradual trend towards a more European model. Growing internationalization of the legal profession has made new legal models available to lawyers in Europe and in the United States. The law on both continents can only benefit from comparing our different experiences.

Chapter 8
Convergence and Mutual Recognition in European Asylum Law

Ida Staffans

8.1 Introduction

It has been said that the asylum policy and the asylum procedures of Europe are undergoing a process of internationalisation.[1] Aside from the jurisprudential implications of internationalisation, there are at least three practical ways in which this statement is true: First, the asylum procedures of Europe are objects of harmonisation and the geographical scope of the legal effects of decisions made within national procedures have expanded regionally and also beyond the borders of Europe.[2] Second, European asylum procedures are increasingly shifting the focus of the decision-making from factors linked to the person present in Europe to general factors in countries outside the region, both countries of origin and other.[3] Third, the field of persons seeking, enjoying or having sought asylum in Europe is continuously being broadened and the decision-makers of Europe's asylum procedures are having to face a much wider range of attitudes and experiences.

I. Staffans (✉)
Institute for International Economic Law, University of Helsinki; Academy of Finland Centre of Excellence in the Foundations of European Law and Polity, Helsinki, Finland
e-mail: ida.staffans@helsinki.fi

[1] For instance McKeever David, Schultz Jessika, Swithern Sophia: *Forreign Territory: The Internationalisation of EU Asylum Policy*, Oxfam Publishing 2005, 1–5.

[2] Readmission agreements, as an example of the expanding scope of judicial decision-making in the union, related to the readmission of amongst others failed asylum seekers have been concluded and are being negotiated with a variety of states outside Europe. *See* Steve Peers: *Readmission Agreements and EC External Migration Law*, Statewatch Analysis no 17, *available at* http://www.statewatch.org/news/2003/may/readmission.pdf (3.8.2007).

[3] *See* articles 26, 27, 29 and 31 of the Council Directive 2005/85/EC of 1 December 2005, OJ (L 326) 13 on Minimum Standard on Procedures in Members States for Granting and Withdrawing Refugee Status, which invoke the concepts of safe third countries, safe countries of asylum and safe countries of origin.

J. Klabbers, M. Sellers (eds.), *The Internationalization of Law and Legal Education*, Ius Gentium: Comparative Perspectives on Law and Justice 2,
DOI 10.1007/978-1-4020-9494-1_8,

This discussion will consider internationalisation as reflected by the impact of supra-national guidelines and norms on national decision-making, the cross-border legal effects of national decisions, and the possibilities for joint processing. An examination of the approach taken by the European Union towards harmonisation or internationalisation will reveal certain weaknesses in existing legislation, and suggest some improvements.

Considering the special nature of asylum as a field of law and the role of national asylum procedures for the states of Europe, the European Union has not been as effective as it should have in encouraging cooperation and convergence among the Member States. The mechanism of mutual recognition offers a better path towards convergence and arguments set out below suggest that a change in vocabulary would strengthen the development of greater conformity in European asylum procedures.

The first part of this argument offers a background to the discussion and looks at the recent developments relating to asylum in the European Union. The second part examines more thoroughly the mechanisms used in the legislative work and analyses the results of harmonisation. Third, mutual recognition is presented as an alternative measure of convergence. And finally, the possibilities for mutual recognition in the field of asylum and immigration in Europe are examined in the light of the ongoing harmonisation.

8.2 The European Asylum Regime

8.2.1 Background: Developments Towards and Reasons for a Common System

The Treaty of Amsterdam transferred legislative competence in the field of asylum to the European Union.[4] This made the asylum practices and legislation of the Member States into objects of unification and europeanisation, and inaugurated the process of the voluntary internationalisation of asylum law.[5]

---

[4] Issues of asylum and migration were with the Treaty of Amsterdam transferred to Title VI of the Treaty on the European Union, which in practice implied that questions linked to asylum and immigration were transferred from the sphere of cooperation government-to-government to the sphere of supra-national, EU, legislative competence. For accounts of the legislative developments in the field of asylum and immigration *see* Steve Peers, *Framework of EC Immigration and Asylum Law in Peers*, Steve and Rogers, N (eds.): *EU Immigration and Asylum Law* Martinus Nijhoff Publishers, 2006 and Hemme Battjes: *European Asylum Law and International Law*, Martinus Nijhoff Publishers, 26–33 (2006).

[5] For an analysis of the concept of Europeanisation *see* Satu Paasilehto, *Constellations a New Approach to Legal Culture and European Integration of Private Law*, Helsinki, 161–165 (2002).

At the time, many different approaches to the task could have been adopted. The European Union chose, however, to pursue for a program of full scale harmonisation, including legislative, practical and judicial-procedural harmonisation, and the Union has persisted in this approach.[6]

The Tampere Conclusions of 1999 firmly state that the objective for the adaptation of the European asylum regime to the needs of the region is the creation of "a common European asylum system" (CEAS) including a common asylum procedure (CEAP) and a uniform status for recognized refugees and persons benefiting from subsidiary protection in Europe.[7] This maxim has become the mantra for those pursuing the European Union integration in the field and has also been reaffirmed by the European Commission as the general goal for future developments.[8]

The objective of a common procedure and a uniform status creates a strong incentive for harmonisation of the member states' asylum and immigration procedures and policies. First, there is the common procedure to be established.[9] It is not quite clear what this common procedure will include, and the Green Paper issued recently by the Commission invites a discussion and further public elaboration of the contents of this common procedure.[10] However, it has become clear that this will include: a common procedural, structural and perhaps also an institutional ground for judicial decision-making in asylum matters; a common understanding and use of the devices and concepts that are inherent to the European discussion on asylum; and possibilities for joint processing and shared technical support-functions, such as databases and sources of country of origin-information. Additionally, persons granted asylum status through the CEAP will receive the same benefits and rights throughout the union, because uniform status that is a part of the CEAS.[11]

---

[6] For general accounts of the harmonisation carried out in the field of asylum in Europe *see* Harlow, Carol and Guild, Elspeth (eds.) *Implementing Amsterdam*, Hart Publications 2001; Rosemary Byme, Noll Gregor & Vedsted-Hansen, Jens: *New Asylum Countries? Migration Control and Refugee Protection in an Enlarged European Union*, Kluwer Law International 2002 and Brinkmann, Gisbert: The Immigration and Asylum Agenda 10 Eur. Law J. 182–199 (2004).

[7] The European Council Summit in Tampere, Finland 1999 set out the practical structures for the work towards harmonisation in the field of Justice and Home Affairs in the European Union. *See* the Presidentiary Conclusions of the Tampere European Council 15–16.10.1999, section 15.

[8] European Commission: *Green Paper on the Future Common European Asylum System*, COM(2007)301 final, 2–3. The green papers issued by the Commission are designed to communicate the views of the Commission and to launch public consultations on the matter regarded.

[9] Ibid., section 13 and Frances Nicholson, *Challenges to Forging a Common European Asylum System in Line with International Obligations* in Peers et al., 2006; Battjes 2006, 195–218 and Vedsted-Hansen, Jens: *Common EU Standards on Asylum*, 7 Eur. J. Migration L. 369–376 (2005).

[10] *Supra* note 8, at 4.

[11] *Supra* note 7, section 14 and Battjes at 447–530 (2006).

Clearly, the prime reason for making the CEAS a primary goal for the regional internationalisation is economic. If a well-functioning common procedure and a uniform asylum status were put in place in Europe, the incentives for asylum seekers to try their luck in numerous jurisdictions would be diminished. Thus, Europe would face fewer total asylum applications and lower the costs that arise from sending and receiving persons between the member countries.[12] Additionally, some of the "administrative" obligations closely connected to national asylum procedures, such as fact-finding and the production of country of origin information, could easily be centralized if the standards and the needs of the procedures regionally were harmonised.

Further reasons for far-reaching harmonisation in the field of asylum and immigration can easily be found in considerations relating to the impact of a CEAS on the self-perception of the Union. Divergences between the Member States in this respect are bound to add to perceptions of inequality and badly distributed burdens. The CEAS also has important implications for the external perception and image of the European Union.

The challenges facing the Union's development towards the CEAS are twofold: On the one hand there are formal and institutional questions to be raised in connection with transfer of powers in the asylum procedure from the purely national to the European level. These questions can be and are often posed irrespective of the substantive area of law effected by the transfer.[13] On the other hand, there are also some implications particular to the subject area of immigration law and especially asylum law. These implications are connected to the bond between the nation state, its sovereignty and judicial decisions that include both the acceptance of a new member in to the national society and a statement on the failure of another state to protect its citizens.[14] As we will see, these challenges have made the task of harmonisation very difficult for the European Union—so difficult that the Union has not been particularly successful in overcoming them.

---

[12] On the economic incentive to burden sharing *see* Eiko R. Thielemann, *Between Interests and Norms: Explaining Burden-Sharing in the European Union*, 16 J. Refugee Studies, 253–273 (2003).

[13] European courts have often been faced with the issue relating to the allocation of the competence to allow for EU competence over national. *See*, for instance the discussion after the famous Maastrich decision, *Manfred Brunner and others v. The European Union Treaty*, BvG 2134/92 & 2159/92, by the German Budesverfassungsgericht in Joachim Wieland, Germany in the European Union – *The Maastricht Decision of the Bundesverfassungsgericht*, 5 Eur. J. Intl. L. 1–8 (1994).

[14] The non-aggressive character of decision making in asylum matters is a principle commonly recognized and accepted in international law. However, this do not imply that considerations relating to effects of a decision outside the host country are absent from the procedure. Atle Grah-Madsen, *The Status of Refugees in International Law II Asylum, Entry and Sojourn*, Sijthoff, Leiden, 26–31 (1972).

8.2.2 Measures of Convergence in the Work Towards the CEAS

The practical aspects of development towards a common procedure and uniform status were divided at the Council meeting in Tampere into two phases: A first phase encompassing the passing of harmonising directives and regulations,[15] ending in 2004, and a second phase ending in 2010 encompassing the practical development and integration of asylum procedures of Europe.[16]

During the first phase, a number of measures were taken and binding community legislation was passed both in relation to the substantive issues of international protection in Europe and in relation to the more formalistic and procedural aspects of their implementation in the Member States. Specific regulations and directives were issued on burden sharing,[17] definitions and eligibility,[18] reception conditions[19] and the procedural aspects of refugee status determination.[20]

These legislative acts and their impact in the Member States are at the moment under evaluation. Prior to the evaluation the Commission established some general goals for enhanced harmonisation during the second phase of legislation. These include enhancing practical cooperation between the Member States by developing technical standards, and requiring a study of the possibility of developing joint processing centres and a pan-European support office to help to implement them.[21]

8.3 Measures of Convergence – Results of the Harmonisation

Having established a background framework for recent developments towards the CEAS, we can now turn to evaluating the mechanisms and

[15] Regulations are legislative acts as such directly binding on the Member States. Directives are not binding, but spell out the binding results or goals that Member States are obliged to reach by measures of their own choice.

[16] On the measures to be taken in each phase *see* Timothy J. Hatton, *European Asylum Policy*, IZA Discussion Paper No. 1721 *available at* http://ssrn.com/abstract=799705 (3.8.2007).

[17] Council regulation 343/2003/EC of 18 February 2003, OJ (L 50).

[18] Council directive 2004/83/EC of 29 April 2004, OJ (L 304) 12.

[19] Council directive 2003/9/EC of 27 January 2003, OJ (l 31) 18.

[20] *Supra* note 3.

[21] *New Structures, New Approaches: Improving the Quality of Decision Making in the Common European Asylum System* Communication from the Commission to the Council and the Parliament on Strengthened Practical Cooperation, COM (2006) 67 final.

legislative approaches used so far, and their (limited) effectiveness in achieving harmonisation.

8.3.1 Outsets

The movement within the European Union with respect to asylum as with law in general has been to develop shared rules and procedures. The aim has been to increase convergence and integration between the legal systems, including the development of common goals and aims and broader, stronger legal norms.

The move towards shared rules can take many different forms, for different reasons and with various aims.[22] The main dichotomy in models of Europeanisation distinguishes between integration through harmonisation and integration through other, looser and softer mechanisms.[23] Of course, there are many variations in both approaches, (which are themselves inseparable).

8.3.2 Harmonisation

Thomas Wilhelmsson distinguishes between three different forms of harmonisation: legal technical, regulatory and ideological.[24] Legal-technical harmonisation includes technical and rather pragmatic rules, often non-binding, for pressing legislative needs. Even when these are technical in their appearance, they may include weighty implicit ideological and political implications. The regulatory approach harmonises corresponding norms in national legislation whose primary aim is some public good beyond unification. Finally, there is the possibility of ideological harmonisation that establishes deeper shared values and presents a common culture to the broader world.

---

[22] For an overview of the measures for integration used in the union *see* Catherin Barnard, *The Substantiate Law of the EU the Four Freedoms*, Oxford University Press, 499–5277 (2007) and Giorgio Gja, Giorgio, Peter Hay, & Ronald Rotunda: Instruments for Legal Integration in the European Community – A Review in Cappelletti Mauro, Monica Seccombe & Joseph Weiler, Integration Through Law Firenze 1986.

[23] This dichotomy is a compromise between the third pillar approach, where the distinction is made between harmonisation and other more formal and rigid methods, and the immigration approach, where the distinction is made between harmonisation and other more politicized tools for harmonisation. *See* Annika Suominen, *Ömsesidigt erkännande av rättsliga beslut som hörnsten i det europeiska straffrättsliga samarbetet*, 142 Tidskrift Utgiven av Juridiska Föreningen i Finland, 607–616 (2006), where the author examines the approaches to harmonisation within the third pillar framework of criminal law.

[24] Thomas Wilhelmsson, *Social Contract Law and European Integration*, Aldershot: Dartmouth, 101–113 (1995).

The distinctions made by Wilhelmsson can also be applied to the analysis of europeanisation in the field of asylum law. The agenda so far has encompassed both ideological and regulatory harmonisation: The union has traditionally through both strategy- and policy papers and through more-or-less spontaneous public debates attempted to create and develop, or merely to identify, the underlying purposes of union action in the fields of asylum and immigration.[25] The union has also been persistent in developing its regulatory regime. Binding legislation has been passed and implemented to cover the legislative needs of the Member States in relation to most issues in the field of asylum and immigration law.

Secondly, the europeanisation of the asylum field can be analysed with the aid of the public law-based formal categorisation of measures of convergence, as presented by Maria Fletcher among others.[26] This approach can be divided into harmonisation through traditional community instruments, harmonisation through measures aiming at flexibility and an open method of coordination. Clearly, this division aims at least partly at exploring the same differences and methods as the model presented by Wilhelmsson, but from a different and perhaps more formal point of view.

Harmonisation through traditional community instruments includes harmonisation pursued both through traditional binding and through non-binding acts of the union. The method of flexibility implies the existence of rules allowing for opt-ins and opt-outs, and other forms of measures of flexibility, which diminish the risk of polarisation in the legislative work or in order to try out different settings and solutions to an issue within the union.[27] Finally, there is the open method of coordination, which sets out to "develop a common approach and objectives, identify best standards and encourage convergence of practice and procedure"[28] through peer-reviews, and other loose structures of cooperation and which is best identified not as a tool of governance and harmonisation but rather as a process of governance.[29]

---

[25] *See* Commission publications COM(2000)755 "Towards a common asylum procedure and a uniform status, valid throughout the Union, for persons granted asylum"; COM(2004)4002 "Area of Freedom, Security and Justice: Assessment of the Tampere programme and future orientations" and MEMO/06/254 "Implementing The Hague Programme: the way forward", where also the fundamental framework for and the goals and aims for the immigration agenda are discussed.

[26] *See* Maria Fletcher, *EU Governance Techniques in the Creation of a Common European Policy on Immigration and Asylum*, 9 Eur. Pub. L. 533–562 (2003).

[27] Ibid., 549–550, recognizes that the outcome of harmonisation through flexibility may be legislative procedures that are more effective, but end results that give unnecessary emphasis to diversity and legal fragmentation.

[28] Ibid., 551.

[29] Damian Chalmers & Martin Lodge, *The Open Method of Co-ordination and the European Welfare State*, Discussion Paper 11, ERSC Centre for Analysis of Risk and Regulation 2003 and Jörg Monar, *Enlarging the Area of Freedom, Security and Justice:*

In the field of asylum traditional legislative acts supply the basis for most efforts at European harmonisation. However, these traditional measures often also include measures aiming at flexibility. The practical implications of the flexibility mechanism in the field are evident in at least two respects: First, there are a number of opt-outs to binding legislation, most famously the possibility for England and Ireland to opt in or opt out of measures taken within the framework of the Schengen agreement.[30] The flexibility mechanism can also be seen in the use of articles 67 and 68, which were used to preserve limited access to the field of asylum for the European Court of Justice (ECJ) and unanimous voting in the council for some years after the treaty was signed.[31]

The open method of coordination can be seen as a supportive measure of convergence and has so far primarily been examined in connection with measures such as peer review and the sharing of best practises in the fields of social policy and employment.[32] However, nothing excludes the concept's applicability to the field of asylum and immigration. Starting with the Tampere conclusions, measures that belong to this category can be identified in statements made about the goals for the europeanisation of asylum law, the discussions held on the subject between Member States and the EU institutions, and in public evaluations of the Europeanized asylum sphere. The latest developments, is a Green Paper published by the Commission, which contemplates possibilities for the future and invites a discussion about the road ahead. The Green Paper can be understood as an example of direct use of the open method of coordination.[33]

8.3.3 The Results of Harmonisation

8.3.3.1 European Asylum Procedures are not Convergent

The methods of Europeanisation mentioned above have, as we have seen, been applied in the asylum context with the aim of creating a common procedure and a uniform status. However, the results of the harmonisation

---

Problems of Diversity and EU Instruments and Strategies in Cambridge Yearbook of European Legal Studies, 322–328 (2001).

[30] On the opt ins and opt outs in the asylum agenda *Battjes*, 183 (2006).

[31] On the restrictions to the harmonisation in terms of voting and the judicial system *see* Steve Peers, *The Future of the EU Judicial System and EC Immigration and Asylum Law*, 7 Eur. J. Migration L. 263–274 (2005) and Steve Peers & Elspeth Guild, *Deference or Defiance? The Court of Justice's Jurisdiction over Immigration and Asylum* in Guild Elspeth et al., 267–290 (2001). Regarding the impacts of the Constitutional Treaty on the role of the ECJ in immigration matters and the future of the unanimous voting scheme *see* the Draft Council Decision, Council Doc 1759/1/07 rev 1.

[32] *See*, e.g., Chalmers (et al.), *supra* note 29 (2003).

[33] *Supra* note 8.

have been meagre and to a large extent unsatisfactory both for the union and for the stakeholders with an interest in European asylum procedures.

The European Council on Refugees and Exiles (ECRE) stated in 2006 that in Europe "the right to seek and enjoy asylum remains a lottery, with [...] dramatic differences in the quality of asylum decisions", and called for strengthened procedural harmonisation in order to increase quality in first instance decision-making organs throughout the region.[34] The organisation also accused Member States of knowingly sabotaging the underlying mechanisms of harmonisation and refusing to cooperate in work towards the CEAS.[35] It has been suggested that in order to achieve the desired goals, the concept of territoriality as understood in EU law must change, opening broader possibilities in the legislative arena.[36]

A study of the recognition rates for 2006 in Europe reveals wide disparities at that time:[37] Whereas Belgium granted asylum in 18.5% of its decisions on asylum applications in the first instance, the rate in the Netherlands was 3.0%. The recognition rate in Austria was 37.5%, in Finland 1.8% and in Portugal 22.8%.[38]

Further, the UNHCR published a report in November 2007 on the effects of one of the most central pieces of harmonising legislation – the qualification directive.[39] The report concludes that even after the implementation of the directive substantial differences exist between the member states included in the study. These were due in part to different approaches to the implementation of the union legislation, and in part due to significantly differing interpretation of the relevant rules and norms.[40]

The union itself has recognised that the current level of harmonisation is not sufficient for a common asylum system to function properly. In the

---

[34] ECRE: *Memorandum to the JHA Council Practical Cooperation – Improving Asylum Systems* AD4/2006/EXT/CN.

[35] ECRE: *Memorandum to the Informal Justice and Home Affairs Council, Tampere, 20–22 Sep. 2006* AD/2006/EXT/RW/PC/CN. *See also* the earlier report by the same organization: *Towards Fair and Efficient Asylum Systems in Europe*, 2005.

[36] Elspeth Guild, *The Europeanisation of Europe's Asylum Policy*, 18 Intl. J. Refugee L. 649 (2006).

[37] The recognition rate is an indicator of how many percent of the asylum seekers in one country are recognised as refugees. It is obvious that not all directives were implemented by the Member States in 2006 and that some of the harmonising measures, thus, are missing from this picture. On the other hand, all relevant directives had entered into force and were thus available at this time, even if they had not been implemented or gained direct effect.

[38] For statistics on the asylum trends in Europe *see* UNHCR: *2007 Global Refugee Trends available at* http://www.unhcr.org/statistics/STATISTICS/4852366f2.pdf (17.9.2008).

[39] *Supra* note 18.

[40] UNHCR: Asylum in the European Union A Study of the Implementation of the Qualification Directive, (Nov. 2007).

Green Paper presented in June 2007 the Commission stressed the need for further harmonisation in order to reach the goals pursued.[41]

8.3.3.2 Challenges for the Harmoniation

It would seem that thus far the challenges posed by harmonisation have been too great for existing legislation to overcome. Measures taken by the union in creating the CEAP have not sufficiently taken the impact of concepts such as sovereignty, territoriality and regional exclusivity into account.[42]

For example, it has been established that refugee status determination and the granting of asylum have an important relationship to state sovereignty. This connection arises from the impact of the decisions made in the procedure – the inclusion of a new member in the society – and from the nature of the institution of asylum as a means of correcting a state's failure to protect its citizens.[43] Refugee status determination is almost as important as criminal law in its implications for state sovereignty in Europe.

The close links between asylum and state sovereignty have also been evident in the legislative process of europeanisation, in which Member States have protected their sovereign powers both on formal and substantive grounds against the growing power of the European Union.

The temporary requirement for unanimous voting in matters relating to asylum and the currently weak position of the European Court of Justice (ECJ), can be seen as manifestations of this reluctance.[44] The troublesome legislative procedures have resulted in lengthy and difficult negotiations on common legislation, the extensive use of measures of flexibility and vast differences in the interpretation and implementation of adopted measures.[45] The extensive use of optional derogations and other measures of flexibility in the harmonising legislation in fact effectively erodes the harmonisation and, thus, may endanger the whole procedure towards the CEAS.[46] It has

---

[41] *Supra* note 8, at 2–4.

[42] *See* Nicholson and Ryszard Cholewinski, *Control of Irregular Migration and EU Law and Policy: A Human Rights Deficit* in Peers et al. (eds.), 899–941 (2006). *See also* Battjes, 211–213 (2006).

[43] For an enlightening historical view on the bond between sovereignty and asylum *see* Beck Robert J.: Britain and the 1933 Refugee Convention: National or State Sovereignty? in 11 Intl. J. Refugee L. 597–624, (1999). *See also* Christian Joppke, *Asylum and State Sovereignty a Comparison of the United States, Germany, and Britain* in 30 Comp. Pol. Studies. 259–298 (1997).

[44] *Supra* note 31.

[45] As an example on the impact of concerns relating to sovereignty on the negotiations on the directives *see* Doede Ackers, *The Negotiations on the Asylum Procedures Directive* in 7 Eur. J. Migration L. 1–33 (2005).

[46] Jens Vedsted-Hansen, *Common EU Standards on Asylum – Optional Harmonisation and Exclusive Procedures?* In 7 Eur. J. Migration L. 372–373 (2005).

become increasingly clear that the quality of the Europeanised legislation has suffered from an ignorance of the bond between asylum, sovereignty and the actions of Member States within the EU.

Furthermore, the differences in implementation of community legislation in the field of asylum law demonstrate the extent to which this is an area with particularly strong implications for national traditions, politics and culture.[47] Combined with the extensive use of mechanisms of flexibility, the heterogeneous implementation of common legislation is yet another difficulty to overcome in establishing the CEAS.

One must remember that the European asylum procedures all are procedures of administrative justice – judicial procedures with a very strong inclination towards national and traditional procedural solutions.[48] Uniform criteria relating to the institutions and procedures surrounding refugee status determination can do little to erode the differences in administrative organisation, culture and tradition that are so evident in the European context.

8.3.3.3 Impact of the Reform Treaty on the Harmonisation in the Field of Asylum and Immigration

The Constitutional Treaty will have important implications for the future of the European asylum system.[49] When (or if) it enters into force, the Constitutional Treaty will give the ECJ competence in matters of immigration and asylum law and will facilitate the transfer from unanimous voting to qualified majority voting in the European Council on matters relating to migration and asylum. Clearly, this will have an impact on efforts towards harmonisation: The expanded ECJ competence may provide much-needed guidance in the interpretation of directives and regulations, and the transfer

---

[47] *Supra* note 40.

[48] A good example of the divergences arising from the administrative environment is the dichotomy between adversarial and inquisitorial procedures – both being used in the asylum procedures of Europe. *See* Giacinto della Cananea, *Beyond the State: the Europeanization and Globalization of Procedural Administrative Law* in 9 Eur. P. L. 563–577 (2003); Jürgen Schwartz, The Convergence of the Administrative Laws of the EU Member States in Snyder, Frances (ed.): *The Europeanisation of Law: The Legal Effects of European Integration*, Oxford 2000 and René Seerden & Frits Stroink, *Administrative Law of the European Union, its Member States and the United States – A Comparative Analysis* Intersentia 2002.

[49] The Constitutional Treaty /Reform Treaty holds within a revised version of the failed constitution for Europe. *See* the Treaty Establishing a Constitution for Europe (2004), OJ 2004 C 310 and the Draft Treaty amending the Treaty on European Union and the Treaty establishing the European Community (2007) CIG 1/07. For an analysis of the impact of the Draft Reform Treaty on issues relating to asylum and immigration, amongst others, *see* Steve Peers, *EU Reform Treaty Analysis 1: JHA provisions*, Statewatch 2007, *available at* http://www.statewatch.org/news/2007/aug/eu-reform-treaty-jha-analysis-1.pdf (24.8.2007).

to qualified majority voting will most certainly reduce the number and impact of compromises in the legislative work.

However, the timetable for the Constitutional Treaty is still unsure, and with a goal of having the CEAS up and running in just a few years, the schedule may well prove to be too vague.[50] The extended ECJ competence still does not reach beyond the scope of the legislation and, thus, leaves unaddressed many of the key issues that directives and regulations do not reach. Abandoning the requirement for unanimous decision making could do little to amend the legislation already agreed upon, which is meant to constitute the basis for the CEAS, nor can the new rules guarantee a harmonised implementation. Hence, it must be concluded that the Constitutional Treaty will not completely solve the difficulties faced by the CEAS.

8.4 Mutual Recognition and Asylum

8.4.1 Mutual Recognition as a Measure of Convergence in the Field of Asylum and Immigration

As we have seen, binding legislation is not the only vehicle through which the European Union has been advancing the process of internationalisation. Another important process is the mechanism of mutual recognition, defined as the free movement of decisions.[51]

Traditionally, the understanding has been that mutual recognition and harmonisation are to be kept far apart and is that they are alternative approaches.[52] Mutual recognition has long been seen as the alternative to harmonisation in fields where harmonisation falls short due to sovereignty or the presence of diverging practises. But there are also important interrelationships between harmonisation and mutual recognition.

---

[50] The EU summit in June 2007 decided that the amendments to the Constitutional Treaty should be agreed by the end of 2007 and that the Reform Treaty should be ratified by June 2009 at the latest. *See* Brussels European Council 21–22.6.2007 Presidentiary Conclusions 11177/1/07 Rev 1, section 11.

[51] Borrowed from professor Dan Frände who used this definition in his speech "Vastavuoroisen tunnustamisen kehittäminen ja edistäminen harmonisoinnin sijasta" at the seminar Rikosoikeudellinen yhteistyö EU:n kolmannen pilarin puitteissa, Helsinki 11.1.2007.

[52] On the development of the understanding of the relationship between mutual recognition and harmonisation *see* Petter Asp, *Ömsesidigt erkännande av europeiska domar och beslut i straffprocessen – erfarenheter och – tillämpningsfrågor* in Forhandlingerne ved Det 37. nordiske Juristmøde i Reykjavík 18–20. (August 2005). Bind I, 68–69.

Mutual recognition implies an obligation for Member States to accept, recognise and implement decisions made in other countries.[53] Referring to the use of the mechanism within the framework of Justice and Home Affairs in the European Union, the motivation is often to avoid the (costly) movement of persons by encouraging the movement of decisions.[54] One of the most discussed situations in which the technique of mutual recognition has been implemented recently is the European Arrest Warrant and the mutual recognition of criminal law decisions that it requires.[55]

Some forms of mutual recognition have also played a part in the europeanisation of immigration and asylum law, although mutual recognition has not usually been thought of as an independent means of integration in this context. Measures of mutual recognition can easily be found in measures taken to develop the CEAS.

A fairly good illustration of the use of mutual recognition in the asylum field is found in the Dublin regulation and the mechanisms for "burden-sharing" implemented by the union within this framework (and before that, in the Schengen framework).[56] The mechanism as invoked by the Dublin regulation states that if a decision-making process has begun in one Member State, the other Member States are *per se* obliged not to interfere with this process. Thus, if an application for asylum is under consideration in an asylum procedure in one Member State, this procedure is considered to be exclusive. Naturally, there are also derogations to this general rule.[57]

The mechanism of mutual recognition as applied in the field of asylum also implies a practice of non-interference with decisions already made on applications for asylum within the EU. According to the directive on asylum procedures member states may dismiss applications if a decision on the same application already has been made within the union.[58] In such circumstances the application is not examined at all. If the Member States considers that circumstances have changed enough to make the matter a new one, then a new application may be made.

It is clear that the form of mutual recognition as implemented by these asylum rules is a soft version of the mechanism, perhaps best understood

---

[53] In opposite of the free movement of persons, goods, services or money, the free movement of decision is not, however, a starting point but a product of the integration. On the backgrounds to mutual recognition as an instrument *see Barnard*, 507–508 (2004).

[54] In the asylum procedure, mutual recognition has been implemented in order to address secondary movements of persons by enforcing the first movement by force.

[55] Council Framework Decision on the European arrest warrant and the surrender procedures between Member States 2002/584/JHA, 13.6.2002.

[56] *Supra* note 17 and Convention determining the State responsible for examining applications for asylum lodged in one of the Member States of the European Communities OC C 254, 19.8.1997.

[57] *Supra* note 17, article 3.

[58] *Supra* note 3, articles 25 (f) and 32.

as an idea rather than as a mechanism. The legislative features described above can be identified and analysed also through concepts other than mutual recognition. Even so it is clear that mutual recognition has a foothold in Europe's existing harmonised asylum procedures.

As with other forms of harmonisation measures in the field of asylum and immigration, the mechanism of mutual recognition has met with some opposition. Discussions of the mutual recognition of procedures to decide on applications for asylum often reveal lack of trust between states and their unwillingness to respect the sufficiency of other states' asylum procedures. Some are also made uncomfortable by the fact that the mutual recognition of asylum procedures has led in practice to an increase in movement of persons.[59]

Notwithstanding the difficulties inevitably involved in implementing mutual recognition and the rather special nature of the concept as invoked in the field of asylum and immigration, the process of mutual recognition has been working comparatively well. This may perhaps be explained by the fact that mutual recognition enables states to make decisions *in casu* on the transfer of powers with respect to individual asylum seekers. This allows for the possibility of exceptions to the rules of transfer and broader margins of appreciation for the Member States, and thus creates a sphere in which states can continue to exercise their sovereign powers. The transfer of powers under a mutual recognition regime remains fairly flexible. There is also symbolic value in allowing most decisions about mutual recognition to be made on the national level.

8.4.2 The Relationship Between Harmonisation and Mutual Recognition

Using mutual recognition as a measure of harmonisation raises the question of the relationship between the two concepts. This arises both in connection with the general movement towards harmonisation, and from the particular point of view of mutual recognition, when it is used as a tool for reaching these goals.

A certain amount of harmonisation seems to be necessary for mutual recognition to be possible at all. It would not be reasonable to expect

[59] *See* for instance the Finnish draft proposal to the Council "Migration management; extended European solidarity in immigration, border controls and asylum policies" *available at* http://www.eu2006.fi/news_and_documents/other_documents/vko36/en_GB/1157615544264/(3.8.2007). *See also* ECRE: *Report on the Application of the Dublin II Regulation in Europe*, ECRE 2006, *available at* http://www.ecre.org/files/ECRE%20Dublin%20Report%2007.03.06%20-%20final.pdf (3.8.2007), and Nicholas Blake, *The Dublin Convention and Rights of Asylum Seekers in the European Union* in Guild et al., 95–120 (2001).

Member States to recognise each other's decisions in any field if the decisions were not themselves built on a common understanding of the general framework.[60] Respect and trust for the other procedures within the system of mutual recognition are vital to the function of the overall mechanism.[61] Mutual recognition in its most basic form also implies that the procedures of decision-making in the Member States in the relevant field of law are at least comparable with one another.

Steve Peers has made the interesting observation that the necessary degree of harmonisation in Europe cannot be reached entirely through Union measures.[62] The level of harmonisation must also be result of coherent traditions and practises that exist without the support of the European Union. When such traditions and practices do not exist they will need to be developed before mutual recognition can function properly.

In the field of asylum and immigration and in the form evident in the Dublin regulation, the mechanism of mutual recognition faces challenges that arise from the lack of a sufficiently harmonised base. The ongoing debates relating to the Dublin regulation are all connected with lack of trust and the correspondingly broad use of exceptions from the ground rule on mutual recognition.[63] The old traditions in refugee status determination arising from international law offer a possible basis for greater harmonisation that might support the mutual recognition regime in the sense suggested by Steve Peers, but this has not, as yet, taken place. Directed European Union measures have also failed sufficiently to provide the necessary support for mutual recognition between the Member States.

Full-scale harmonisation will neither be possible without some form of mutual recognition. Harmonisation should be viewed as an end in itself, as well as a means towards other goals. This would seem to entail mutual recognition in the relevant fields of law. Of course, mutual recognition is not the only available mechanism for achieving harmonisation, but other harmonisation measures often themselves require mutual recognition to be in place before they will be effective.

---

[60] *See* Steve Peers, *Mutual Recognition and Criminal Law in the European Union: Has the Council Got it Wrong?* 41 Common Market L. Rev. 5–36 (2004).

[61] Valsamis Mitsilegas, *The Constitutional Implications of Mutual Recognition in Criminal Matters* in the EU 43 Common Market L. Rev. 1277–1311 (2006), the author asks whether the trust needed in order for mutual recognition to work actually can be rendered between the Member States due to the constitutional implications of mutual recognition both in criminal matters and on a more general level.

[62] Peers, *supra* note 60, at 20.

[63] *Supras* note 30–31.

8.4.3 The Possibilities for Mutual Recognition

As we have seen, measures taken so far to advance the harmonsation of European asylum law have not yet had the intended effect. Despite the legislation passed at the union level regarding most aspects of the asylum procedures, the outcome has been disappointing and the standards reached still provide an inadequate basis for a common asylum procedure. The existing level of harmonisation does not even reach the level necessary for mutual recognition to function properly.[64]

The European Union's lack of success in implementing the harmonisation of asylum procedures raises the question whether other measures might be more effective than those that are currently in place. Specifically, might not mutual recognition offer a better mechanism for convergence in the field of asylum than some of the more "traditional" measures of harmonisation that have been favoured by the European Union?

Mutual recognition has never been explicitly acknowledged as an independent means of harmonisation in the asylum debate, but this has not prevented its successful use, avoiding many of the shortcomings connected with the "general harmonisation" in the field.[65] Perhaps the technique would be even more effective if it received greater conscious attention and support.

As we have seen, mutual recognition first requires a state to recognise decisions taken elsewhere in the union to accept and process an application for asylum.[66] Decisions made on applications for asylum are objects of

---

[64] As we have seen, the Dublin scheme is one of the most prominent examples of the implementation of mutual recognition in the European asylum policy. As both the report from ECRE, the European Council of Refugees and Exiles, and official documents of evaluation from the Commission clearly show, the Dublin system has, nevertheless, failed to produce the effect of mutual recognition that was anticipated. Only a fraction of the cases that are intended to be transferred through the scheme are actually subjected to mutual recognition. All evaluations also conclude that the greatest issue is the lack of trust, not only between the Member States but also between the legislator and the Member States. Ibid and ECRE: *Report on the Application of the Dublin II Regulation in Europe available at* http://www.ecre.org/files/ECRE%20Dublin%20Report%2007.03.06%20-%20final.pdf (3.8.2007) and Commission Staff Working Paper: *Revisiting the Dublin Convention* SEC (2005)522 *available at* http://www.arena.uio.no/sources/jpa/dublin/com/paper/2000/SEC522.pdf (3.8.2007).

[65] The problems persisting in relation towards mutual recognition seem often to be connected to the lack of a harmonized base as opposite of to the measure of mutual recognition itself.

[66] The Dublin Regulation, *supra* note 17, article 4(1) states that the "process of determining the Member State responsible under this Regulation shall start as soon as an application for asylum is lodged", which implies that the lodging of an application is enough to trigger the mechanisms of mutual recognition. The application will, namely, not be processed until it is clear in which state the procedure shall take place, according to the mutual recognition procedure. *See* for instance the Aliens Act of Finland

mutual recognition, precluding multiple proceedings in different Member States. This requires some administrative cooperation, including the mutual recognition of various procedural decisions.[67] The directive on mutual recognition of decisions on expulsion enforces mutual recognition of negative decisions, which include decisions on expulsion, which can be quite contentious.[68]

Mutual recognition offers far-reaching means for cooperation and must be seen as an important part of the CEAS. However, the lack of an adequately harmonised base effects also this sector, encouraging exceptions to the rule of mutual recognition many and making practical implementation difficult. This is evident both when looking at how Member States use the discretion awarded by relevant directives, and when looking at how the parts of the harmonised asylum procedure requiring mutual recognition have been implemented.[69]

The CEAS envisages a common procedure and shared decision-making. This quite clearly reaches beyond mutual recognition by obliging Member States to entrust decision-making, to foreign officials. The CEAP would require greater cooperation on the practical side of the decision-making than can be achieved if mutual recognition were restricted to procedural questions.[70] The implementation of a common procedure would be a harmonising measure in itself, strengthening ideological harmonisation and developing the European identity simply by being in existence.

The value added by full-scale harmonisation, going beyond mutual recognition, would be primarily on this ideological level. There is also a hope the CEAS would facilitate the management of asylum-seekers, and simplify the overall procedural complexity of the process.

8.5 The Choice for Mutual Recognition

Those who wish to strengthen the Europeanisation of the asylum process have two primary options. The Union must either accept the need to adopt

(301/2004), which in section 103(2) states that an application for asylum will be left without investigation when another Member State is responsible for the processing of the application.

67 *Supra* note 17, article 21.

68 Directive on Mutual Recognition of Decisions on Expulsion of Third Country Nationals 2001/40/EC of 28 May 2001, OJ (L 149).

69 *Supra* note 04.

70 *See* the Commission Green Paper on the Future of the European Migration Network COM(2005)606, 7–9. *See also* the Communication from the Commission to the Council and the European Parliament on strengthened practical cooperation – New structures, new approaches: improving the quality of decision making in the common European asylum system COM(2006)67.

new means of europeanisation, or reformulate its aims to accept more limited objectives.

As we have seen, the problem is that legal technical and regulatory harmonisation without deeper forms of cooperation have lead to a harmonisation without a base. The asylum regime presents such a difficult and contentious set of problems, that the means of harmonisation must be carefully chosen. If indeed the European Union does opt to strengthen its harmonisation in the field of asylum, there may be a need for new and more subtle techniques.

One such technique would be greater mutual recognition of decision made in other Member States. Mutual recognition suits the special requirements of the subject area, while also strengthening and deepening cooperation between states. The growing popularity of mutual recognition could make it a vital tool for harmonisation leading up gradually to the development of more comprehensive common procedures throughout the Union.

Placing mutual recognition in the forefront of harmonisation of the asylum field in this way would clearly require that the method be given the opportunity to works toward a common understanding of the CEAP. Even so, mutual recognition alone will not be enough on its own to achieve the goal of establishing a common procedure across Europe.

If, however, the European Union chooses instead to amend its goals for the harmonisation of the asylum and immigration sector in Europe and decides that the added value of a common procedure does not make up for the costs of reaching the required level of harmonisation, then mutual recognition offers a working and already well-established alternative to full-scale harmonisation. It is clearly possible to identify a valuable goal in mutual recognition itself. In either case, mutual recognition cannot provide the basis for a successfully harmonised procedure without a certain amount of initial harmonisation to support mutual recognition itself.

Chapter 9
Copyright Protection for Works of Foreign Origin

Tyler T. Ochoa

9.1 Introduction

Copyright law is premised on the principle of territoriality, under which a nation's intellectual property laws apply only to conduct occurring within its own borders.[1] With globalization, of course, it has long been necessary for nations to make arrangements with each other to accommodate the flow of information and copyrighted works across international borders. The gradual evolution of United States law to provide copyright protection for works of foreign origin illustrates some of the challenges still presented by the continuing globalization of copyright law.

For the first hundred years of its existence, the United States did not provide any copyright protection to works of foreign origin.[2] When it finally agreed to extend such protection on a reciprocal basis, questions arose regarding how existing requirements, such as the requirement of copyright notice, applied to works first published abroad.[3] An ambiguity in the 1909 Copyright Act exacerbated the difficulty, resulting in uncertainty that persists today regarding works first published abroad prior to 1978.[4]

T.T. Ochoa (✉)
High Technology Law Institute, Santa Clara University School of Law, Santa Clara, CA, USA
e-mail: ttochoa@scu.edu

[1] *See* 2 Sam Ricketson and Jane C. Ginsburg, International Copyright and Neighboring Rights: The Berne Convention and Beyond §20.15 at 1301 (2d ed. 2005) (It is "a widely held concept of international copyright law . . . that there is not international copyright law as such, but rather a collection of national copyright laws."); Paul Goldstein, International Copyright Law §3.1.2. at 65 (2001) ("Territoriality, the principle that a country's prescriptive competence ends at its borders, is the dominating norm in international copyright cases.").

[2] *See* notes 6–33 and accompanying text.

[3] *See* notes 34–49 and accompanying text.

[4] *See* notes 50–102 and accompanying text.

J. Klabbers, M. Sellers (eds.), *The Internationalization of Law and Legal Education*, Ius Gentium: Comparative Perspectives on Law and Justice 2,
DOI 10.1007/978-1-4020-9494-1_9,

As illustrated by a recent case, this uncertainty can result in copyright terms that differ by as much as one hundred years depending on how the ambiguity is resolved.[5]

9.2 1790–1908

When the U.S. enacted its first Copyright Act in 1790, it specifically provided that copyrights would only be granted to "citizens or residents" of the United States:

> [T]he author or authors of any map, chart, book or books..., being a citizen or citizens of these United States, or resident therein,...shall have the sole right and liberty of printing, reprinting, publishing and vending such map, chart, book or books...[6]

At the time, of course, every nation that had a copyright statute offered protection only to its own citizens or residents.[7] There was no point in granting an exclusive right to citizens or residents of other nations; doing so would harm the balance of trade by increasing the royalty payments that would flow to foreign authors and publishers.[8] It was therefore very much in the national interest to restrict copyright to a nation's own citizens and residents. But just to make sure that the effect of that restriction was absolutely clear, the Copyright Act of 1790 added the following proviso:

> [N]othing in this act shall be construed...to prohibit the importation or vending, reprinting, or publishing within the United States, of any map, chart, book or books, written, printed, or published by any person not a citizen of the United States, in foreign parts or places without the jurisdiction of the United States.[9]

As the U.S. was primarily an English-speaking country, the principal effect of this restriction was that books by British authors could be freely copied and disseminated in the U.S., which provided U.S. citizens and residents with a large quantity of reading material at cheap prices.[10] The restriction of copyright protection to U.S. citizens and residents was carried forward in the Copyright Act of 1831.[11]

---

[5] *See* notes 103–124 and accompanying text.

[6] Copyright Act of 1790, c. 15, §1, 1 Stat. 124.

[7] *See* 1 Ricketson & Ginsburg, *supra* note 1, §1.20 at 19 ("unauthorized reproduction and use of foreign works...[continued] for a considerable period after the adoption of national copyright laws by most countries....[W]hile protecting the works of their national authors, [most countries] did not regard the unauthorized exploitation of foreign works as either unfair or immoral.").

[8] *Cf.* 1 Ricketson & Ginsburg, *supra* note 1, §1.22 at 21.

[9] Copyright Act of 1790, c. 15, §5, 1 Stat. 125.

[10] *See* William Briggs, The Law of International Copyright 46–47 (1906).

[11] Copyright Act of 1831, c. 16, §1, 4 Stat. 436 ("[A]ny person or persons, being a citizen or citizens of these United States, or resident therein, who shall be the author or authors

Beginning in the 1820s, however, European nations began to enter into bilateral treaties on the basis of mutual reciprocity.[12] This arrangement would benefit both nations if the balance of trade in copyrighted works between them was relatively equal. Later, in 1852, France decided to unilaterally offer copyright protection in France to all authors, regardless of nationality or domicile, in the hope that it would encourage other countries to grant similar protection to French authors.[13] This move eventually led to the adoption in 1886 of the Berne Convention for the Protection of Literary and Artistic Works,[14] under which member nations agreed to provide copyright protection to the citizens and residents of other member nations on the basis of "national treatment," meaning that each nation would provide copyright protection to the citizens of other Berne nations on terms that were no less favorable than those it provided to its own citizens.[15]

The United States sent an observer to the diplomatic conference that adopted the Berne Convention,[16] but it chose not to become a member of the Berne Union for more than a hundred years.[17] There were a number of reasons for this extraordinary delay. First, in the beginning it was simply not in the national interest to offer copyright protection to foreign citizens. At the time, the U.S. produced very few

---

of any book, books, map, chart, or musical composition,. . .or who shall invent, design, etch, engrave, [or] work. . .any print or engraving, shall have the sole right and liberty of printing, reprinting, publishing, and vending such book or books, map, chart, musical composition, print, cut, or engraving. . . ."); Id., §8, 4 Stat. 438 ("[N]othing in this act shall be construed. . .to prohibit the importation or vending, printing, or publishing, of any map, chart, book, musical composition, print or engraving, written, composed, or made, by any person not being a citizen of the United States, nor resident within the jurisdiction thereof.").

[12] *See* 1 Ricketson & Ginsburg, *supra* note 1, §§1.29–1.31 at 27–32, 40.

[13] *See* Decree of March 28, 1852 (Fr.); 1 Ricketson & Ginsburg, *supra* note 1, §1.24 at 22; Goldstein, *supra* note 1, §2.1.1. at 17.

[14] *See* 1 Ricketson & Ginsburg, *supra* note 1, §§2.05–2.52 at 44–83.

[15] *See* Berne Convention for the Protection of Literary and Artistic Works, Sept. 9, 1886, art. 2 ("Authors who are subjects or citizens of any of the countries of the Union. . .shall enjoy in the other countries for their works. . .the rights which the respective laws do now or may hereafter grant to natives."). The most recent revision of the Berne Convention provides for national treatment in Art. 5. *See* Berne Convention for the Protection of Literary and Artistic Works, Paris Text, July 24, 1971, art. 5 ("Authors shall enjoy, in respect of works for which they are protected under this Convention, in countries of the Union other than the country of origin, the rights which their respective laws do now or may hereafter grant to their nationals.").

[16] *See* 1 Ricketson & Ginsburg, *supra* note 1, §2.39 at 74–75, §2.51 at 82.

[17] *See* Goldstein, *supra* note 1, §2.1.2.1 at 23 ("The United States was the single, commercially most important country to remain outside the Berne Union for its entire first century."). The United States eventually adhered to the Berne Convention effective March 1, 1989. *See* World Intellectual Property Organization, Contracting Parties, Berne Convention, *available at* http://www.wipo.int/treaties/en/ShowResults.jsp?lang=en&treaty_id=15 (last visited Sept. 18, 2007).

copyrighted works that would be of interest to readers in other nations, so the economic benefit it would have received from a reciprocal arrangement was very small;[18] and the cost to the balance of payments, in terms of the royalties that would have flowed overseas, would have been very high.[19] It therefore very much remained in the national interest that U.S. citizens would continue to have a supply of reading material at cheap prices, regardless of the diplomatic cost of foreign authors complaining about U.S. "piracy."[20] Thus, for most of the 19th Century, the U.S. chose to remain what China is today: the biggest "pirate" of copyrighted works in the world.

Second, even when trade in copyrighted works began to even out, U.S. law had a number of features which were incompatible with membership in the Berne Convention. For example, because U.S. law was based primarily on a utilitarian theory of copyright, under which copyright is offered as a financial incentive to encourage authors and publishers to create and disseminate new works of authorship,[21] it made little sense to offer copyright protection to an author (or publisher) unless that author affirmatively claimed that he or she wanted the benefit of copyright protection; otherwise, the government was simply giving away a right to royalties without receiving anything in return. Thus, U.S. law had always required formalities, such as registration and notice, as a condition of copyright protection.[22] But because European countries were influenced more by author's rights theories of copyright, under which an author has a natural right to the economic fruits of his or her creative labor, the 1908 revision of the Berne

---

[18] *See* United Dictionary Co. v. G. & C. Merriam Co., 208 U.S. 260, 264 (1908) ("in 1802, there was little ground to anticipate the publication of American works abroad. As late as 1820 Sydney Smith, in the Edinburgh Review, made his famous exclamation, 'In the four quarters of the globe, who reads an American book?' ").

[19] *Cf.* Goldstein, *supra* note 1, §2.3 at 47 ("International copyright and international trade are inherently linked. Any time one country undertakes...to protect works originating in another country, it makes at least implicitly a calculation of the decision's implications for the balance of trade.").

[20] *Cf.* Briggs, *supra* note 10, at 47 (with regard to the United States, "little can be expected from the pressure of external interest, for America's capacity for self-support, due mainly to its geographic position, gives it the power in many matters to dictate its own terms.").

[21] Thus, the 1790 Copyright Act was titled "An act for the encouragement of learning, by securing the copies of maps, charts, and books, to the authors and proprietors of such copies, during the times therein mentioned." 1 Stat. 124. *See also* Harper & Row Publishers, Inc. v. Nation Enterprises, 471 U.S. 539, 558 (1985) ("By establishing a marketable right to the use of one's expression, copyright supplies the economic incentive to create and disseminate ideas.").

[22] *Cf.* Wheaton v. Peters, 33 U.S. 591, 663–64 (1834) ("when the legislature are about to vest an exclusive right in an author or inventor, they have the power to prescribe the conditions on which such right shall be enjoyed; and...no one can avail himself of such right who does not substantially comply with the requisitions of the law.").

Convention prohibited the imposition of any formalities as a condition of copyright protection.[23] For similar reasons, the delegates that adopted the Berne Convention recommended the adoption of a minimum duration of 30 years after the death of the author,[24] which was usually much longer than the then-maximum U.S. duration of 42 years after first publication.[25] In the 1908 revision of the Berne Convention, a minimum duration of 50 years after the death of the author was recommended,[26] and that minimum duration was made mandatory in 1948.[27] As a result, the U.S. could not join the Berne Convention until it was willing to make major changes in its fundamental approach to copyright protection.

Throughout the 19th Century, foreign authors (British authors in particular) regularly petitioned Congress to extend copyright protection to foreigners, but those pleas fell on deaf ears.[28] Thus, the Copyright Act of 1870 carried forward the limitation that only U.S. citizens or residents were eligible for copyright protection.[29] It was not until the United States could boast of some authors of international prominence that it finally became in the national interest to extend copyright protection to citizens of other nations on a reciprocal basis. Those U.S. authors who could reasonably expect to earn royalties from publication of their works overseas added their voices to the chorus of foreign authors clamoring for some kind of international copyright protection in the United States.[30] In addition, even

---

[23] *See* Berne Convention for the Protection of Literary and Artistic Works, Berlin Text, Nov. 13, 1908, art. 4 ("The enjoyment and the exercise of these rights shall not be subject to any formality."); Goldstein, *supra* note 1, §2.1.2.1 at 23 ("Political pressure to retain formalities . . ., which were prohibited since 1908 by the Berlin Text, was one reason the United States declined to join Berne.").

[24] *See* Ricketson & Ginsburg, *supra* note 1, §§9.14–9.15 at 536–38.

[25] Act of July 8, 1870, c. 230, §§87–88, 16 Stat. 212, codified at Rev. Stat. §§4952–54, 18(I) Stat. 957 (consisting of an initial term of 28 years, plus a renewal term of 14 years).

[26] *See* Berne Convention for the Protection of Literary and Artistic Works, Berlin Text, Nov. 15, 1908, art. 7.

[27] *See* Berne Convention for the Protection of Literary and Artistic Works, Brussels Text, June 26, 1948, art. 7(1).

[28] *See generally* James J. Barnes, Authors, Publishers and Politicians: The Quest for an Anglo-American Copyright Agreement, 1815–1854 (1974); Richard Rodgers Bowker, Copyright: Its History and Its Law 341–64 (1912); George Haven Putnam, *The Contest for International Copyright*, in George Haven Putnam, ed., The Question of Copyright 376–98 (1891).

[29] Act of July 8, 1870, c. 230, §86, 16 Stat. 212 ("any citizen of the United States, or resident therein"), codified at Rev. Stat. §4952, 18(I) Stat. 957; Act of July 8, 1870, c. 230, §103, 16 Stat. 213 ("nothing herein contained shall be construed to prohibit the printing, publishing, importation, or sale of any [work] . . . written, composed, or made by any person not a citizen of the United States nor resident therein."), codified at Rev. Stat. §4971, 18(I) Stat. 960.

[30] Among the prominent U.S. authors who lobbied Congress for an international copyright bill were James Fenimore Cooper, Ralph Waldo Emerson, Washington Irving, Henry Wadsworth Longfellow, Walt Whitman, John Greenleaf Whittier, and Mark Twain. *See*

U.S. authors whose works were only popular domestically were tired of competing for business with cheap imports from Great Britain.[31] Finally, in 1891, the U.S. adopted the Chace Act, which extended copyright protection to citizens and residents of foreign nations when those nations agreed to provide copyright protection to U.S. citizens and residents:

> Provided further, That this act shall only apply to a citizen or subject of a foreign state or nation when such foreign state or nation permits to [U.S.] citizens...the benefit of copyright [by national treatment], or when such foreign state or nation is a party to an international agreement which provides for reciprocity in the granting of copyright [to which the U.S. is also a party].[32]

As a direct result of the Chace Act, the U.S. quickly entered into reciprocal copyright agreements with its major European trading partners, including the United Kingdom, France, and Germany.[33]

But even though a major barrier had been breached, the U.S. still made it difficult for foreign authors to obtain copyright protection in the United States. First, in a blatant protectionist measure, the U.S. simultaneously adopted the so-called "manufacturing clause," which provided that in order to obtain copyright protection in the U.S., foreign works had to be printed from plates manufactured or type set in the United States.[34] This requirement was gradually relaxed over the years, but in some form it was retained as a part of U.S. copyright law until 1986.[35]

Second, the U.S. still required foreign authors to comply with the formalities imposed by U.S. law. One of these formalities was the condition that the work be registered in the United States before it was published anywhere in the world.[36] Thus, a foreign author who published a work in

---

Bowker, *supra* note 28, at 347, 355, 359; W.E. Simonds, *International Copyright (Report of the House Committee on Patents)*, in Putnam, *supra* note 28, at 145–47.

[31] *See* Briggs, *supra* note 10, at 98–99.

[32] Act of March 3, 1891, c. 565, §13, 26 Stat. 1110.

[33] *See* Goldstein, *supra* note 1, §2.1.1 at 18; 1891 Pres. Proc. No. 3, 27 Stat. 981–82 (Belgium, France, Great Britain, Switzerland); 1892 Pres. Proc. No. 24, 27 Stat. 1021–22 (Germany).

[34] *See* Act of March 3, 1891, c. 565, §3, 26 Stat. 1107, codified at Rev. Stat. §4956 ("Provided, That in the case of a book, photograph, chromo, or lithograph, the two [deposit] copies...shall be printed from type set within the limits of the United States, or from plates made therefrom, or from negatives, or drawings on stone made within the limits of the United States, or from transfers made therefrom. During the existence of such copyright the importation into the United States of any book, chromo, lithograph or photograph, so copyrighted, or any edition or editions thereof, or any plates of the same not made within the limits of the United States, shall be, and is hereby prohibited [with certain exceptions].").

[35] *See* Copyright Act of 1909, c. 320, §§15–16, 35 Stat. 1078–79 (renumbered §§16–17 in 1947, repealed 1978); 17 U.S.C. §601 (eff. Jan. 1, 1978; setting a sunset date of July 1, 1986).

[36] Act of March 3, 1891, c. 565, §3, 26 Stat. 1107, codified at Rev. Stat. §4956 ("No person shall be entitled to a copyright unless he shall, on or before the day of publication in

his or her domestic market before thinking about doing so in the United States irrevocably lost the opportunity to obtain copyright protection here. Another one of these formalities, dating back to 1802, was the requirement that copyright notice be inserted in all published copies of the work.[37] Thus, the 1870 Copyright Act required that:

> No person shall maintain an action for infringement of his copyright unless he shall give notice thereof by inserting in the several copies of every edition published. . .the following words, viz.: "Entered according to act of Congress, in the year -----, by A.B., in the office of the librarian of Congress, at Washington."[38]

In 1874, an amendment allowed the simplified short form of the notice that is familiar to us today: the word "Copyright," the date of first publication, and the name of the author or copyright claimant.[39] Failure to include the copyright notice on published copies meant than an author forfeited any U.S. copyright protection for his or her work.

The notice requirement was retained without discussion when copyright was extended to foreign authors in 1891. This immediately led to a question of interpretation: was copyright notice required only when the work was published in the United States? Or did an author also have to include a copyright notice when the work was published outside the United States, at the risk of losing his or her copyright protection?

When the question finally reached the U.S. Supreme Court in 1908, the Court, in *United Dictionary Co. v. G. & C. Merriam Co.*,[40] held that notice was only required on copies published in the United States: "We are satisfied that the statute does not require notice of the American copyright on books published abroad and sold only for use there."[41] Writing for the Court, Justice Holmes reasoned that "it is unlikely that [Congress] would make requirements of personal action beyond the sphere of its control. . .[or] that it would require a warning to the public against the infraction of a law beyond the jurisdiction where that law was in force."[42] The

---

this or any foreign country, deliver at the office of the Librarian of Congress. . .a printed copy of the title of the [work]. . .for which he desires a copyright, no unless he shall also, not later than the day of publication thereof in this or any foreign country, deliver at the office of the Librarian of Congress. . .two copies of such [work].").

37 *See* Act of Apr. 29, 1802, c. 36, §1, 2 Stat. 171.

38 Act of July 8, 1870, c. 230, §97, 16 Stat. 214, codified at Rev. Stat. §4962, 18(I) Stat. 959.

39 Act of June 18, 1874, c. 301, §1, 18(III) Stat. 78–79. The use of the familiar © symbol in lieu of the word "Copyright" was first allowed for certain categories of works in the 1909 Act, *see* Copyright Act of 1909, c. 320, §18, 35 Stat. 1079 (renumbered §19 in 1947), and was extended to all works in an amendment that became effective in 1955. P.L. 83–743, c. 1161, §1, 68 Stat. 1031 (codified at former 17 U.S.C. §9(c) (repealed 1978)); id. §3, 68 Stat. 1032 (codified at former 17 U.S.C. §19 (repealed 1978)).

40 208 U.S. 260 (1908).

41 Id. at 266.

42 Id. at 264.

court also noted that when the notice requirement was added in 1802, international copyright relations did not exist. "If a publication without notice of an American copyright did not affect the copyright before the days when it was possible to get an English copyright also, it is not to be supposed that Congress, by arranging with England for that possibility, gave a new meaning to the old [statute], increasing the burden of American authors, and attempted to intrude its requirements into any notice that might be [required] by the English law."[43]

Although the *United Dictionary* decision resolved an important question under U.S. law, it bears emphasizing that the scope of that opinion was limited. Before 1978, a work was protected by a state common-law copyright before it was published;[44] once it was published, the state common-law copyright expired, and unless a federal statutory copyright was obtained, the work entered the public domain.[45] In *United Dictionary*, the work in question was first published in the United States with a proper copyright notice, and the plaintiff took all the necessary steps to obtain a federal statutory copyright, before a revised version of the work was subsequently published in England without notice.[46] The question, therefore, was whether the lack of notice in the English edition divested the plaintiff of a federal

[43] Id. at 265.

[44] *See, e.g.*, Wheaton v. Peters, 33 U.S. 591, 657 (1834) ("That an author, at common law, has a property in his manuscript, and may obtain redress against anyone who deprives him of it, or by improperly obtaining a copy endeavours to realise a profit by its publication, cannot be doubted; but this is a very different right from that which asserts a perpetual and exclusive property in the future publication of the work, after the author shall have published it to the world."); Caliga v. Inter Ocean Newspaper Co., 215 U.S. 182, 188 (1909) At common law an author had a property in his manuscript, and might have an action against anyone who undertook to publish it without authority.").

[45] *See, e.g.*, Caliga, 215 U.S. at 188 ("At common law, the exclusive right to copy existed in the author until he permitted a general publication. Thus, when a book was published in print, the owner's common-law right was lost."); Tribune Co. of Chicago v. Associated Press, 116 F. 126, 126 (C.C.N.D. Ill. 1900) ("Literary property is protected at common law to the extent only of possession and use of the manuscript and its first publication by the owner. . . .With voluntary publication the exclusive right is determined at common law, and the statutory copyright is the sole dependence of the author or owner for a monopoly in the future publication.").

[46] 208 U.S. at 263. The facts are more clearly stated in the Court of Appeals opinion, which states that the work was first published simultaneously in the United States and England on Aug. 9, 1892; and that the work "was subsequently published commercially in England under an agreement. . .entered into on July 18, 1894." G. & C. Merriam Co. v. United Dictionary Co., 146 F. 354, 355 (7th Cir. 1906), *aff'd*, 208 U.S. 260 (1908). The court noted that there was "an exact and literal compliance with the United States statute in regard to all books published or circulated by or with the consent of [the plaintiff] in the United States," id., and that the two editions were identical except for the first 3 and last 34 pages, id. at 355, 359.

statutory copyright which it had obtained in the United States.[47] In the more usual case, however, a work is first published abroad without notice, and only later is it published in the United States. In such a situation, the relevant authorities were clear: if the work was published anywhere in the world (with or without notice) *before* being registered in the United States, the work lost its common-law copyright, thereby placing it in the public domain and rendering it permanently ineligible for a federal statutory copyright.[48] Because British law required first publication in Great Britain, the result was that publishers had to publish works simultaneously in Great Britain and the United States in order to obtain copyright in both countries.[49]

9.3 1909–1978

To complicate the matter further for foreign authors, one year after *United Dictionary* Congress adopted the 1909 Copyright Act, which contained language that reintroduced an ambiguity in the question of whether some foreign copies had to bear copyright notice. Prior to the 1909 Act, copyright protection was secured initially by registering the work (before publication) with the Copyright Office;[50] only after obtaining copyright protection by registration did the requirement of placing notice on published copies begin.[51] But under the 1909 Act, it was the act of publication with proper copyright notice that invested copyright protection in the first place. Section 9 of the 1909 Act provided:

> Any person entitled thereto by this title may secure copyright for his work by publication thereof with the notice of copyright required by this title; and such notice shall be affixed to each copy thereof published or offered for sale in the United States by authority of the copyright proprietor..."[52]

---

[47] 208 U.S. at 263 ("The question is whether omission of notice of the American copyright from the English publication, with the assent of the appellee, destroyed its rights.").

[48] *See* Eaton S. Drone, A Treatise on the Law of Property in Intellectual Productions in Great Britain and the United States 295–96 (1879) ("there can be no doubt that...an author forfeits his claim to copyright in this country by a first, but not by a contemporaneous, publication of his work abroad."); *Tribune Co.*, 116 F. at 128 ("As the exclusive right of publication at common law terminates with the publication in London, no protection then exists beyond that expressly given by the statute.").

[49] *See* Briggs, *supra* note 10, at 93–94; George Haven Putnam, *Analysis of the Provisions of the Copyright Law of 1891*, in Putnam, *supra* note 28, at 177; *Tribune Co.*, 116 F. at 128 ("Before the amendment authorizing copyright in America on foreign publications, under prescribed conditions *where the publication is simultaneous*, such foreign property was left unprotected.") (emphasis added).

[50] *See* note 36, *supra*.

[51] *See* note 38, *supra*.

[52] Copyright Act of 1909, c. 320, §9, 35 Stat. 1077 (renumbered §10 in 1947, repealed 1978).

The second clause of section 9 was consistent with the U.S. Supreme Court's holding in the *United Dictionary* case: after copyright protection was secured, it was clear that only copies of the work published in the U.S. had to bear copyright notice; and if copies of the work without notice were published in a foreign country after U.S. copyright protection was secured, it would not divest the copyright owner of his or her U.S. copyright.

But if that proposition was clear, it was now unclear what steps needed to be taken in order to secure U.S. copyright protection initially. If a work was published initially in a foreign country with whom the United States had treaty relations, did the work have to bear a U.S. copyright notice in order to secure federal copyright protection? If so, did the initial publication in that foreign country without proper notice place the work in the public domain, thereby forfeiting the right to subsequently obtain a federal statutory copyright?[53] Or was the foreign publication without notice simply to be ignored, as if it had never occurred?[54] Alternatively, was mere publication of the work in that foreign country, without any notice at all, sufficient to secure U.S. copyright protection for the foreign work?[55] Or did the work have to be republished in the United States with proper copyright notice (as the manufacturing clause seemingly required) in order to obtain U.S. copyright protection?[56]

The proper interpretation of section 9 was made even more cloudy by the legislative history of the 1909 Act. As initially drafted, section 9 read as follows:

---

[53] This view was taken in Basevi v. Edward O'Toole Co., 26 F. Supp. 41, 46 (S.D.N.Y. 1939) ("publication of a book. . .in a foreign country without notice of United States copyright thereon, will prevent the owner of the book from subsequently securing a valid copyright thereof in the United States."). *See also* Universal Film Mfg. Co. v. Copperman, 212 F. 301, 303 (S.D.N.Y. 1914) ("Because, therefore, there was a publication in Europe before registration [or publication] in the United States, the bill [alleging infringement] must be dismissed."), *aff'd on other grounds*, 218 F. 511 (2nd Cir. 1914), *cert. denied*, 235 U.S. 704 (1914); American Code Co. v. Bensinger, 282 F. 829, 833 (2d Cir. 1922) ("Publication of an intellectual production without copyrighting it causes the work to fall into the public domain. It becomes by such publication dedicated to the public, and any person is therefore entitled to publish it for his own benefit.")

[54] This view was taken in Italian Book Co. v. Cardilli, 273 F. 619, 620 (S.D.N.Y. 1918) ("publication in Italy [with reservation of rights in Italian but without U.S. copyright notice]. . . did not prevent the subsequent American copyright, if (as is the case here) there had been no publication in the United States prior to that of the copyright owner.").

[55] *See* Heim v. Universal Pictures Co., 154 F.2d 480 (2d Cir. 1946), discussed *infra* at notes 61–68 and accompanying text.

[56] *See* Twin Books v. Walt Disney Co., 83 F.3d 1162 (9th Cir. 1996), discussed *infra* at notes 80–96 and accompanying text. For yet a further view, taking the position that the initial publication of the work had to occur in the United States, *see* Arthur W. Weil, American Copyright Law 273–76 (1917); *but see* Richard C. DeWolf, An Outline of Copyright Law 38 (1925) (disagreeing with Weil on this point).

> Any person entitled thereto by this title may secure copyright for his work by publication thereof *in the United States* with the notice of copyright required by this title; and such notice shall be affixed to each copy thereof published or offered for sale by authority of the copyright proprietor . . ."[57]

As initially drafted, the statute was relatively clear: a work had to be published in the United States with proper copyright notice in order to obtain a federal statutory copyright, and notice had to be inserted in each published copy; there was nothing to suggest that the notice requirement did not apply to copies published outside the United States. In the final version, however, the phrase "in the United States" was moved from the first clause to the second. "This change made it clear that a work duly copyrighted in the United States did not lose protection merely because there might be an edition subsequently published abroad without notice,"[58] as the *United Dictionary* case had held; but it also suggested that a work did not have to be published in the United States in order to obtain U.S. copyright protection. Thus, publication *with* notice outside the United States, in a country with whom the United States had treaty relations, was now deemed sufficient to obtain a U.S. copyright.[59] But ambiguity remained with respect to the effect of an initial publication outside the United States *without* a proper copyright notice.[60]

When the issue reached the Second Circuit in 1954, the court split on the proper interpretation of Section 9. In *Heim v. Universal Pictures Co.*,[61] the work at issue, a popular song, was first published in Hungary in 1935, but the copyright notice stated that the date of first publication was 1936 (the date that the work was registered and first published in the United States as part of a Hungarian motion picture).[62] Under U.S. law, notice with an incorrect date was tantamount to publication without any notice at all.[63] Nonetheless, the majority held that the error was immaterial:

---

[57] The original draft is quoted in Herbert G. Howell, The Copyright Law 73 (2d ed. 1948), and in 2 William F. Patry, Patry on Copyright, §6:44, at 6–56 (2007).

[58] Patry, *supra* note 57, §6:44, at 6–56.

[59] *See* DeWolf, *supra* note 56, at 38 ("it seems probable, at least, that publication in a foreign country with the statutory notice is sufficient to initiate copyright protection, even if it takes place in advance of publication in the United States.").

[60] A leading treatise published in 1938 took the view that "no person is entitled to claim statutory copyright under the Act, unless, when first publishing the work abroad or in the United States, he has affixed the statutory notice." 2 Stephen P. Ladas, The International Protection of Literary and Artistic Property §324 at 698 (1938).

[61] 154 F.2d 480 (2d Cir. 1946).

[62] Id. at 481.

[63] More precisely, if the date in the notice was *later* than the actual date of first publication or registration, then the notice and the copyright were invalid, because the error would have had the effect of lengthening the term of the copyright; but if the date in the notice was *earlier* than the actual date of first publication or registration, then the error did not affect the validity of the copyright, but only shortened its duration. *See* Callahan v. Myers, 128 U.S. 617, 657–58 (1888); American Code Co. v. Bensinger, 282 F. 829, 836 (2d Cir. 1922); Baker v. Taylor, 2 Fed. Cas. 478, 478–49 (No. 782) (C.C.S.D.N.Y. 1848).

> We construe the statute, as to publication in a foreign country by a foreign author . . ., not to require, as a condition of obtaining or maintaining a valid American copyright, that any notice be affixed to any copies whatever published in such foreign country, regardless of whether publication first occurred in that country or here, or whether it occurred before or after registration here.
>
> It seems to be suggested by some text-writers that. . .where publication abroad precedes publication here, the first copy published abroad must have affixed to it the notice described. . . . Such a requirement would achieve no practical purpose, for a notice given by a single copy would obviously give notice to virtually no one. . . .[T]he most practicable and, as we think, the correct interpretation, is that publication abroad will in all cases be enough, provided that, under the laws of the country where it takes place, it does not result in putting the work in the public domain.[64]

The majority nonetheless affirmed the trial court's conclusion that no copying had occurred.[65] Concurring in the result, Judge Clark criticized the majority for upholding the validity of the copyright:

> The opinion holds that American copyright is secured by publication abroad without the notice of copyright admittedly required for publication here. This novel conclusion, suggested here for the first time, seems to me impossible in the face of the statutory language.[66]

Neither opinion focused on the specific language of the relevant treaty between the United States and Hungary, which stated:

> The enjoyment and exercise of the rights secured by the present Convention are *subject to the performance of the conditions and formalities* prescribed by the laws and regulations of the country where protection is claimed under the present Convention.[67]

Although this language could be considered a mere tautology, it is more likely that it was intended to require that Hungarian citizens comply with the same formalities with which U.S. authors were required to comply.[68]

After the *Heim* decision, the U.S. Copyright Office began to accept copyright registrations for works that had first been published outside the United States without notice under its "rule of doubt,"[69] although it

---

[64] 154 F.2d at 486–87.

[65] Id. at 488.

[66] Id. at 488 (Clark, J., concurring).

[67] United States – Hungary Copyright Convention, Jan. 30, 1912, art. 2, 37 Stat. 1631 (eff. Oct. 15, 1912) (emphasis added).

[68] After a comprehensive review of the statute and other relevant authorities (not including the United States – Hungary Copyright Convention), a prominent copyright practitioner reluctantly reached the conclusion that "the copyright law, as currently drafted, require[s] notice of copyright in works [first] published abroad." *See* Arthur S. Katz, *Is Notice of Copyright Necessary in Works Published Abroad? A Query and a Quandary*, 1953 Wash. U. L.Q. 55, 87.

[69] *See* Abraham L. Kaminstein, ©: *Key to Universal Copyright Protection*, in Theodore R. Kupferman & Mathew Foner, eds., Universal Copyright Convention Analyzed 23, 32 (1955). Under the "rule of doubt," "no claim should be disapproved if an Examiner has

continued to instruct foreign authors to include notice when publishing their works abroad.[70] However, after the United States adhered to the Universal Copyright Convention in 1955, the Copyright Office reversed course and adopted a regulation providing that published copies had to bear copyright notice even if the work was first published outside the United States.[71] The Office reasoned that otherwise, the notice requirement of the U.C.C. (which provided that all formalities were deemed to be satisfied if the work was published with proper copyright notice[72]) would be rendered a nullity.[73] This requirement is carried forward for pre-1978 works in the current Copyright Office Regulations.[74]

---

a reasonable doubt about the ultimate action which might be taken under the same circumstances by an appropriate court." Id. at 32 n. 18.

[70] *See* U.S. Copyright Office, Form A-B (Foreign), *quoted in* Katz, *supra* note 68, at 87 n. 98 ("Publish the work with the statutory notice of copyright. . . .After publication with the notice of copyright, . . .send all the required items to the Register of Copyrights."). In addition, it should be noted that many of the then-existing bilateral treaties specifically required compliance with U.S. formalities as a condition of bilateral protection. *See* Katz, *supra* note 68, at 80; George D. Cary, *The United States and Universal Copyright: An Analysis of Public Law 743*, in Kuperfman & Foner, *supra* note 69, at 83, 93 & n. 21.

[71] *See* 37 C.F.R. §202.2(a)(3) (1959) ("Works first published abroad, other than works eligible for ad interim registration, must bear an adequate copyright notice at the time of their first publication in order to secure copyright under the law of the United States."), in 24 Fed. Reg. 4956.

[72] *See* Universal Copyright Convention, Sept. 6, 1952, Art. III(1) ("Any Contracting State which, under its domestic law, requires as a condition of copyright, compliance with formalities . . .shall regard these requirements as satisfied with respect to all works protected in accordance with this Convention, and first published outside its territory and the author of which is not one of its nationals, if from the time of first publication all the copies of the work published with the authority of the author or other copyright proprietor bear the symbol © accompanied by the name of the copyright proprietor and the year of first publication placed in such a manner and location as to give reasonable notice of claim of copyright.").

[73] *See* George D. Cary, *Proposed New Copyright Office Regulations*, 6 Bull. Copyr. Soc'y USA 213, 213 (1959) (regulation "is intended to make clear that the Office no longer considers the dictum in the [*Heim*] case . . .as controlling its action . . .[because] the subsequent enactment of the so-called 'U.C.C. amendments' to the copyright law in effect amounted to a Congressional expression, contrary to the dictum, that foreign works, in order to obtain the benefit of U.S. copyright law, must, at the time of first publication, contain the form of notice provided for in the U.C.C."). *See also* Kaminstein, *supra* note 69, at 33; George D. Cary, *The United States and Universal Copyright: An Analysis of Public Law 743*, in Kuperfman & Foner, *supra* note 69, at 83, 91–94. The author agrees with this analysis; but it should be noted that two respected commentators have concluded otherwise. *See* 2 Melville B. Nimmer and David Nimmer, Nimmer on Copyright, §7.12[D][2][a], at 7–105 to 7–106 (2007); 1 Paul Goldstein, Goldstein on Copyright §3.7.2, at 3:114 (3rd ed. 2005).

[74] *See* 37 C.F.R. §202.2(a)(3) (2007) ("Works first published abroad before January 1, 1978, other than works for which ad interim copyright has been obtained, must have borne an adequate copyright notice. The adequacy of the copyright notice for such

9.4 1978 to the Present

In the 1976 Copyright Act, Congress dramatically changed the requirements for obtaining federal copyright protection. Instead of requiring publication with notice, the 1976 Act provided that a federal statutory copyright would arise as soon as a work was "fixed in any tangible medium of expression."[75] At the same time, however, Congress not only retained the notice requirement for published copies, but it also unambiguously extended the notice requirement to all copies of the work, published anywhere in the world. As enacted, Section 401 of the 1976 Act stated:

> Whenever a work protected under this title is published in the United States *or elsewhere* by authority of the copyright owner, a notice of copyright as provided by this section shall be placed on publicly distributed copies from which the work can be visually perceived, either directly or with the aid of a machine or device.[76]

It was not until March 1, 1989, the effective date of U.S. adherence to the Berne Convention, that the notice requirement was finally made optional rather than mandatory, by changing the word "shall" to the word "may."[77]

Thus, for works published on or after January 1, 1978 (the effective date of the 1976 Act),[78] it has been clear what the effect of publication without notice in a foreign country is on the federal statutory copyright in the United States. Ambiguity remains, however, regarding works first published abroad before January 1, 1978; and since some copyrights obtained under the 1909 Act will remain in effect until at least December 31, 2072,[79] we have another 65 years to go before we can declare the ambiguity to be no longer material. It is important, therefore, to consider the subsequent history of the 1909 Act in the courts.

In *Twin Books Corp. v. Walt Disney Co.*,[80] the work at issue was the children's book *Bambi, A Life in the Woods*, written by an Austrian citizen, Felix Salten.[81] *Bambi* was written in German and was first published in Germany in 1923 without any copyright notice.[82] In 1926, *Bambi* was republished in Germany with U.S. copyright notice, and the work was

---

works is determined by the copyright statute as it existed on the date of first publication abroad.").

[75] 17 U.S.C. § 102(a).

[76] *See* 17 U.S.C. §401(a), as enacted in P.L. 94–553, Title I, §101, 90 Stat. 2576–77 (1976).

[77] *See* 17 U.S.C. §401(a), as amended by Berne Convention Implementation Act, P.L. 100–568, §7(a), 102 Stat. 2857 (1988).

[78] *See* P.L. 94–553, Title I, §102, 90 Stat. 2598–99 (1976).

[79] *See* 17 U.S.C. §304(a) (providing for an initial term of 28 years and a renewal term of 67 years, for a maximum duration of 95 years from the date of first publication).

[80] 83 F.3d 1162 (9th Cir. 1996).

[81] Id. at 1164.

[82] Id.

registered in the U.S. in 1927.[83] In 1954, the copyright was renewed by Salten's heir.[84] The question presented was straightforward: when did U.S. copyright protection for *Bambi* commence? If U.S. copyright protection commenced in 1923, when the work was first published in Germany, then the 1954 renewal came too late, because the work had entered the public domain in 1951 when its first 28-year term expired.[85] But if U.S. copyright protection did not commence until 1926, when the work was republished in Germany with notice, then the renewal in 1954 was valid.

The Ninth Circuit held that, under the doctrine of territoriality, notice was not required when a work was first published abroad, and therefore "the 1923 publication of *Bambi* in Germany did not put *Bambi* in the public domain in the United States...[and] did not preclude the author from subsequently obtaining copyright protection in the United States by complying with the 1909 Copyright Act."[86] The court relied heavily on *Heim* in support of its holding.[87] However, the court ignored *Heim* in holding that the U.S. copyright did not commence until 1926, when the book was republished with U.S. copyright notice.[88] What was the status of the book during the intervening three years? According to the Ninth Circuit, the book was in some sort of copyright limbo:

> During 1923, 1924, and 1925, anyone could have sold the *Bambi* book in the United States or made some derivative movie of the *Bambi* book, and the author Salten would have had no recourse under the United States copyright law.[89]

The Ninth Circuit's holding in *Twin Books* is internally inconsistent. If during 1923–1926, "anyone could have sold the Bambi book in the United States," then the book had lost its common-law copyright when it was first published in Germany, and if it did not simultaneously obtain a federal statutory copyright, it was therefore in the public domain in the United States.[90] But earlier in its opinion, the Ninth Circuit expressly held that the

---

[83] Id.

[84] Id.

[85] Under the 1909 Act, a copyright had an initial duration of 28 years, and it could obtain a renewal term of an additional 28 years only if a renewal registration was made during the final year of the initial term. Former 17 U.S.C. §23 (1909; renumbered §24 in 1947; repealed 1978). The renewal term for pre-1978 works was extended to 47 years in 1976, for a maximum duration of 75 years from first publication. *See* 17 U.S.C. §304(a), §304(b), as enacted in P.L. 94–553, Title I, §101, 90 Stat. 2573–74 (1976). The renewal term for such works was further extended to 67 years in 1998, for a maximum duration of 95 years from first publication. *See* 17 U.S.C. §304(a), §304(b) (as amended).

[86] 83 F.3d at 1167.

[87] Id. at 1166–67.

[88] Id. at 1167–68.

[89] Id. at 1167.

[90] *See* notes 45 & 48 and accompanying text, *supra*.

book was *not* in the public domain,[91] probably because the public domain had traditionally been considered to be irrevocable.[92] Instead, the court held that a U.S. copyright arose upon publication with notice in 1926, even though the common-law copyright in the work had expired three years earlier. The Ninth Circuit also mischaracterized *Heim* when it paraphrased that case as holding that "publication abroad with no notice or with an erroneous notice would not preclude *subsequently* obtaining a valid United States copyright."[93] That is not what *Heim* held; instead, *Heim* held that a valid United States copyright arose upon publication abroad with no notice or with an erroneous notice.[94] Yet two pages later, the *Twin Books* court states: "Disney cites no authority, nor could it, for the proposition that publication abroad without notice of copyright secures protection under the 1909 Act."[95] The authority that so holds is *Heim*, which *Twin Books* purported to rely on.[96]

The result reached in *Twin Books* would have made more sense if the court had held instead that publication in a foreign country simply didn't count at all for purposes of common-law copyright (even though that conclusion would have contradicted a century of precedent).[97] If the court had so ruled, then during 1923–1926, the work would still have been protected in the United States under common-law copyright as an unpublished work (that is, as a work unpublished in the United States), and then the work would have validly obtained a federal statutory copyright when it was published with notice in a country with whom the U.S. had treaty relations.[98]

Alternatively, the *Twin Books* court could have relied on copyright restoration. Effective January 1, 1996,[99] in accordance with Art. 18 of the Berne Convention,[100] Congress restored the copyrights in works of foreign

---

[91] *See* note 86, *supra*.

[92] *See* Tyler T. Ochoa, *Origins and Meanings of the Public Domain*, 28 U. Dayton L. Rev. 215, 262–66 (2003); *but see* Tyler T. Ochoa, *Patent and Copyright Term Extension and the Constitution: A Historical Perspective*, 49 J. Copyr. Soc'y USA 19, 48–49 (2001) (noting individual instances of Congress restoring copyright in works in the public domain); id. at 61–72 (describing Congressional restoration of patent protection to inventions in the public domain).

[93] *Twin Books*, 83 F.3d at 1166 (emphasis added).

[94] *Heim*, 154 F.2d at 486–87; id. at 488 (Clark, J., concurring).

[95] *Twin Books*, 83 F.3d at 1168.

[96] *See also* 1 Nimmer on Copyright, *supra* note 73, §4.01[C][1], at 4–8 n. 35.11.

[97] *See* note 48, *supra; see also* Carte v. Duff (The Mikado Case), 25 F. 183, 184 (C.C.S.D.N.Y. 1885) ("Common law rights of authors run only to the time of the publication of their manuscripts without their consent. . . *It is immaterial whether the publication be made in one country or another.*") (emphasis added).

[98] *See Twin Books*, 83 F.3d at 1168 ("Disney is correct publication in a foreign country with notice of United States copyright secures United States copyright protection.").

[99] *See* 17 U.S.C. §104A(h)(2)(A).

[100] *See* Berne Convention for the Protection of Literary and Artistic Works, 1971 Paris Text, Art. 18(1) ("This Convention shall apply to all works which, at the moment of its

origin that had entered the public domain in the United States for failure to comply with formalities, such as notice and renewal, but had not yet entered the public domain in their source countries.[101] Had the court taken this copyright restoration statute into account, it could have found that the copyright in *Bambi* commenced in 1923, under *Heim*; and that *Bambi* had lost its U.S. copyright in 1951, when Salten's heir failed to file a renewal; but that *Bambi* had its U.S. copyright restored in 1996. Alternatively, it could have held that *Bambi* had been placed in the public domain in 1923 when it was published without notice, but that it had its U.S. copyright restored in 1996. In either case, however, Disney would have been treated as a "reliance party" and would have been entitled to continue exploiting its movie version during the remainder of the copyright term on payment of a reasonable royalty.[102]

9.5 An Illustrative Case

The incoherence of *Twin Books* becomes all the more apparent when it is applied in a more typical factual setting, one in which publication of the work with notice does not occur until many years later, if at all. That is the situation that arose in *Société Civile Succession Richard Guino v. Beseder, Inc.*,[103] a case which involved eleven sculptures created in France between 1913 and 1917 by Pierre August Renoir and Richard Guino.[104] The sculptures were first published in 1917 in France as works of Renoir;[105] and they were republished in France in 1974 and in 1983 as works of Renoir and Guino.[106] The works were registered in the United States in 1984;[107] but there was no evidence that the works had ever been published with authorization in the United States. When the defendants reproduced the

---

coming into force, have not yet fallen into the public domain in the country of origin through the expiry of the term of protection.").

[101] *See* 17 U.S.C. §104A(h)(6)(B), 17 U.S.C. §104A(h)(6)(C)(i).

[102] *See* 17 U.S.C. §104A(h)(4) (defining "reliance party"); 17 U.S.C. §104A(d)(3)(A) (defining rights of reliance parties in derivative works created before enactment of the Uruguay Round Agreements Act).

[103] 414 F. Supp. 2d 944 (D. Ariz. 2006).

[104] Id. at 946 & n. 3 (listing the eleven sculptures).

[105] Id. at 946.

[106] Id. The opinion is a little unclear on this point. It states that "[t]he sculptures were published as Renoir-Guino works in 1974, in an exhibition for sale held at the Bristol Hotel in Paris, France." Id. Later, however, it states that "the sculptures were not first published as Renoir-Guino works until 1983." Id.

[107] Id. ("Plaintiff registered the copyright to the sculptures with the Copyright Office in the United States on June 11, 1984.").

sculptures and advertised them for sale at their art gallery in Arizona, the plaintiffs sued for copyright infringement.[108]

This case starkly demonstrates the differences between the *Heim* and *Twin Books* approaches to the formality of notice under the 1909 Act. If *Heim* is correct, then the sculptures obtained a U.S. statutory copyright no later than 1917, when the sculptures were first published in France, a country with whom the U.S. had reciprocal copyright relations.[109] Those copyrights would have expired 28 years later, in 1945, when no renewals were filed for in the United States.[110] When the 1976 Act came into effect, the works would have been in the public domain, and they would have been ineligible for further copyright protection.[111] Even assuming hypothetically that renewals had been made, the copyrights would have been remained valid for another 28 years until 1973. All such subsisting copyrights were extended temporarily pending the enactment of the 1976 Act,[112] when 19 years were added to the renewal term.[113] The copyrights would therefore have expired at the end of 1992,[114] placing the works in the public domain, and rendering them ineligible for either the 1996 restoration of copyright for works of foreign origin[115] or the 1998 term extension.[116]

---

[108] Id.

[109] *See* 1891 Presidential Proclamation No. 3, 27 Stat. 981–82.

[110] *See* former 17 U.S.C. §23 (1909, renumbered §24 in 1947, repealed 1978) (author or his heirs are entitled to renewal only "when application for such renewal and extension shall have made to the copyright office and duly registered therein within one year prior to the expiration of the original term of copyright.").

[111] *See* P.L. 94–553, Title I, §103, 90 Stat. 2599 (1976) ("This Act does not provide copyright protection for any work that goes into the public domain before January 1, 1978.").

[112] *See* P.L. 92–566, 86 Stat. 1181 (1972) (extending all subsisting copyrights to Dec. 31, 1974); P.L. 93–573, §104, 88 Stat. 1873 (1974) (extending all subsisting copyrights to Dec. 31, 1976).

[113] *See* former §304(b), as enacted by P.L. 94–553, Title I, §101, 90 Stat. 2574 (1976) ("The duration of any copyright, the renewal term of which is subsisting at any time between December 31, 1976, and December 31, 1977, inclusive, . . .is extended to endure for a term of seventy-five years from the date copyright was originally secured."); *see also* id. §102, 90 Stat. 2598–99 (providing that §304(b) "take[s] effect upon enactment of this Act.").

[114] *See* 17 U.S.C. §305 ("All terms of copyright provided by sections 302 through 304 run to the end of the calendar year in which they would otherwise expire.").

[115] *See* 17 U.S.C. §104A(h)(6)(C) (restoration applies only if the work is in the public domain for one of the specified reasons, not including expiration of maximum period of duration); *see also* 17 U.S.C. §104A(a)(a)(B) ("Any work in which copyright is restored under this section shall subsist for the remainder of the term of copyright that the work would have otherwise been granted in the United States if the work had never entered the public domain in the United States.").

[116] *See* 17 U.S.C. §304(b) (as amended) ("Any copyright in its renewal term *at the time that the Sonny Bono Copyright Term Extension Act become effective* shall have a copyright term of 95 years from the date copyright was originally secured.") (emphasis added). The CTEA became effective on Oct. 27, 1998, *see* P.L. 105–298, §106, 112

Under *Twin Books*, however, the 1917 publication of the sculptures in France did *not* place the works in the public domain, nor did it secure a federal statutory copyright. Thus, when the 1976 Act came into effect, the sculptures would have been eligible for protection under section 303, as works "created before January 1, 1978, but not theretofore in the public domain or copyrighted."[117] Under this section the works are entitled to the copyright term given to new works, life of the longest-surviving author plus 70 years, subject to a statutory minimum.[118] Since Guino died in 1973, the copyrights would endure until the end of 2043.[119] However, since the works were "published on or before December 31, 2002," the statutory minimum term provides that "the term of copyright shall not expire before December 31, 2047."[120]

Thus, application of *Heim* would result in the copyright having expired in 1945 (or 1992, if hypothetically renewed), and being ineligible for copyright restoration; whereas application of *Twin Books* would result in the copyright enduring to the end of 2047, a difference of over 100 years! Not surprisingly, although the district court was located in the Ninth Circuit and was bound to follow *Twin Books*, it did criticize *Twin Books* in its opinion, expressing the view that it had been decided incorrectly.[121]

But it is not as simple a matter as choosing between these two alternatives, because there are two additional possibilities that must be considered (although in this case, they lead to the same two results). First, under the Copyright Office's interpretation of the 1909 Act,[122] publication without notice in France in 1917 placed the works in the public domain, instead of investing them with a federal statutory copyright. Again, however, the works would have been ineligible for copyright restoration in 1996, because the term they otherwise would have enjoyed but for the notice and renewal requirements would have expired in 1992.[123] Alternatively, one could take the (historically incorrect) view that foreign publication simply

Stat. 2829, so any works already in the public domain at that time did not have their copyrights extended.

117 17 U.S.C. §303(a). As an aside, it is clear that Congress intended for §303 to apply only to unpublished works. *See* notes 126–30, *infra*. It is only the Ninth Circuit's erroneous holding that publication without notice abroad *neither* placed the work in the public domain *nor* invested it with statutory copyright that allows such works to fall within the literal language of § 303.

118 *See* 17 U.S.C. § 303(a).

119 *See Société Civile Succession Richard Guino*, 414 F. Supp. 2d at 952.

120 17 U.S.C. §303(a). Recall that the court found that the works had been published in 1983. *See* note 106 and accompanying text, *supra*. The court and the litigants apparently overlooked the effect of this publication in making the works eligible for the statutory minimum term.

121 *See Société Civile Succession Richard Guino*, 414 F. Supp. 2d at 949–51.

122 *See* notes 69–74 and accompanying text, *supra*.

123 *See* 17 U.S.C. §104A(a)(1)(B).

did not count as a "publication" at all for purposes of divesting a work of its common-law copyright. If that was the case, then the work was neither "in the public domain [n]or copyrighted" on January 1, 1978, and section 303 would again be applicable, resulting in a valid copyright (under the statutory minimum) through the end of 2047.[124]

So which of these four interpretations of the 1909 Act is correct? The statute is ambiguous, and the legislative history is unclear, leaving us to rely primarily on policy arguments for making our decision.

The least likely interpretation is the one expressed in *Twin Books*, for three reasons. First, no court before or since has suggested that a work could be freely copied in the United States (having lost its common-law copyright by virtue of publication without notice abroad), but somehow not be in the public domain in the United States, and instead be in some sort of copyright limbo from which it could obtain a federal statutory copyright by subsequent publication with notice.[125] Second, it is clear from the legislative history of the 1976 Act that section 303 was intended to apply only to works which were unpublished on January 1, 1978.[126] The phrase "not in the public domain or copyrighted" was intended to exclude all published works, which either had been published with notice (and were therefore "copyrighted")[127] or had been published without notice (and were therefore in the public domain).[128] It was also intended to exclude those few unpublished works which had nonetheless been registered under the 1909 Act (and were therefore "copyrighted").[129] The notion that there were works which had been published, but which were neither in the public domain nor

---

[124] *See* 17 U.S.C. § 303(a).

[125] The one case that reached a similar result, Italian Book Co. v. Cardillli, 273 F. 619 (S.D.N.Y. 1918), was apparently predicated on the view that under the 1909 Act (unlike under previous Acts), a work's common-law copyright was not lost by foreign publication without notice. Id. at 620. Under that view, however, the work could not have been freely copied in the United Staes prior to its re-publication in the United States, since it still would have been subject to common-law copyright.

[126] The House Report stated that the purpose of §303 was "to substitute statutory for common law copyright for everything now protected at common law." H.R. Rep. No. 94–1476, at 139 (1976), reprinted in 1976 U.S.C.C.A.N. 5755. But as indicated above, common-law copyright only applied to unpublished works, and publication anywhere in the world divested a work of its common-law copyright. *See* notes 44–49 and accompanying text.

[127] *See* former 17 U.S.C. §9 (1909, renumbered §10 in 1947, repealed 1978) ("any person entitled thereto by this Act may secure copyright for his work by publication of notice thereof with the notice of copyright required by this Act.").

[128] *See* notes 45–48 and accompanying text, *supra*.

[129] *See* former 17 U.S.C. §11 (1909, renumbered §12 in 1947, repealed 1978) ("copyright may also be had of the works of an author, of which copies are not reproduced for sale, by the deposit, with claim of copyright, of one complete copy of such work.").

copyrighted, simply did not exist in the minds of the legislature.[130] Third, as the district court noted in the *Guino* case, Congress intended the 1996 copyright restoration to apply to works of foreign origin which were in the public domain in the United States for failure to comply with formalities (such as copyright notice).[131] If *Twin Books* is correct, however, many fewer works would have needed copyright restoration, because works of foreign origin never published in the United States would not have entered the public domain in the United States in the first place.[132]

It is also unlikely that Congress intended that publication without notice abroad simply would not count for purposes of common-law copyright. Although this alternative avoids the first two of the problems identified for *Twin Books*, it does not avoid the third; many fewer works would have needed copyright restoration if this rule had been in effect. In addition, as noted above, this alternative contradicts some 100 years of precedent that held that common-law copyright was divested by *any* publication, either here or abroad;[133] and it also requires that a court treat publication abroad in two different ways, depending on whether notice was used or not. Publication with notice would count as a "publication," but publication without notice would not.

The *Heim* rule has some merit, in that it is at least arguably consistent with the ambiguous language of the statute. The 1909 Act stated that copyright protection is secured "by publication thereof with the notice required by this title";[134] but since "this title" only required notice on copies of

---

130 *Cf.* H.R. Rep. No. 94–1476, at 129, 1976 U.S.C.C.A.N. at 5745 ("Instead of a dual system of 'common-law copyright' for unpublished works and statutory copyright for published works, which has been the system in effect in the United States since the first copyright statute in 1790, the bill adopts a single system of Federal statutory copyright from creation. . . .Common law copyright protection for works coming within the scope of the statute would be abrogated, and the concept of publication would lose its all-embracing importance as the dividing line between common law and statutory protection *and between both of these forms of legal protection and the public domain*.") (emphasis added).

131 *See* 17 U.S.C. §104A(h)(6)(C)(i); *Société Civile Succession Richard Guino*, 414 F. Supp. 2d at 950–51 ("The *Twin Books* rule would prevent a foreign work published without notice from being eligible for copyright restoration under §104A, which expressly provides copyright restoration for foreign works published without notice of copyright.").

132 *See Société Civile Succession Richard Guino*, 414 F. Supp. 2d at 951 ("A prerequisite to restoration under §104A is that a work is in the public domain, for enumerated reasons, in the United States. . . .The *Twin Books* rule provides that a work published in a foreign country without copyright notice is not in the public domain in the United States, unduly preventing copyright restoration of such work"); 1 Nimmer on Copyright, *supra* note 73, §4.01[C][1] at 4–9 to 4–10.1.

133 *See* notes 45 & 48, *supra*.

134 Former 17 U.S.C. §9 (1909; renumbered §10 in 1947, repealed 1978). As enacted, this section used the word "Act" instead of the word "title"; the word "title" was substituted when the statute was codified and renumbered in 1947.

the work published in the United States, arguably works first published abroad without any notice were published "with the notice required by this title."[135] Again, however, if one could secure a U.S. copyright by publishing abroad without notice, fewer works would have needed to have their copyrights restored in 1996, because they already would have had a copyright[136] (if properly renewed).[137] In addition, any third parties that began exploiting such works without permission before 1996 would not be treated as reliance parties, because the works technically would have been "subject to copyright protection" and would not have been in the public domain.[138] Instead, they would simply be longstanding (but newly discovered) infringers. Finally, one must admit that it is a strange reading of the statute to say that publication without any notice at all is the equivalent of publication "with the notice required by this title."[139]

That leaves us with the fourth alternative: that initial publication without notice in a foreign country placed the work in the public domain in the United States, even though it would not have done so if the work had previously been published with notice. This solution is consistent with the language of the statute; and unlike *Heim*, it is also consistent with the regulation adopted by the U.S. Copyright Office in 1959 and still in effect today.[140] It is subject to the criticism that it would be pointless to require only that the initial copy sold abroad bear notice;[141] but as a practical matter, that would be unlikely to happen. If the foreign author or publisher wanted

---

[135] This is the interpretation advocated by Nimmer. *See* 2 Nimmer on Copyright, *supra* note 73, §7.12[D][2][a] at 7–103 to 7–104.

[136] *See* Vincent A. Doyle, George D. Cary, Marjorie McCannon & Barbara Ringer, Copyright Law Revision Study No. 7, Notice of Copyright 14 (1957) ("the doctrine of the *Heim* case would mean that the bulk of works by foreign authors first published abroad are effectively protected under U.S. copyright law without the observance of any formalities.").

[137] Admittedly, the formality of renewal would have caused most of these works to enter the public domain at the end of their initial 28-year term, since only those copyright owners who were aware of the *Heim* decision would have bothered to apply for renewal of copyright in their works. These works would therefore benefit from copyright restoration. This fact makes the *Heim* approach clearly the second-best alternative in terms of making copyright restoration meaningful.

[138] *See* 17 U.S.C. §104A(h)(4)(A) (defining "reliance party" as "any person who . . . with respect to a particular work, engages in acts, before the source country of that work becomes an eligible country, which would have violated section 106 if the restored work had been subject to copyright protection, and who, after the source country becomes an eligible country, continues to engage in such acts.").

[139] *See Heim*, 154 F.2d at 488 (Clark, J., concurring) ("This novel conclusion . . . seems to me impossible in the face of the statutory language."); *Twin Books*, 83 F.3d at 1168 ("There is absolutely no way to interpret that language to mean that an author may secure copyright protection for his work by publishing it without any notice of copyright.").

[140] *See* notes 71–74 and accompanying text.

[141] *See Heim*, 154 F.2d at 487 ("Such a requirement would serve no practical purpose, for a notice given by a single copy would obviously give notice to virtually no one."). Note, however, that a sale of only a single copy would not likely be deemed to

to secure a U.S. copyright without publishing the work in the United States, it is more likely that the entire first edition sold abroad would have a copyright notice, even if subsequent editions did not.[142] And since the 1909 Act had a manufacturing clause, requiring that deposit copies be printed from type set in the United States,[143] it is likely that Congress envisioned (or desired) that most works would be published domestically first, or else that they would simultaneously be published in the United States and abroad, in order to secure United States copyright protection.[144] Finally, those works which *were* first published abroad without notice would still be eligible for the copyright restoration enacted by Congress in 1994 (effective January 1, 1996).[145] This solution would also allow parties who began exploiting such works before 1996 to be treated as reliance parties under the copyright restoration statute.[146]

It should be noted that, because of copyright restoration, the last two alternatives will today always reach the same results in terms of validity and expiration of the copyright. The only meaningful difference between them is that the Copyright Office's interpretation would allow third parties who began exploiting such works before 1996, and which continue to do so today, to be treated as reliance parties under the statute; whereas under the *Heim* approach, there can be no reliance parties for those few works which were registered under the "rule of doubt" and were subsequently renewed.

9.6 Conclusion

Copyright practitioners should be dismayed that an important question of interpretation of the 1909 Act is still unresolved nearly 100 years after

---

constitute a "publication." *See* 17 U.S.C. §101 (defining "publication" as "the distribution of copies. . .of the work to the public").

142 That was the case in *Heim* itself, where the entire first edition published in Hungary bore a U.S. copyright notice. 154 F.2d at 481. It was only the error in the date in the notice that made it necessary for the court to determine whether publication without notice was sufficient to obtain copyright protection. Id. at 486. *See also* Katz, *supra* note 68, at 68 ("In practice, English language works and periodicals published abroad tend to carry the notice of copyright in the initial printing. Astute foreign publishers of foreign language works have long made the initial publication bear the appropriate United States copyright notice.").

143 *See* notes 34–35 and accompanying text, *supra*.

144 This is particularly true when one considers the sole express exception to the notice requirement. Works first published abroad in English could secure an *ad interim* copyright by depositing one complete copy of the foreign edition, giving the copyright owner a short time to comply with the manufacturing clause and to deposit and register the complying copies. *See* Copyright Act of 1909, §§21–22 (renumbered §§22–23 in 1947; repealed 1978); Katz, *supra* note 68, at 60 (making this argument).

145 *See* 17 U.S.C. §104A(h)(6)(C).

146 *See* 17 U.S.C. §104A(h)(4)(A).

its enactment, and that choosing the proper interpretation will still be a material issue for another 65 years in the future. Indeed, anyone who believes that laws should be clear and consistent and easily applied should be appalled by this state of affairs. Copyright scholars have already noted the difficulty of determining whether a given work is in the public domain;[147] when the work was first published abroad without notice, the difficulties are insurmountable.[148]

While I believe that the solution outlined above is the correct one, it is perhaps even more important that a single solution be agreed upon, so that copyright owners and users in different parts of the country are not tempted to shop for a favorable forum in which to obtain the result they desire. Thus, if the *Guino* case is appealed, the Ninth Circuit should take the case *en banc* and overturn its nonsensical decision in *Twin Books*. The court should then either adopt the reasoning in *Heim*, harmonizing its law with the plausible but second-best interpretation of the Second Circuit; or it should adopt the correct solution outlined above, leaving it to the U.S. Supreme Court to grant certiorari and decide the question once and for all.

---

[147] *See, e.g.*, Kenneth D. Crews, *Copyright Duration and the Progressive Degeneration of a Constitutional Doctrine*, 55 Syracuse L. Rev. 189 (2005); Elizabeth Townsend Gard, *January 1, 2003: The Birth of the Unpublished Public Domain and Its International Implications*, 24 Cardozo Arts & Ent. L.J. 687 (2006); *see generally* Tyler T. Ochoa, *Copyright Duration: Theories and* Practice, in Peter K. Yu, ed., Intellectual Property and Information Wealth 133, 148–53 (2007).

[148] For another example demonstrating these difficulties, *see* Elizabeth Townsend Gard, *Vera Brittain, Section 104(a) and Section 104A: A Case Study in Sorting Out the Duration of Foreign Works Under the 1976 Copyright Act*, Tulane Public Law Research Paper No. 07–09 (draft), *available at* http://papers.ssrn.com/sol3/papers.cfm?abstract_id=1015575 (last visited Sept. 23, 2007).

Chapter 10
The Internationalization of Internet Law

Paul Przemysław Polański

Originally dominated by North American users, the growth of the internet has spread all over the world. In November 2007 there were nearly 1.3 billion of internet users worldwide. The largest population of internet users is currently located in Asia (36,6%), followed by Europe (27,7%), North America (18,8%), Latin America (9,7%), Africa (3,5%), the Middle East (2,7%) and Australia (1,5%).[1]

This internationalization of the internet has had a discernable impact on global trade and international law, as internet businesses have created a new international marketplace for goods and services. Globally recognised brands such as EBay, Google and Amazon, along with popular Web 2.0 websites such as MySpace and Facebook have not only provided transnational platforms for exchanging products or information but also empowered the enormous growth of web advertising. At the same time, global peer-to-peer networks have contributed to the creation of a file sharing culture, creating enormous copyright tensions in some jurisdictions, particularly in the United States.

Facing these rapid new developments and challenges, international lawmakers has responded very slowly. Although there have been some important developments in international electronic commerce law, no globally binding written norms have been established so far.

The first important instrument was the 1996 UNCITRAL Model Law on Electronic Commerce, a non-binding template that helps draft technology-focused regulations. However, this instrument has at least two major downsides: first, it is not binding; and second, it was drafted in the pre-web era, which does not make it a good model to guide the regulation of modern electronic commerce.

P.P. Polański (✉)
Department of European Law, Warsaw University Faculty of Law, Warsaw, Poland
e-mail: ppolanski@wpia.uw.edu.pls

[1] http://www.internetworldstats.com/stats.htm, (last visited October 10, 2008).

J. Klabbers, M. Sellers (eds.), *The Internationalization of Law and Legal Education*, Ius Gentium: Comparative Perspectives on Law and Justice 2,
DOI 10.1007/978-1-4020-9494-1_10,

The 2005 United Nations Convention on the Use of Electronic Communications in International Contracts (UNECIC or the UN Convention) is the most likely candidate for providing usable transnational norms for electronic commerce. However, it is not binding and only contains very general provisions that will not be helpful in solving many internet disputes. Compared with the 1980 Vienna Convention on Contracts for the International Sale of Goods (CISG or the Vienna Convention), which provides detailed regulation of parties' rights and obligations, the UNECIC is not as flexible and comprehensive. On the other hand, the Vienna Convention was drafted at the end of the 1970s, and therefore favors the use of telexes and faxes. Because this convention does not take into account the growing importance of computer networks, it is unsuitable for regulating web-based commerce.

Although there have been interesting international developments in the areas of cybercrime and intellectual property law, these conventions are not directly relevant in the area of e-commerce regulation. For example, the 2001 Convention on Cybercrime, although comprehensive, is addressed primarily to European states and a few other countries. The 1996 WIPO Treaties only dealt with intellectual property in a general context, instead of with e-commerce more broadly. Although some provisions reflect concerns of the drafters on the potential impact of the internet on the rights of reproduction and distribution and the need to protect intellectual works in the digital era, because these treaties were also drafted in the pre-Web era, they do not address the key contemporary challenges to the copyright regime, such as peer-to-peer networks or open source software.

The discussion presented here will consider the most important developments in international internet law, in particular the 2005 United Nations Convention, the Convention on Cybercrime, and the 1996 WIPO Treaties.

10.1 The 2005 United Nations Convention on the Use of Electronic Communications in International Contracting

10.1.1 General Information

On November 23, 2005, the United Nations General Assembly adopted a new Convention on the Use of Electronic Communications in International Contracting (UNECIC).[2] Drafted by the UNCITRAL Working Group IV over six sessions since 2002, the UNECIC is the most important and long awaited

---

[2] United Nations (23 November 2005) *United Nations Convention on the Use of Electronic Communications in International Contracts*, A/60/515: http://www.uncitral.org/pdf/english/texts/electcom/2005Convention.pdf, (last visited August 7, 2006). See also UNCITRAL (23 November 2005) *General Assembly adopts new Convention on the Use*

development in international electronic commerce law. Available in Arabic, Chinese, English, French, Russian and Spanish, all of its versions are equally authentic.[3]

From 16 January 2006 to 16 January 2008, any state can sign the UNECIC at the United Nations Headquarters in New York.[4] During this period, a total of 18 states signed it, including: the Central African Republic, China, Columbia, Honduras, Iran, Lebanon, Madagascar, Montenegro, Panama, Paraguay, Philippines, the Republic of Korea, the Russian Federation, Saudi Arabia, Senegal, Sierra Leone, Singapore and Sri Lanka.[5] Three ratifications are still required before the Convention will enter into force.

The United States has not yet signed the Convention, nor have any of the European Union Member States or the European Union itself (although the Convention is open for signature by regional economic integration organisations[6]).[7] A reason for European hesitation might be that there are some overlaps with EU directives concerning electronic commerce and electronic signatures.

10.1.2 Aim of the Convention

The aim of the UN Convention is to remove legal obstacles to electronic commerce, including those which arose under other instruments, on the basis of the principle of functional equivalence.[8] Furthermore, the treaty aims to provide a common solution in a manner acceptable to states with differing legal, social and economic systems.[9] Its unique contribution can be found in Article 20, which has the goal of removing obstacles to e-commerce found in earlier conventions:

---

of Electronic Communications in International Contracting, http://www.un.org/News/Press/docs/2005/ga10424.doc.htm, (last visited December 3, 2005).

[3] Art. 25(2).

[4] Art. 16(1).

[5] http://www.uncitral.org/uncitral/en/uncitral_texts/electronic_commerce/2005Convention_status. html, (last visited January 20, 2008).

[6] Art. 17.

[7] See W. Kilian (2007), *The UN-Convention on the Use of E-Communications in International Contracts*, CRi 4/2007, p. 102.

[8] UNCITRAL (11- 22 October 2004) *A/CN.9/571 – Report of the Working Group on Electronic Commerce on the work of its forty-fourth session*, Vienna, http://daccessdds.un.org/doc/UNDOC/GEN/V04/589/92/PDF/V0458992.pdf?OpenElement, (last visited February 1, 2006), para. 14.

[9] United Nations (23 November 2005) *United Nations Convention on the Use of Electronic Communications in International Contracts*, A/60/515, http://www.uncitral.org/pdf/english/texts/electcom/2005Convention.pdf, (last visited August 7, 2006). See Preamble, 6th passage.

The provisions of this Convention apply to the use of electronic communications in connection with the formation or performance of a contract to which any of the following international conventions, to which a Contracting State to this Convention is or may become a Contracting State, applies:

Convention on the Recognition and Enforcement of Foreign Arbitral Awards (New York, 10 June 1958);

Convention on the Limitation Period in the International Sale of Goods (New York, 14 June 1974) and Protocol thereto (Vienna, 11 April 1980);

United Nations Convention on Contracts for the International Sale of Goods (Vienna, 11 April 1980);

United Nations Convention on the Liability of Operators of Transport Terminals in International Trade (Vienna, 19 April 1991);

United Nations Convention on Independent Guarantees and Stand-by Letters of Credit (New York, 11 December 1995);

United Nations Convention on the Assignment of Receivables in International Trade (New York, 12 December 2001).[10]

Since the UN Convention applies to the listed conventions to which a Contracting State is, or may become, a party, it may have a significant effect on existing legal rules. For example, the term "writing" as used in Article 13 of CISG would be given a new meaning when a Contracting State to CISG becomes a Contracting State to the new Convention. The provisions of the Convention also apply to other conventions related to international trade, but a Contracting State may declare that it will not bound by that provision.[11] Such a declaration by a Contracting State can be made, changed and withdrawn at any time,[12] unlike reservations, which are not permitted under this Convention.[13]

10.1.3 Organization

The UN Convention contains a Preamble and 25 articles. It is organised into four chapters. Chapter delineates the convention's scope of application. Chapter 1 contains general provisions, including the definitions of the terms used. Chapter 2.3, covering the "use of electronic communications in international contracts," contains provisions on the legal recognition of electronic communications, form requirements of a contract or a communication, time and place of electronic communications, invitation to make offers, use of automated systems for contract formation, availability of contract terms, and treatment of input error. Chapter 3.4 contains some final provisions.

---

[10] Art. 20(1).

[11] See Art. 20(2).

[12] Arts. 21(1) and (4).

[13] Art. 22.

The drafters of the Convention were heavily influenced by the 1980 Vienna Convention and the Model Laws on Electronic Commerce and Electronic Signatures. The influence of the Vienna Convention is clearly visible in the first chapter of the Convention, and to a lesser extent in the remaining parts. The impact of the Model laws is noticeable in the third chapter.

10.1.4 Sphere of Application

The scope of application of the UN Convention extends to the use of electronic communications in connection with the formation or performance of a contract between parties whose places of business are in different states,[14] and therefore, is wider than that of the CISG, which is applicable only to contracting states. However, Article 19 of the UN Convention permits contracting states to limit its application to other contracting states or when the parties agree that it applies, they might limit its application only to contracting states. Recently, Connoly and Ravindra pointed out that this provision 'has the potential to re-introduce the very legal ambiguities that the Convention is designed to avoid.'[15]

The Convention defines "electronic communication" as "any communication that the parties make by means of data messages". "Data message", in turn, means "information generated, sent, received or stored by electronic, magnetic, optical or similar means, including, but not limited to, electronic data interchange, electronic mail, telegram, telex or telecopy." Although applications such as the World Wide Web or peer-to-peer networks are not expressly mentioned, the definition is broad enough to cover all existing and emerging information processing technologies.[16]

By applying the Convention to all electronic communications, the scope of the Convention is made very broad. Coverage extends not only to contracts, but also to electronic negotiations and contracts formed partially by digital means. The nationality or character of the parties is irrelevant.[17] Place of business is defined as "any place where a party maintains a non-transitory establishment to pursue an economic activity other than the temporary provision of goods or services out of a specific location."[18] A party's place of business is presumed to be the location indicated by that

---

[14] Art. 1(1). See also Art. 1(2) which repeats Art. 1(2) of CISG.

[15] Connoly, C. and Ravindra, P. (2006), *First UN Convention on eCommerce finalized*, p. 33.

[16] For a critique of this approach, see Polański, P. P. (July 2003) *Custom as a Source of Supranational internet Commerce Law (PhD Thesis)*, The University of Melbourne, http://eprints.unimelb.edu.au/, (last visited June 1, 2007), s. 46.

[17] Art. 1(3).

[18] Art. 4(h).

party,[19] and not that where the technological equipment is located or where an information system can be accessed. It may also appear from any previous dealings or from information disclosed by the parties.[20] If a party does not indicate its place of business, or has more than one, then the place of business will be determined under the "closest relationship" test. However, the Convention makes it clear that a domain name or electronic mail address connected to a specific country does not create a presumption that a given party has a place of business in that country.[21]

The UN Convention differs from the Vienna Convention in many respects. First, the UN Convention is not limited to contracts for the sale of goods and applies to transactions other than sales such as barters. More importantly, it also applies to transactions regarding services and information. This is a fundamental and long-awaited change. Thanks to this new provision, international electronic services have finally been given legal recognition.

Second, the UN Convention applies to contracts between parties located in two different states, even if one or both are not Contracting States. The wording of this provision has been influenced by the 1964 Hague Convention relating to a Uniform Law on the International Sale of Goods,[22] and suggests a universal character of the Treaty, but in application, it has produced two conflicting interpretations.[23] The prevailing view is that the Convention should only apply when the laws of a contracting state apply to the underlying transaction.[24] Therefore the Convention applies only so long as the law of a Contracting State applies to the dealings of the parties. The other view holds that any Contracting State may declare that it will apply the Convention only when the states are Contracting States or when parties have agreed that it applies.[25]

---

[19] Art. 6(1). It should appear from any previous dealings, contract or information disclosed by the parties. See Arts. 1(2) and 1(3).

[20] Art. 1(3).

[21] Art. 6(5). This provision not only limits the freedom of adjudicator but also ignores the fact that these days ccTLDs give strong indication of parties' location. Although in theory a business can easily register a domain name in another country, modern online entrepreneurs nearly always try to register a domain name in a country where they actually run a business. The current wording seems to have been influenced by early fears in this regard. See, for example Johnson, D. R. i Post, D. (May 1996) *Law and Borders – The Rise of Law in Cyberspace*, Stanford Law Review 48 Section B.

[22] UNCITRAL Working Group IV (Electronic Commerce) (2005) *A/60/17 – Report of the United Nations Commission on International Trade Law on the work of its thirty-eighth session, 4–15 July 2005*, United Nations, http://daccessdds.un.org/doc/UNDOC/GEN/V05/868/63/PDF/V0586863.pdf?OpenElement, (last visited November 5, 2005), para. 19.

[23] Ibid., para. 22.

[24] Ibid., paras. 18–22.

[25] Art. 21(1).

The autonomous character of the UN Convention is reflected in the provision on interpretation, which repeats Article 7 of the Vienna Convention. Therefore, its provisions should be interpreted with due regard to its international character and the need to promote uniformity and the observance of good faith in international trade. Any gaps are to be settled in conformity with the general principles on which the UN Convention is based, such as the principles of functional equivalence and technological neutrality, which are expressly referred to in the Preamble. Only in the absence of such principles should questions not expressly settled in the UN Convention be answered by virtue of the general rules of private international law.

The UN Convention does not contain any regulation of trade usages akin to the formulation found in Article 9 of the Vienna Convention.[26] The lack of such a provision might imply that trade usages continue to apply as usual. Some entrepreneurs might have objections to the absence of explicit recognition of trade usages. A restrictive interpretation of the UN Convention might undermine the flexibility of the conventional norms. The best interpretation of this convention would allow the continued application of trade usages, even in the absence of a specific reference to the Convention. This would allow continued access to commercial custom, which is one of the fundamental sources of international commercial law.

In general, the scope of application of the UN Convention is much broader than that of the Vienna Convention. However, the UN Convention does not apply to consumer contracts, electronic financial services and international transferable documents such as bills of exchange.[27] As under the Vienna Convention, parties to the UN Convention may exclude its application or derogate from or vary the effect of any of its provisions.[28]

10.2 Principles

10.2.1 Recognition of Electronic Contracting

With respect to the norms regarding electronic communications, a contract or a communication[29] can be made or evidenced in any particular

[26] UNCITRAL Model Law on Electronic Commerce, which also used narrow interpretation of the term 'law' and 'the rule of law'. UNCITRAL (11–22 October 2004) *A/CN.9/571 – Report of the Working Group on Electronic Commerce on the work of its forty-fourth session*, Vienna, http://daccessdds.un.org/doc/UNDOC/GEN/V04/589/92/PDF/V0458992.pdf?OpenElement, (last visited February 1, 2006), para. 58.

[27] Art. 2.

[28] Art. 3.

[29] Art. 4(a). 'Communication' means any statement, declaration, demand, notice or request, including an offer and the acceptance of an offer, that the parties are required to make or choose to make in connection with the formation or performance of a contract.

form.[30] The wording of this provision has been influenced by the Vienna Convention and is broad enough to cover electronic contracts. However, the Treaty on e-contracting specifically recognises such contracts as functionally equivalent to paper-based ones:

> A communication or a contract shall not be denied validity or enforceability on the sole ground that it is in the form of an electronic communication.[31]

In addition, a contract formed by a computer system and a natural person, or by the interaction of automated message systems,[32] shall not be denied validity or enforceability on the sole ground that no natural person reviewed or intervened in each of the individual actions carried out by the automated message systems or the resulting contract.[33] Parties' agreement to use electronic communications can be inferred from the party's conduct.[34]

10.2.2 Electronic Writing, Signatures and Originals

The UN Convention specifies the requirements for electronic writing, signature and originality based on Articles 6–8 of the Model Law on Electronic Commerce. The requirement of writing is met by an electronic communication if the information contained therein is accessible to be usable for subsequent reference.[35]

The requirement of signature is met if a method is used that identifies the party, indicates its intention and is as reliable as appropriate for its purpose (or proven in fact to have fulfilled the above functions).[36] The definition of signature is open to embrace different kinds of signatures, such as digital signatures or signatures based on biometric methods.

The requirement of originality is met if the integrity of information is reliably assured from the time when it is first generated in its final form and the information can be displayed to the person requesting it.[37] The integrity of information is assured if it has remained complete and unaltered, apart from any changes that arise in the normal course of electronic data transfer.

---

[30] Art. 9(1).
[31] Art. 8(1).
[32] Art. 4(g). 'Automated message system' means a computer program or an electronic or other automated means used to initiate an action or respond to data messages or performances in whole or in part, without review or intervention by a natural person each time an action is initiated or a response is generated by the system.
[33] Art. 12.
[34] Art. 8(2).
[35] Art. 9(2).
[36] Art. 9(3).
[37] Art. 9(4).

The standard of reliability shall be assessed in the light of the purpose for which the information was generated and all relevant circumstances,[38] including trade usages.

10.2.3 Time and Place of Dispatch and Receipt of Electronic Communications

The UN Convention's provisions on time and place of dispatch and on receipt of electronic messages differ in comparison to those of the Model Law on Electronic Commerce.[39] As a rule of thumb, the place of business designates the place where the information was dispatched or received, even if the supporting information system is located elsewhere.[40] The time of dispatch is considered to be the time when a message leaves the computer system of a sender, whereas the time of receipt is the time it becomes capable of being retrieved by the addressee at a designated electronic address. The message is presumed to be capable of being retrieved when it reaches the addressee's electronic address.[41]

The correct electronic address is important, because the time of receipt at another address is when the addressee becomes aware that a message has been sent and that it can be retrieved. This provision is well-suited to e-mail and EDI-based electronic commerce, but may not be so easy to establish in case of web-based commerce, where such information would usually be recorded only by one automated system. This provision is not intend to establish rules for ascertaining the time and place of contract formation.

10.2.4 Invitation to Make Offers

The UN Convention also contains novel principles on invitations to make offers. Article 11 contains the following presumption with regards to the status of interactive ordering systems:

A proposal to conclude a contract made through one or more electronic communications which is not addressed to one or more specific parties, but is generally accessible to parties making use of information systems, including proposals that make use of interactive applications for the placement of orders through such information systems, is to be considered as

---

38 Art. 9(5).
39 Art. 10.
40 See Art. 6.
41 Art. 10(2), third sentence.

an invitation to make offers, unless it clearly indicates the intention of the party making the proposal to be bound in case of acceptance.[42]

This presumption is of particular importance for web-based electronic shops. Therefore, unless the online merchant making the proposal clearly indicates his or her intention on a website, his electronic catalogue will not be treated as a definite offer. However, one should note that this presumption is only valid provided that a proposal is not addressed to one or more specific parties. The drafters may have failed to notice that after a customer logs into an interactive ordering system, the proposal is always specifically addressed to him or her, which can be easily ascertained if a system has implemented shopping cart technology. In consequence, from the moment of log-in, proposals should be treated as offers as they are customarily very specific, addressed to a registered user and allow for immediate placement of an order. Clearly, the provision of Article 11 could have been better formulated. It fails to take into account the fact that registration in any online system can be regarded as a communication addressed to a specific person. Furthermore, it does not define what constitutes an invitation to treat and how it is to be distinguished from an offer.[43] Finally, it uses the confusing term "interactive applications for the placement of orders" rather than "automated message system" used elsewhere in the text, which might lead to unnecessary problems of interpretation.[44]

10.2.5 Electronic Mistake

The UN Convention also regulates the consequences of a contractual mistake. When a person makes an input error on an interactive website and is not given the opportunity to correct it, he or she has the right to withdraw that portion of the electronic communication if he or she:

> (a) (...) notifies the other party of the error as soon as possible; and (b) (...) has not used or received any material benefit or value from the goods or services, if any, received from the other party.[45]

This provision spurred a great deal of controversy. Critics argued that such a provision might conflict with well-established contract law principles; that it is more appropriate for consumer transactions; and that it

---

[42] Art. 11.

[43] See the discussion on this topic under Vienna Convention heading and Contract law section *above*.

[44] See an even more confusing explanation for this choice in UNCITRAL Working Group IV (Electronic Commerce) (2005) *A/60/17 – Report of the United Nations Commission on International Trade Law on the work of its thirty-eighth session, 4–15 July 2005*, United Nations, http://daccessdds.un.org/doc/UNDOC/GEN/V05/868/63/PDF/V0586863.pdf?OpenElement, (last visited November 5, 2005), para. 87.

[45] Art. 14(1).

would create serious difficulties for trial courts, since the only evidence of the error would be the assertion of the interested party that he or she made an error. The proponents argued that this type of error is specific to electronic communication and therefore deserves special treatment; that it provides a much-needed uniform rule in view of the differing and possibly conflicting national rules; and that it does not in any way aggravate the evidentiary difficulties that already exist in a paper-based environment, because the courts would have to assess all the circumstances anyway.[46] The proponents won, but the purpose of this provision is not entirely clear. It only provides for consequences of input error, but does not oblige online entrepreneurs to introduce systems of error identification and correction, despite the fact that it is a customary practice to do so.[47] The drafters felt that such a prescriptive provision would be incompatible with "the enabling nature" of the Convention.[48] Furthermore, no time limit was set for the exercise of the right of withdrawal, thereby introducing legal uncertainty.

10.2.6 Summary

The UN Convention is certainly the most important recent international development in electronic commerce law. Focusing primarily on the formation of electronic contracts, it recognises the value of electronic communications and modernises the terminology of older conventions to embrace the impact of digital technologies. Another advantage of the UN Convention is its broader scope of application. Compared to that of the Vienna Convention, the UN Convention goes beyond sales and covers trade in goods, services and information. It also confirms widely recognised principles such as that of functional equivalency or irrelevancy of the location of information systems.

The UN Convention increases the certainty of electronic contracting by expressly recognising this form of transaction. It could be said that

---

[46] UNCITRAL (11–22 October 2004) *A/CN.9/571 – Report of the Working Group on Electronic Commerce on the work of its forty-fourth session*, Vienna, http://daccessdds.un.org/doc/UNDOC/GEN/V04/589/92/PDF/V0458992.pdf?OpenElement, (last visited February 1, 2006), ss. 185–186. UNCITRAL Working Group IV (Electronic Commerce) (2005) *A/60/17 – Report of the United Nations Commission on International Trade Law on the work of its thirty-eighth session, 4–15 July 2005*, United Nations, http://daccessdds.un.org/doc/UNDOC/GEN/V05/868/63/PDF/V0586863.pdf?OpenElement, (last visited November 5, 2005), paras. 96–105.

[47] See Chapter IX.

[48] UNCITRAL (11–22 October 2004) *A/CN.9/571 – Report of the Working Group on Electronic Commerce on the work of its forty-fourth session*, Vienna, http://daccessdds.un.org/doc/UNDOC/GEN/V04/589/92/PDF/V0458992.pdf?OpenElement, (last visited February 1, 2006), para. 184.

the convention attaches special importance to automated message systems such as online marketplaces, interactive electronic shops or EDI. It also removes a barrier to electronic commerce by specifying requirements for the recognition of electronic writing, signature and original documents. By using a rather generic language, it allows different technologies to meet conventional criteria. Finally, it offers a useful definition of the parties' place of business, specifies the time and place of electronic communication, and provides novel regulations on invitation to treat and input error.

However, the UN Convention also has some shortcomings. Although it has a broader scope than the Vienna Convention, this new treaty nevertheless excludes fundamental areas of e-commerce where uniform, international regulation is really necessary. Consumer trade is excluded even though online consumers might need better protection that is offered by their domestic legal systems. Financial transactions are excluded even though their international regulation remains obscure. Electronic bills of lading and other transferable documents are excluded despite an interesting regulation of criteria for the recognition of originals. The relationship between this and other conventions may also be a source of confusion.

The lack of explicit recognition of trade usages might cause problems in the application of the conventional norms, as parites will have to rely on general principles underlying the Convention. Furthermore, some of the conventional norms are vague and do not recognize common practices that have emerged in electronic commerce, such as order confirmation or encryption of transactions. Unnecessarily confusing terminology is sometimes used as in the case of "automated message system" and "interactive systems for placing orders". In certain areas, the UN Convention is not as comprehensive as the CISG or the European Union e-commerce directives.

These weaknesses in the treaty reflect inadequacies in the drafting process. UNCITRAL underestimated the value of public consultations with the internet community. Only states and interested international organizations were invited to participate fully in the preparation of the draft Convention.[49] The absence of the internet community during the drafting process or even to express opinions on UNCITRAL's website violated the spirit of the internet, which continues to be developed through open sharing of information. Global internet regulations should at least be consulted with the users.

Despite its shortcomings, this treaty on e-contracting represents a major step forward in the international regulation of electronic commerce. Therefore, all states ought to ratify the UN Convention in order to bring more certainty and predictability to modern international trade.

---

[49] A60/515 p. 7.

10.3 2001 Convention on Cybercrime

10.3.1 General Information

The Convention on Cybercrime is the other important new instrument dedicated solely to internet activities. Written under the auspices of the Council of Europe and signed in Budapest on 23 November 2001, it is so far the only international convention dealing with fighting internet-related crime. The Convention entered into force in July 2004.

As of January 2008, 43 European states and 4 non-European states have signed the Convention; among these, 21 European states and the United Staes have already ratified it. The accession of non-European states is possible by virtue of Article 37 of the Convention, which states that:

> the Committee of Ministers of the Council of Europe, after consulting with and obtaining the unanimous consent of the Contracting States to the Convention, may invite any state not a member of the Council and which has not participated in its elaboration to accede to this Convention.

The Cybercrime Convention is a success. It became binding on the United States on January 1, 2007. Other states that have ratified the Convention include: Albania, Armenia, Bosnia and Hercegovina, Bulgaria, Croatia, Cyprus, Denmark, Estonia, Finland, France, Hungary, Iceland, Latvia, Lithuania, the Netherlands, Norway, Romania, Slovakia, Slovenia, the former Yugoslav Republic of Macedonia and Ukraine.

European states that have signed the Convention but not ratified it yet include: Austria, Belgium, the Czech Republic, Germany, Greece, Ireland, Italy, Luxemburg, Malta, Moldova, Montenegro, Poland, Portugal, Serbia, Spain, Sweden, Switzerland and United Kingdom. Non-European states that have signed it include Japan, Canada and South Africa.

10.3.2 Organization

The Cybercrime Convention consists of 48 articles, divided into four chapters, with an additional protocol concerning the criminalisation of acts of a racist or xenophobic nature committed through computer systems.

The first part of the Cybercrime Convention contains only one article defining four key terms ("computer system", "computer data", "service provider" and "traffic data"). There are no provisions outlining the aim and scope of the Convention, exclusions or any of the other typical provisions usually found in modern conventions. There are also no provisions dealing with the interpretations of the Convention, although the Convention's Preamble is helpful in this regard.

The most important part of the Convention is the second part. It is divided into two sections covering substantive criminal law and procedural criminal law. Rather than addressing individuals and companies, the Convention addresses states-signatories and requires them to implement the required provisions. The following discussion will limit itself to considering the section devoted to the substantive law. The substantive section defines computer crimes, grouped into four categories: offences against the confidentiality, integrity and availability of computer data and systems, computer-related offences, content-related offences and offences related to infringements of copyright and related rights).

The Convention does not contain a definition of "cybercrime". The term 'cyber' implies the internet or at least a networked environment. That would suggest that the Convention deals only with internet-related offences. But its scope is (intentionally or unintentionally) broader and also covers computer-related offences such as computer forgery and fraud.

The Convention may not ever fully achieve a harmonised system of cybercrime law, as in most cases it allows for qualification of the definitions of computer offences. In all cases except system interference[50] and computer-related forgery,[51] the provisions of domestic law implementing the Convention can be substantially modified and may either require additional conditions to be satisfied or can be derogated from.

The Convention also penalises intentional attempts as well as the aiding or abetting of the commission of any of the above listed offences,[52] and establishes the liability of legal persons. The Convention does not contain any specific sanctions for the specified crimes and leaves it to the states to ensure that the criminal offences "are punishable by effective, proportionate and dissuasive sanctions, which include deprivation of liberty."[53]

In addition to its substantive provisions, the Convention also contains procedural provisions such as those related to the expedited preservation and partial disclosure of traffic data[54] or real-time collection of traffic data.[55] Member states must empower their competent authorities to search or access a computer system or computer-data storage medium in which computer data may be stored in its territory. Part three of the Convention deals with international co-operation with respect to fighting online crime.

---

[50] Art. 5.
[51] Art. 7.
[52] Art. 11.
[53] Art. 13.
[54] Art. 17.
[55] Art. 20.

10.3.3 Selected Provisions

Although the scope of this discussion does not extend to all of the computer crimes listed in the Convention, some of the most controversial deserve comment.

10.3.4 Misuse of Devices

One such controversial offence is described in Article 6 under the heading of 'misuse of devices'. According to this article, making available software, hardware or computer access codes with the intent that it be used for the purpose of committing illegal access or interception or data or system interference constitutes a cybercrime. In consequence, producers of programs creating Trojan horses or hacking software can be held liable, and so can their distributors, importers and other parties. Individuals or corporations behind websites that make freely available software keys, key-generators and cracks are also cyber offenders under the Convention.

The Convention goes even further by outlawing the mere possession of such software, hardware or access codes with the intent to illegally access, intercept data or cause data or system interference. The problem is especially apparent if one realises that in today's online world, the computers of users can easily be infected with dangerous software, which can commit unlawful acts without the user's knowledge or intent. The intent required as an element of cyber crime, may be difficult to establish. The Convention provides that a state:

> may reserve the right not to apply paragraph 1 of this Article, provided that the reservation does not concern the sale, distribution or otherwise making available of the items referred to in paragraph 1(a)(2).[56]

10.3.5 Child Pornography

Other controversial provisions relate to the problem of child pornography. It is commonly accepted that pornography is one of the most profitable business models on the internet. Unfortunately, porn websites also sell or sometimes even publicly advertise child pornography. This raises the question how best to combat such practices.

Article 9 of the Convention lists several forms of child pornography. It provides a very wide definition of child pornography, which includes pornographic material that visually depicts a minor (a person under eighteen years of age) engaged in sexually explicit conduct; a person appearing to be

---

[56] Art. 6(3).

a minor engaged in sexually explicit conduct; or realistic images representing a minor engaged in sexually explicit conduct. Such a broad definition creates many problems as, for example, which criteria should be used to ascertain whether a given image depicts a person appearing to be a minor.[57] Many legal systems outlaw sexual contact with a person below fifteen years of age, but the Convention also protects older under-age persons. This conflict could lead to serious complications.

The Convention outlaws the production of child pornography for the purpose of its distribution through a computer system; offering or making available child pornography through a computer system; and distributing or transmitting child pornography through a computer system. However, it also outlaws procuring child pornography through a computer system for oneself or for another[58] and even possessing child pornography in a computer system or on a computer data storage medium.[59] These provisions have generated heated debate and are probably the reasons the Convention allowed for derogation from penalising purchasing child pornography for oneself or for another, as well as the possession of child pornography.[60]

10.4 1996 WIPO Intellectual Property Treaties

More than a decade ago, the World Intellectual Property Organization (WIPO), the organization best known for its activities concerning domain name dispute resolution, adopted two very important intellectual property-related treaties: the Copyright Treaty (WCT) and Performances and the Phonograms Treaty (WPPT). The WCT entered into force on 6 March 2002 and the WPPT on 20 May 2002. Since both contain similar provisions, this discussion will focus on the WCT.

10.4.1 General Information

The WIPO Copyright Treaty has been signed by 91 states from all over the world. List of signatories include: Albania, Argentina, Armenia, Australia, Austria, Azerbaijan, Bahrain, Belarus, Belgium, Benin, Bolivia, Botswana, Bulgaria, Burkina Faso, Canada, Chile, China, Colombia, Costa Rica, Croatia, Cyprus, the Czech Republic, Denmark, the Dominican Republic, Ecuador, El Salvador, Estonia, the European Community, Finland, France, Gabon, Georgia, Germany, Ghana, Greece, Guatemala, Guinea,

[57] Arts. 9(2) and 9(3).
[58] Art. 9(1(d)).
[59] Art. 9(1(e)).
[60] Art. 9(3).

Honduras, Hungary, Indonesia, Ireland, Israel, Italy, Jamaica, Japan, Jordan, Kazakhstan, Kenya, Kyrgyzstan, Latvia, Liechtenstein, Lithuania, Luxembourg, Mali, Mexico, Moldova, Monaco, Mongolia, Montenegro, Namibia, the Netherlands, Nicaragua, Nigeria, Oman, Panama, Paraguay, Peru, the Philippines, Poland, Portugal, Qatar, the Republic of Korea, Romania, Saint Lucia, Senegal, Serbia, Singapore, Slovakia, Slovenia, South Africa, Spain, Sweden, Switzerland, The former Yugoslav Republic of Macedonia, Togo, Ukraine, the United Arab Emirates, the United Kingdom, the United States of America, Uruguay and Venezuela. It is binding in 64 of those states, including the United States.

The WCT consists of the Preamble and 25 articles to which no reservations are admitted.[61] It extends the Berne Convention for the Protection of Literary and Artistic Works, constituting "a special agreement" within the meaning of Article 20 of the Berne Convention.[62] Together with the TRIPS Agreement, the WCT is considered to be one of the most important treaties dealing with the impact of modern information technologies on the copyright regime. Unfortunately, the Convention was drafted in the very early age of the internet, and does not take newer developments sufficiently into account. The WCT was adopted in Geneva on 20 December 1996. Since then, many important technological developments have taken place, such as file-sharing systems, which enable unconstrained swapping of music and video files. Even more important has been the rapid growth of internet-based commerce and the rise of the Open Source Movement.

10.4.2 Analysis of Selected Provisions

Article 2 of the Treaty confirms the scope of copyright protection:

> Copyright protection extends to expressions and not to ideas, procedures, methods of operation or mathematical concepts as such.

Technological influence is certainly visible in Articles 4 and 5, which extend copyright protection to computer programs and databases. However, in the case of databases, protection does not extend to the data or the material itself. This does not mean that such data or material, if already protected by copyrights, loses its protection.

Articles 6 to 8 enumerate three rights of authors of artistic and literary works including software programs and databases: the right of distribution, the right of rental, and the right of communication to the public. The right of communication to the public is of particular importance in the internet age, because it entails the exclusive right of the author to authorise:

---

[61] Art. 22.
[62] Art. 1(1–2).

> any communication to the public of their works, by wire or wireless means, including the making available to the public of their works in such a way that members of the public may access these works from a place and at a time individually chosen by them.

The Treaty gives the author of the webpage the exclusive prerogative of making copyrighted material available to the public. An infringement of this right would occur when the act of a person other than the author would result in making such material available to the public. Such an infringement would usually be passive (a link to a copyrighted material on a website, a file uploaded to an FTP server or made available on a hard disk for other P2P users).[63] In this sense, Article 8 applies to the potential of making available copyrighted material on the internet, via a website, newsgroups, file-sharing systems, File Transfer Protocol or some other procedure. Sending material in an e-mail might conceivably be considered to be an infringement of Article 8.

Since internet Service Providers (ISPs) actually enable public access to such communication, it was important to clarify whether such companies can be liable for copyright infringement. Agreed statements concerning Article 8 clearly remove the liability of ISPs:

> It is understood that the mere provision of physical facilities for enabling or making a communication does not in itself amount to communication within the meaning of this Treaty or the Berne Convention.

Therefore the passive provision of electronic services as in the case of ISPs does not infringe the right of communication to the public.

Technological influence is also visible in Article 11 which forces Contracting Parties to:

> provide adequate legal protection and effective legal remedies against the circumvention of effective technological measures that are used by authors in connection with the exercise of their rights under this Treaty or the Berne Convention and that restrict acts, in respect of their works, which are not authorized by the authors concerned or permitted by law.

Circumventions of effective technological measures are greatly facilitated by the use of technological tools, which are mainly software-related. Circumventions are also powered by the ease of distribution through online channels. (The DVD Jon case is the primary example of the ease of circumventing technological measures). This is further elaborated in Article 12 which concerns the obligations of Contracting States concerning the removal or alteration of any electronic rights management information without authority, or the distribution of works (or copies of works) without authority.[64] The remaining parts of the Treaty deal primarily with

---

[63] See Chapter X.

[64] Art. 12.

institutional aspects of managing the monitoring and enforcement of the Treaty and for this reason will not be further elaborated.

10.4.3 Summary

WIPO Treaties provide a very important framework for a more detailed regulation of the copyright regime in national legal systems. The new framework provides important enhancements of the existing copyright regime in the interest of copyright holders. However, certain problems remain to be dealt with, such as technology-related copying or "ephemeral copying", such as caching. Problems arising from the linking of various resources will continue to create legal problems. Other important aspects of internet-related IP issues not covered in the Treaty include: the status of file-sharing systems; the relation to Open Source initiatives and the large number of licensing schemes connected with the idea of freely available software; technological security innovations such as watermarking or the problem of the admissibility of patenting software; and e-commerce novel practices such as Amazon's famous One-click technology.

WIPO treaties have been transposed into the legal framework of the European Union in Directive 2001/29/EC on the harmonisation of certain aspects of copyright and related rights in the information society.[65]

10.5 Conclusion

All of these developments illustrate the movement towards the internationalisation of internet laws. This is especially visible in the harmonisation and unification efforts of UNCITRAL, WIPO and the Council of Europe. There is also a trend towards self-regulation, which opposes the top-down regulation of internet law. This approach is especially visible in the Open Source Movement, which relies more on contracts and various normative documents issued by internet commerce participants than on rules or documents generated by governments or governmental bodies. This approach gives rise to difficulties of its own. Prominent among them is the fact that it will not lead to the development of globally binding internet laws. Also, if an agreement does not cover all the issues at hand, parties to the dispute will remain uncertain of the outcome.

Finally, there is the possibility of combining the self-regulatory scheme with an official public law arrangement. This approach will probably prevail

---

[65] OJ L 167/10 (22.06.2001) *Directive 2001/29/EC of the European Parliament and of the Council of 22 May 2001 on the harmonisation of certain aspects of copyright and related rights in the information society.*

as it offers both the certainty of the harmonisation movement and the self-regulation of more detailed matters in agreements. None of these approaches, however, will provide the globally binding norms necessary to solve present internet disputes. The regulatory approach fails to do so, because there are as yet no global written laws. The self-regulation approach fails to do so because it only binds the parties to the agreement.

The widespread adoption of a global internet convention could potentially help to solve this problem. The new Convention on the Use of Electronic Communications in International Contracting may ultimately provide the solution. However, the new Convention would have to be accepted by every country interested in the use of the internet, which seems unachievable in the near future. It would also have to be revised to reflect changes in technology, which is also a very difficult task. At best the Convention will provide a general framework, leaving detailed norms to be decided by others, and providing only a limited measure of legal certainty.

Index

Breinigsville, PA USA
23 April 2010
236698BV00001B/16/P

9 781402 094934